MICROWAVE
COOKING

MICROWAVE COOKING

Contributing editor
Sarah Brown

The Reader's Digest Association, Inc.
Pleasantville, New York

This is an RD Home Handbook
specially created for The Reader's Digest Association, Inc.,
by Dorling Kindersley Limited.

First American edition, 1990
Copyright © 1990 by Dorling Kindersley Limited, London
Text copyright © 1990 by Sarah Brown and
Dorling Kindersley Limited, London

Published in the United States
by The Reader's Digest Association, Inc.,
Pleasantville, N.Y.
Published in Great Britain
by Dorling Kindersley Limited, London
Printed in Singapore

Designed and edited by Swallow Books,
260 Pentonville Road, London N1 9JY

Library of Congress Cataloging in Publication Data

Microwave cooking / contributing editor, Sarah Brown. — 1st American ed.
  p. cm. — (RD home handbooks)
  ISBN 0-89577-348—1
  1. Microwave cookery.   I. Brown, Sarah.   II. Reader's Digest
Association.   III. Series.
TX832.M493   1990
641.5′882—dc20   89-70347
                                                                     CIP

CONTENTS

INTRODUCTION

To those new to microwaves, cooking without any source of direct heat is a strange concept which seems to entail a whole new set of rules. With a gadget like a food processor, for example, it's obvious what it will and will not do. With a microwave oven, however, you not only have to get used to a new piece of equipment, but also to an entirely new method of cooking.

In reality, there is nothing difficult about it, but it does take some time to adjust initially. Techniques such as stirring, arranging and covering foods are all far more crucial in the microwave than in conventional cooking. For this reason this book includes a section on these techniques, on pages 196-203.

Timing is essential in microwave cooking. With some dishes it is vital to watch the seconds pass, while others can be left to stand and finish cooking until you are ready. This book starts with a comprehensive ingredients section which describes just how long you need to cook specific quantities of each. As in the recipes that follow, cooking times are given for the three standard power settings.

Once you have become familiar with microwaves, you will find that they are ideal for most types of cooking. They are excellent for vegetables, preserving the maximum number of nutrients because so little water is used. The flavors are fresh, and the colors remain rich, while the texture can be firm and tender. They are just as good for most varieties of fish, as they cook them quickly with less chance of the fish drying out or breaking up. The only disadvantage with cooking meat in a microwave is that, though it is cooked through, it is not browned; but for appearance sake it can be finished in a conventional oven or browning agents can be added.

There is a particular emphasis on healthy cooking in this book, in keeping with modern thinking about diet and nutrition. This might mean that very occasionally there is an ingredient that you are not familiar with, but if that is the case it will be available from larger supermarkets or from a health food store. Microwaves are good for production of healthy food as shorter cooking times can mean less destruction of vitamins.

Finally, although it is hoped that this book will provide new straightforward recipes to tempt your tastebuds, using a microwave does not mean abandoning old, tried and tested favorites, and advice on converting recipes is given on pages 168–170.

COOKING
TIMES AND
TECHNIQUES

This section gives you all the information necessary to cook meat, poultry and game, fish and vegetarian ingredients in the microwave. Cooking times have been given, where appropriate, for fresh, frozen and dried products in 500W, 600W and 700W ovens. With large amounts of food, increase the timings by a third to a half. Look at foods often when they are in the microwave and check after the minimum cooking time.

All meat and poultry can be cooked in the microwave, but some types are more successful than others. Chops, sausages and hamburgers, for example, will look more attractive if they are cooked in a browning dish. Fish only needs to be cooked for a short time in the microwave and remains tender and flavorsome.

The shortest cooking time has been given for vegetables so that they remain crunchy; if you prefer a softer texture, just increase the cooking time slightly. To reheat canned foods, place in a dish and cook on HIGH for 2-4 mins. 600W (1-3 mins. 700W, 3-5 mins. 500W) stirring once or twice. Other ingredients like pasta and dried beans cook well in the microwave and create less mess, although often no real time is saved.

Fresh and frozen vegetables

Always choose fresh-looking vegetables and
avoid any that are wilting or yellowing. For
best results cook vegetables for only a short
time to prevent them from overcooking and
becoming soggy.

BRUSSELS SPROUTS

Fresh

Quantity	Cooking time on HIGH in minutes		
	500W	**600W**	700W
½lb (1½ cups)			
	5-6	**4-5**	3-4
1lb	8-10	**7-8**	6-7

Cooking technique Wash and trim.
Cut a cross in each bottom, then
place in a bowl. Add 2 tablespoons
water. Cover and cook, stirring once
or twice. Allow to stand for 2-3 mins.

Frozen

Quantity	Cooking time on HIGH in minutes		
	500W	**600W**	700W
½lb	8-9	**6-7**	5-6

Cooking technique Place in a bowl
and cover. Stir 2 or 3 times. Allow to
stand for 3-5 mins.

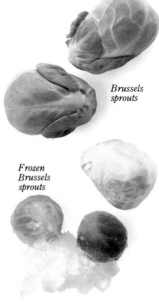

Brussels sprouts

Frozen Brussels sprouts

CAULIFLOWER

Fresh

Quantity	Cooking time on HIGH in minutes		
	500W	**600W**	700W
½lb (2¼ cups)			
	6-8	**4-6**	3-5
1lb	10-12	**8-10**	6-8

Cooking technique Wash and break
into even-sized flowerets. Place in a
bowl with 2-3 tablespoons water and
cover. Stir during cooking. Stand for
2-3 mins. To cook whole, trim off
outer leaves and stem. Cut a cross in
the bottom. Place in a plastic bag,
secure loosely and put on a plate,
bottom up. Turn over halfway
through and half turn the plate every
30 secs. Stand for at least 3 mins.

Frozen

Quantity	Cooking time on HIGH in minutes		
	500W	**600W**	700W
½lb	6-10	**5-8**	4-6

Cooking technique Cook covered but
stir or shake twice. Allow to stand
for 3-5 mins.

Fresh green cauliflower

Frozen cauliflower

Chinese cabbage

CHINESE CABBAGE

Fresh

Quantity	Cooking time on HIGH in minutes		
	500W	**600W**	700W
½lb (3 cups)	3-5	**2-4**	2-4
1lb	8-10	**6-8**	5-7

Cooking technique Wash and remove any damaged leaves. Trim the stems and shred the leaves. Place in a dish and add 1 tablespoon water. Cook covered, stirring once or twice. Allow to stand for 2-3 mins.

BROCCOLI

Fresh

Quantity	Cooking time on HIGH in minutes		
	500W	**600W**	700W
½lb (2½ cups)			
	5-6	**4-5**	3-4
1lb	6-10	**5-8**	4-7

Cooking technique Wash, remove any tough stems and cut a slit in mature stems. Arrange in a bowl with the heads toward the center. Add 2 tablespoons water and cover. Rearrange slightly halfway through the cooking time. Allow to stand for 2-3 mins.

Frozen

Quantity	Cooking time on HIGH in minutes		
	500W	**600W**	700W
½lb	8-11	**6-9**	5-8

Cooking technique Place in a bowl and cover. Stir or shake once or twice during the cooking time. Allow to stand for 3-5 mins.

Fresh broccoli

Frozen broccoli

CABBAGE (All varieties)

Fresh

Quantity	Cooking time on HIGH in minutes		
	500W	600W	700W
½lb (2½ cups)	3-5	2-4	2-4
1lb	8-10	6-8	5-7

Cooking technique Discard any damaged leaves. Wash and shred. Place in a bowl with 2 tablespoons water. (Omit the water when cooking young, green cabbage.) Stir once during cooking. Allow to stand for 2-4 mins. Alternatively, cook in a little margarine in a covered bowl. Stir once during cooking and stand for 2 mins. When stewing red cabbage, extend the cooking time by about 2 mins.

Fresh spinach

Frozen spinach

Fresh Savoy cabbage

Fresh red cabbage

Fresh green cabbage

SPINACH

Fresh

Quantity	Cooking time on HIGH in minutes		
	500W	600W	700W
½lb (8½ cups)	2-5	2-4	2-3
1lb	4-8	3-6	2-5

Cooking technique Wash and rinse well, discarding any damaged leaves. Cook covered without adding any water. Stir halfway through. Allow to stand for 2-3 mins.

Frozen

Quantity	Cooking time on HIGH in minutes		
	500W	600W	700W
½lb	6-9	5-7	4-6
1lb	9-11	7-9	6-8

Cooking technique Place in a dish and cover. Do not add water. Stir once during cooking.

Asparagus

ASPARAGUS

Fresh

Quantity	Cooking time on HIGH in minutes		
	500W	**600W**	700W
½lb	6-10	**5-8**	4-6
1lb	8-12	**7-10**	6-8

Cooking technique Trim off woody stalks and arrange on a dish with the tender tips pointing toward the center. Sprinkle with 1 tablespoon water. Cover and cook. Rearrange the spears, keeping the tips to the center of the plate, halfway though the cooking time. Thicker ends should be tender when pierced with a knife. Allow to stand for 3 mins.

Frozen

Quantity	Cooking time on HIGH in minutes		
	500W	**600W**	700W
10oz	8-11	**6-9**	5-8

Cooking technique Place on a plate and cover. Separate and rearrange during the cooking time, keeping the tips in the center. Allow to stand for 5 mins.

Belgian endive

BELGIAN ENDIVE

Fresh

Quantity	Cooking time on HIGH in minutes		
	500W	**600W**	700W
4 heads	7-10	**6-8**	5-7

Cooking technique Trim the heads, discarding any damaged leaves. Slice in two lengthwise and arrange in a casserole dish, narrower ends to the center. Add 1 tablespoon lemon juice and 1 tablespoon water. Cover and cook. Rearrange halfway through cooking, moving heads from the edge to the center of the dish. Allow to stand for 3 mins.

KOHLRABI

Fresh

Quantity	Cooking time on HIGH in minutes		
	500W	**600W**	700W
1lb (3½ cups)	10-12	**8-10**	6-8

Cooking technique Peel and chop into even-sized pieces. Add ¼ cup water and cook covered. Stir once during the cooking time. Stand for 3 mins.

Kohlrabi

Celery

Sliced celery

LEEKS

Fresh

Quantity	Cooking time on HIGH in minutes		
	500W	**600W**	700W
½lb (1⅓ cups)			
	3-6	**3-5**	2-4
1lb	6-8	**5-7**	4-6

Cooking technique Wash, trim and slice evenly. Add 2 tablespoons water, cover and cook. Stir once during cooking. Allow to stand for 3-5 mins. before serving.

Leek

Sliced leek

CELERY

Fresh

Quantity	Cooking time on HIGH in minutes		
	500W	**600W**	700W
½lb (1½ cups)			
	6-8	**5-7**	4-6
1lb	10-12	**8-10**	6-8

Cooking technique Separate the stalks. Wash, trim and cut into ½-inch pieces. Add ¼ cup water and cover. Stir halfway through the cooking time. Allow to stand for 3 mins.

FENNEL

Fresh

Quantity	Cooking time on HIGH in minutes		
	500W	600W	700W
½lb	5-7	4-6	3-5
1lb	7-10	6-8	5-6

Cooking technique Trim and wash leaves. Slice in half lengthwise. Place in a dish or bag with 2 tablespoons water. Cover and cook, stirring twice. Leave to stand for 3 mins. This method results in a crisp vegetable. Cook for 1 or 2 mins. longer for a softer texture.

Onions

Frozen onion rings

ONIONS

Fresh

Quantity	Cooking time on HIGH in minutes		
	500W	600W	700W
½lb (2 cups)	4-6	3-5	2-4

Cooking technique Peel and slice. Add 2 tablespoons water or cook in 1 tablespoon oil, preheated for 1 min. Cover and stir once during cooking. Extend the cooking time by a few minutes when cooking larger quantities or if stewing until soft. To bake whole with a stuffing, cook uncovered for double the time and stand for 3 minutes.

Frozen

Quantity	Cooking time on HIGH in minutes		
	500W	600W	700W
½lb (2 cups)	5-7	4-6	3-5

Cooking technique Place in a dish and cover. Shake or stir once. Leave to stand for 3 mins.

Fennel

ARTICHOKES

Fresh

Quantity	Cooking time on HIGH in minutes		
	500W	600W	700W
1 head	6-7	5-6	4-5
2 heads	9-10	7-8	6-7

Cooking technique Wash, cut off stalk and lower leaves. Snip leaf tips. Place in a large roasting bag or covered dish with ¼ cup water and 2 tablespoons lemon juice. Turn once during the cooking time. Test if ready by removing one of the leaves—it should come away easily. Drain and stand for 3-5 mins. before serving with butter or margarine.

Globe artichoke

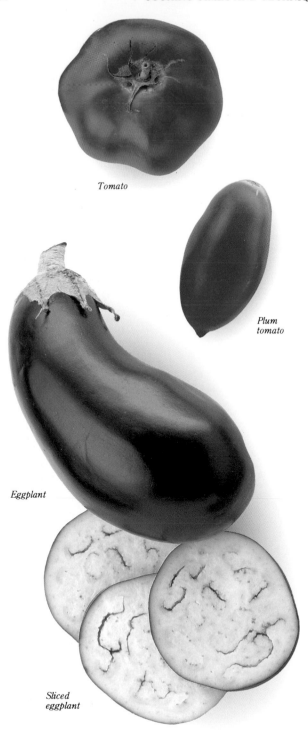

Tomato

Plum tomato

Eggplant

Sliced eggplant

TOMATOES

Fresh

Quantity	Cooking time on HIGH in minutes		
	500W	**600W**	700W
½lb	3-6	**3-5**	2-4
1lb	6-8	**5-7**	4-6

Cooking technique Cut in half or into slices. Flavor with black pepper and basil, marjoram, thyme or oregano. Cover and stir once during cooking. Large tomatoes make excellent containers for savory stuffings.

EGGPLANT

Fresh

Quantity	Cooking time on HIGH in minutes		
	500W	**600W**	700W
½lb (heaped 1 cup)	3-6	**3-5**	2-4
1lb	6-10	**5-8**	4-6

Cooking technique To stew sliced eggplants, cover and cook in 1 tablespoon heated oil or water, following above timings. Stir once during cooking. Season with salt, pepper and fresh herbs. Allow to stand for 4 mins. To cook whole, trim, then pierce skin. Wrap in paper towels. Turn over and rearrange once during cooking. Allow to stand for 4 mins. Serve whole, sliced or mashed with lemon juice. For stuffed eggplants, cook for minimum time and stand. Scoop out the flesh and mix with a cooked grain and vegetable or ground beef filling before replacing in the shell. Reheat for 2-4 mins. before serving.

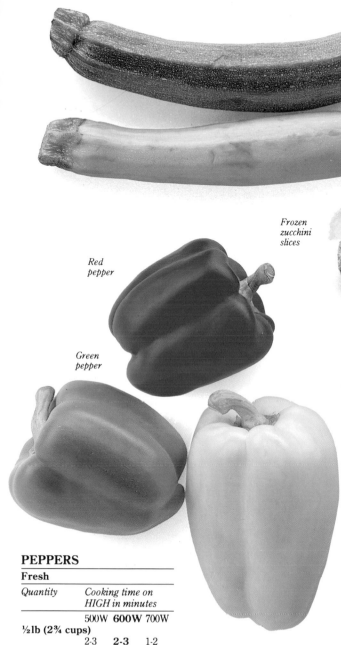

Zucchini and yellow squash

Frozen zucchini slices

Red pepper

Green pepper

Yellow pepper

ZUCCHINI

Fresh

Quantity	Cooking time on HIGH in minutes		
	500W	**600W**	700W
½lb (2¾ cups)			
	5-7	**4-6**	3-5
1lb	7-10	**6-8**	5-7

Cooking technique Cut into strips or rings. Dot with margarine or allow to stew in own juices. Add herbs and ground black pepper for extra flavor. Cover and stir once during cooking. Simply cut the ends off baby zucchini and cook whole. Allow to stand for 3 mins. before serving.

Frozen

Quantity	Cooking time on HIGH in minutes		
	500W	**600W**	700W
½lb	8-11	**7-9**	6-7
1lb	11-14	**9-11**	7-9

Cooking technique Place in bag; pierce. Shake during cooking. Stand for 3 mins.

PEPPERS

Fresh

Quantity	Cooking time on HIGH in minutes		
	500W	**600W**	700W
½lb (2¾ cups)			
	2-3	**2-3**	1-2
1lb	5-7	**4-6**	3-5

Cooking technique Remove the central rib and seeds. Cut into slices. Cook, covered, in 1 tablespoon water or preheated oil. Stir or rearrange once during cooking.

SUMMER SQUASH

Fresh

Quantity	Cooking time on HIGH in minutes		
	500W	**600W**	700W
½lb (1⅔ cups)			
	5-7	**4-6**	3-5
1lb	7-10	**6-8**	5-7

Cooking technique Peel if the skin is tough. Slice in half and remove seeds and fibrous flesh. Cut into cubes. Add herbs and ground black pepper to enhance the flavor. Cover and allow to stew in own juices. Stir once during cooking. Stand for 3 mins.

Summer Squash

PUMPKIN

Fresh

Quantity	Cooking time on HIGH in minutes		
	500W	**600W**	700W
1lb	7-10	**6-8**	5-6

Cooking technique Halve and remove stem and bottom so each half can sit on a plate. Cover with paper towels and cook one half at a time. Test for tenderness as timing will depend on age and size. Allow to stand for 2 mins. before scooping out the seeds and pith. Purée the flesh with ground coriander and garlic.

Pumpkin

ITALIAN-STYLE GREEN BEANS

Fresh

Quantity	Cooking time on HIGH in minutes		
	500W	**600W**	700W
½lb (2 cups)	6-8	**5-7**	4-6
1lb	8-11	**7-9**	6-8

Cooking technique String and slice. Add 2 tablespoons water and cover. Stir 2-3 times during cooking. Leave to stand for 2 mins. Allow more time for larger beans.

GARDEN PEAS

Fresh

Quantity	Cooking time on HIGH in minutes		
	500W	**600W**	700W
½lb (1½ cups)	6-8	**5-7**	4-6
1lb	10-12	**8-10**	7-8

Cooking technique Shell. Add 2 tablespoons water. Cover and stir during cooking. Allow to stand for 3-5 mins.

Frozen

Quantity	Cooking time on HIGH in minutes		
	500W	**600W**	700W
½lb	5-6	**3-4**	3-4
1lb	9-10	**7-8**	6-7

Cooking technique Add 1 tablespoon butter or margarine and cover. Stir during cooking. Allow to stand for 2-3 mins.

Fresh Italian-style green beans

Fresh peas

Frozen peas

PETIT POIS

Frozen

Quantity	Cooking time on HIGH in minutes		
	500W	**600W**	700W
½lb	4-6	**3-5**	2-4
1lb	7-10	**6-8**	5-7

Cooking technique Add 1 tablespoon of butter and cover. Stir once during cooking. Allow to stand for 2 mins.

Frozen petit pois

SNOW PEAS

Fresh

Quantity	Cooking time on HIGH in minutes		
	500W	**600W**	700W
½ lb	7-9	**6-7**	5-6
1 lb	10-11	**8-9**	6-7

Cooking technique Wash and trim. Add 2 tablespoons water and cover. Stir during cooking. Allow to stand for 2-3 mins.

Fresh snow peas

GREEN BEANS

Fresh

Quantity	Cooking time on HIGH in minutes		
	500W	**600W**	700W
½ lb	6-9	**5-7**	4-6
1 lb	9-11	**7-9**	6-8

Cooking technique Wash and trim. Add 3 tablespoons water and cover. Stir once during cooking. Allow to stand for 3 mins.

LIMA BEANS

Fresh

Quantity	Cooking time on HIGH in minutes		
	500W	**600W**	700W
½ lb (1½ cups)	8-10	**6-8**	5-7
1 lb	11-12	**9-10**	8-9

Cooking technique Shell. Add 3 tablespoons water and cover. Stir after 3 mins. and test after 5 mins. Dot with butter or margarine and allow to stand for 5 mins.

Frozen

Quantity	Cooking time on HIGH in minutes		
	500W	**600W**	700W
½ lb	9-10	**7-8**	6-7
1 lb	12-15	**10-12**	8-10

Cooking technique Add 1 tablespoon butter or margarine or 2-4 tablespoons water and cover. Stir once or twice during cooking. Allow to stand for 5 mins.

GREEN BEANS

Frozen

Quantity	Cooking time on HIGH in minutes		
	500W	**600W**	700W
½ lb	8-10	**7-8**	6-7
1 lb	10-11	**9-10**	8-9

Cooking technique Add 1 tablespoon butter or margarine or 3-4 tablespoons water. Cover. Stir once during cooking. Allow to stand for 5 mins.

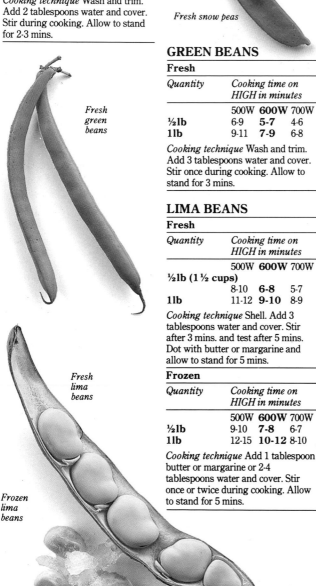

Fresh green beans

Fresh lima beans

Frozen lima beans

Frozen green beans

French-style green beans

FRENCH-STYLE GREEN BEANS

Fresh

Quantity	Cooking time on HIGH in minutes		
	500W	**600W**	700W
½ lb	5-6	**4-5**	3-4
1 lb	6-9	**5-7**	4-6

Cooking technique Wash and trim. Add 2 tablespoons water and cover. Stir during cooking. Allow to stand for 2-3 mins.

Fresh okra

CORN-ON-THE-COB

Fresh

Quantity	Cooking time on HIGH in minutes		
	500W	**600W**	700W
1 ear	5-6	**4-5**	3-4
2 ears	8-10	**6-8**	5-7
4 ears	10-12	**8-10**	7-9

Cooking technique Trim and wash. Add 1 tablespoon water per ear and cover. Turn over during cooking. Leave to stand 2-3 mins. Serve with butter or margarine. Alternatively, wrap in waxed paper. Turn over and rearrange halfway through the cooking time.

Frozen

Quantity	Cooking time on HIGH in minutes		
	500W	**600W**	700W
1 ear	4-5	**3-4**	2-3
2 ears	8-9	**6-7**	5-6

Cooking technique Dot with butter or margarine and wrap in waxed paper. Turn over and rearrange halfway through cooking. Leave to stand for 3-5 mins.

Frozen corn kernels

CORN KERNELS

Frozen

Quantity	Cooking time on HIGH in minutes		
	500W	**600W**	700W
½lb	5-8	**4-6**	3-5
1lb	9-10	**7-8**	6-7

Cooking technique Add 2 tablespoons water or 1 tablespoon of butter or margarine. Cover and stir during cooking. Allow to stand for 3 mins.

OKRA

Fresh

Quantity	Cooking time on HIGH in minutes		
	500W	**600W**	700W
½lb (2 cups)	8-9	**6-7**	5-6
1lb	10-11	**8-9**	7-8

Cooking technique Trim and wash. Cook whole or cut into 1-inch pieces. Add ¼ cup water or 1 tablespoon preheated oil. Cover. Turn the bowl halfway through the cooking time. Stand for 3 mins.

Frozen corn-on-the-cob

Fresh baby cob

Fresh corn-on-the-cob

Fresh sweet potatoes

SWEET POTATOES

Fresh

Quantity	Cooking time on HIGH in minutes		
	500W	**600W**	700W
1lb (2-3 potatoes)	8-10	**6-8**	5-7

Cooking technique Select small, even-shaped potatoes. Scrub and remove any long tail parts. Pierce all over and space around the edge of a plate. Cover and cook, turning over and rearranging halfway through the cooking time. Allow to stand for 2-3 mins., then dot with butter or margarine, chopped fresh parsley or mint. Serve whole or sliced.

POTATOES

Fresh

Quantity	Cooking time on HIGH in minutes		
	500W	**600W**	700W
1lb (2-3 potatoes)	10-15	**8-10**	6-8

Cooking technique Choose even-sized potatoes and scrub well before cooking. Pierce all over and wrap in paper towels. Arrange in an evenly spaced circle on a plate and cook. Turn over and rearrange halfway through the cooking time. Allow to stand for 5 mins. Serve whole or sliced thinly as required.

BEETS

Fresh

Quantity	Cooking time on HIGH in minutes		
	500W	**600W**	700W
1lb (9 beets)	12-15	**10-12**	8-10

Cooking technique If cooking large beets, peel and cut into even-sized chunks. Cook covered for about half the length of time. Scrub small ones and remove their stems and bottoms. Pierce well on all sides, then cook in a plastic bag. Turn over and rearrange halfway through the cooking time. Allow to stand for 3-5 mins., then scrape off skins. Serve whole or diced. Delicious served as a hot vegetable or chilled in salads.

Fresh, raw beet

Fresh potatoes

Fresh turnips

PARSNIPS

Fresh

Quantity	Cooking time on HIGH in minutes		
	500W	**600W**	700W
1lb (about 5 parsnips)			
	6-10	**5-8**	4-7

Cooking technique Peel, cut in half or cut into even-sized chunks or julienne strips and place in a dish. If cooking halves, arrange with the thinner ends toward the center. Add 2 tablespoons water and a few drops of lemon juice. Cook covered and stir or rearrange halfway through cooking. Allow to stand for 2-3 mins., then drain. Toss in butter or margarine.

CARROTS

Fresh

Quantity	Cooking time on HIGH in minutes*		
	500W	**600W**	700W
1lb (about 5 carrots)			
	8-10	**6-8**	5-7

Cooking technique Wash and prepare as usual. Leave baby carrots whole but slice larger ones into julienne strips or slices. Place in a dish and add 2-3 tablespoons water. Cover and cook, stirring once or twice. Allow to stand for 2-3 mins.

Frozen

Quantity	Cooking time on HIGH in minutes		
	500W	**600W**	700W
½lb	6-8	**5-7**	4-6

Cooking technique Pour the carrots into a dish and cover. Cook, stirring once or twice during the time. Allow to stand for 2-3 mins.

TURNIPS

Fresh

Quantity	Cooking time on HIGH in minutes		
	500W	**600W**	700W
1lb (3⅓ cups)			
	10-12	**8-10**	6-8

Cooking technique Peel and slice evenly, but leave baby turnips whole. Add 2 tablespoons water and cook covered until tender, stirring twice. Leave to stand for 3-5 mins. Drain well before serving.

Fresh baby carrots

Fresh carrot slices

Fresh carrot julienne strips

Frozen carrots

Fresh parsnips

Frozen rutabaga

Fresh rutabaga

CELERY ROOT

Fresh

Quantity	Cooking time on HIGH in minutes		
	500W	**600W**	700W
1lb (3 cups)	8-10	**6-8**	4-6

Cooking technique Scrub, trim and peel. Cut into julienne strips and place in a dish with 3 tablespoons water. Cover and cook, stirring once or twice during cooking. Drain well and toss in lemon juice. To blanch celery root, cook for half the length of time, stirring every minute. Then drain and toss in lemon juice and serve with a dressing.

RUTABAGA

Fresh

Quantity	Cooking time on HIGH in minutes		
	500W	**600W**	700W
1lb (3¼ cups)	10-12	**8-10**	7-9

Cooking technique Peel and dice. Place in a bowl with 2 tablespoons water. Cover and cook until tender, stirring once or twice. Drain well. Serve sprinkled with black pepper and chopped parsley. Rutabaga is also delicious mashed with some butter or margarine, yogurt and ground black pepper.

Frozen

Quantity	Cooking time on HIGH in minutes		
	500W	**600W**	700W
½lb	12-15	**10-12**	8-10

Cooking technique Place in a dish and add ¼ cup water. Cover and cook, stirring halfway through the time. Stand for 2 mins, then drain. See serving ideas above.

Fresh celery root

Fresh and frozen fruit

Fruit cooks extremely well in the microwave. It can be cooked quickly to retain its color, flavor and texture. If a recipe calls for a soft puree, just cook the fruit for a few minutes longer.

Frozen apple slices

Fresh cooking apple

Fresh blueberries

Fresh apple

Frozen blueberries

Frozen blackberries

Fresh blackberries

APPLES

Fresh

Quantity	Cooking time on HIGH in minutes		
	500W	**600W**	700W
1 large	3-5	**3-4**	2-3
2 large	7-10	**6-8**	5-7

Cooking technique Pare, core and slice. Sprinkle with lemon juice and a little honey, if preferred. Cover and stir once during cooking. Allow to stand for 3 mins. To cook whole apples, use the same cooking times, but remember that they will vary according to the size of the apples. Core and fill with a mixture of dried fruit, chopped nuts and a little margarine. Score around the center to prevent bursting. Arrange in a circle and rearrange halfway through the cooking. Allow to stand for 2 mins. Cook 2 mins. if required.

Frozen

Quantity	Cooking time on HIGH in minutes		
	500W	**600W**	700W
½lb	2-5	**2-4**	2-3
1lb	6-10	**4-8**	5-7

Cooking technique Add a knob of butter or margarine and cover. Stir the apples during cooking. Leave to stand for 5 mins.

BLACKBERRIES

Fresh

Quantity	Cooking time on HIGH in minutes		
	500W	**600W**	700W
½lb (1 ½ cups)	2-5	**2-4**	2-3
1lb	3-6	**2-5**	2-4

Cooking technique Hull and wash. Cover. Stir the berries once. Allow to stand for 3 mins.

Frozen

Quantity	Cooking time on HIGH in minutes		
	500W	**600W**	700W
½lb	3-6	**3-5**	2-4
1lb	4-7	**4-6**	3-5

Cooking technique Cover. Stir the fruit once. Allow to stand for 5 mins.

BLUEBERRIES AND BLACK CURRANTS

Fresh

Quantity	Cooking time on HIGH in minutes		
	500W	**600W**	700W
½lb (1 ½ cups)	2-5	**2-4**	2-3
1lb	3-6	**3-5**	2-4

Cooking technique Wash the fruit. Add 1 tablespoon honey, if preferred. Cover the fruit and stir once. Allow to stand for 3 min.

Frozen

Quantity	Cooking time on HIGH in minutes		
	500W	**600W**	700W
½lb	3-6	**3-5**	2-4
1lb	4-7	**4-6**	3-5

Cooking technique Place frozen fruit in a covered container. Stir once during cooking. Stand for 5 mins.

Frozen black currants

Fresh black currants

RED CURRANTS

Fresh

Quantity	Cooking time on HIGH in minutes		
	500W	**600W**	700W
½lb (1 ½ cups)	2-5	**2-4**	2-3
1lb	3-6	**2-5**	2-3

Cooking technique Wash. Cover and stir once during cooking time. Red currants add color to poached fruit; or try them with pears or peaches, in mixed fruit compotes.

Frozen

Quantity	Cooking time on HIGH in minutes		
	500W	**600W**	700W
½lb	3-6	**3-5**	2-4
1lb	4-7	**4-6**	3-5

Cooking technique Cover and stir once during cooking. Stand for 5 mins.

Frozen red currants

Fresh red currants

GREENGAGES

Fresh

Quantity	Cooking time on HIGH in minutes		
	500W	**600W**	700W
½lb (1 ½ cups)	3-5	**3-5**	2-4
1lb	5-7	**4-6**	3-5

Cooking technique Wash, cut in half and remove pits. Add 1 tablespoon water, or orange juice for a different flavor. Cover and cook, stirring once during the cooking time. Allow to stand for 3 mins.

Fresh nectarines

Fresh peach

NECTARINES

Fresh

Quantity	Cooking time on HIGH in minutes		
	500W	**600W**	700W
1lb (about 3 nectarines)	5-7	**4-6**	3-5

Cooking technique Wash, cut in half and remove pits. Slice, quarter or leave as halves. Add 2 tablespoons water or fruit juice. Cover. Stir or rearrange once during cooking. Allow to stand for 3 mins.

Fresh greengages

PEACHES

Fresh

Quantity	Cooking time on HIGH in minutes		
	500W	**600W**	700W
1lb (about 3 peaches)	5-7	**4-6**	3-5

Cooking technique Wash, cut in half and remove pits. Slice, quarter or leave as halves. Add 2 tablespoons water or fruit juice. Cover. Stir or rearrange once during cooking. Allow to stand for 3 mins.

PLUMS

Fresh

Quantity	Cooking time on HIGH in minutes		
	500W	**600W**	700W
½lb (1 ½ cups)	3-6	**3-5**	2-4
1lb	5-7	**4-6**	3-5

Cooking technique Wash, then slice each fruit in half and remove pit. Add a touch of cinnamon and grated lemon peel for extra flavor, or cook in 1-2 tablespoons red wine. Cover and stir the plums once during cooking. Allow to stand for 5 mins.

Fresh plums

Fresh apricots

PEARS

Fresh

Quantity	Cooking time on HIGH in minutes		
	500W	**600W**	700W
1lb (about 3 pears)			
	6-8	**5-7**	4-6

Cooking technique Peel, then cut in half lengthwise and remove the cores. Arrange in a round dish with the broadest ends at the outer edge. Pour over 2 tablespoons orange juice and sprinkle in some ground ginger. Cover and cook until tender, rearranging halfway through. Allow to stand for 3 mins.

Fresh pears

APRICOTS

Fresh

Quantity	Cooking time on HIGH in minutes		
	500W	**600W**	700W
1lb (about 12 apricots)			
	7-10	**6-8**	5-7

Cooking technique Wash, halve and remove pits. Leave halved or cut into slices. Add 1 tablespoon apple juice and some grated lemon peel, if preferred. Cover and stir once. Allow to stand for 3 mins.

BANANAS

Fresh

Quantity	Cooking time on HIGH in minutes		
	500W	**600W**	700W
2	2-3	**2-3**	1-2
4	3-5	**3-4**	2-3

Cooking technique Use firm bananas. Peel and place in a dish. Mix together the juice of 1 lemon and 1-2 tablespoons honey and pour it over the bananas. Cook uncovered and leave to stand for 2 mins. Serve with yogurt or flambé with rum. Heating liquor in the microwave can be dangerous as it may ignite, so flambé conventionally.

RHUBARB

Fresh

Quantity	Cooking time on HIGH in minutes		
	500W	**600W**	700W
½lb (1¾ cups)			
	5-7	**4-6**	3-5
1lb	7-11	**6-9**	5-8

Cooking technique Trim, wash and cut into even 1-inch pieces. Place on a plate and sprinkle with grated orange peel or some ground ginger. Cover. Stir twice during cooking. Allow to stand for 3 mins.

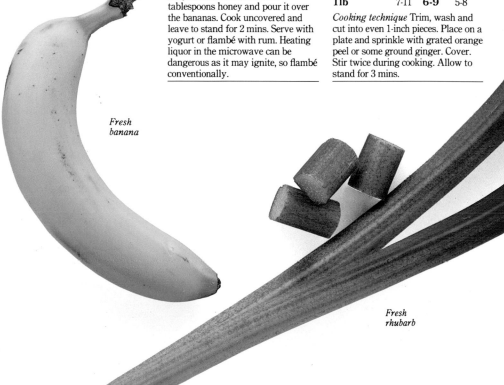

Fresh banana

Fresh rhubarb

Dried fruit

Dried apricots

Hunza apricot

Dried fruit are ideal for microwave cooking as they quickly plump and soften, taking away the need for long hours of pre-soaking. The longer you leave the fruit to stand after cooking, the richer the flavors.

Dried figs

DRIED APRICOTS

Quantity	Cooking time on HIGH in minutes		
	500W	**600W**	700W
1 cup	6-10	**5-8**	5-8

Cooking technique Place in a bowl and cover with 2½ cups boiling water. Cover and cook, stirring once. Allow to stand for 10-30 mins.

HUNZA APRICOTS

Quantity	Cooking time on HIGH in minutes		
	500W	**600W**	700W
2 cups	6-10	**5-8**	5-8

Cooking technique Place in a bowl and cover with 3¾ cups boiling water. Cover and cook, stirring once. Allow to stand for 10-30 mins.

Prunes

PRUNES

Quantity	Cooking time on HIGH in minutes		
	500W	**600W**	700W
2¼ cups	10-12	**10-12**	10-12

Cooking technique Place in bowl with 2½ cups boiling water. Cover and cook, stirring once or twice. Leave to stand for 15-30 mins.

DRIED BANANAS

Quantity	Cooking time on HIGH in minutes		
	500W	**600W**	700W
2¼ cups	10-12	**10-12**	10-12

Cooking technique To make an interesting purée or spread, chop the bananas finely, then place in a bowl with 2½ cups boiling water. Cover and cook, stirring once or twice. Stand until cool, then drain and purée with orange or lemon juice added to taste.

Dried dates

DRIED DATES

Quantity	Cooking time on HIGH in minutes		
	500W	**600W**	700W
1¼ cups	4-6	**3-5**	3-5

Cooking technique Place in a bowl with ⅔ cup boiling water. Cover and cook, stirring once. Leave to stand for 10-15 mins. Cook with fresh fruit to add sweetness.

DRIED APPLES AND PEACHES

Quantity	Cooking time on HIGH in minutes		
	500W	**600W**	700W
1 cup	6-10	**5-8**	5-8

Cooking technique Place in a bowl with 2½ cups boiling water. Cover and cook, stirring once. Allow to stand for 10-30 mins.

DRIED FIGS

Quantity	Cooking time on HIGH in minutes		
	500W	**600W**	700W
1½ cups	8-10	**8-10**	8-10

Cooking technique Place in a bowl and cover with boiling water. Cover and cook, stirring once or twice. Leave the figs to stand for 30 mins. to soften.

Dried pear

Dried apple ring

DRIED PEARS

Quantity	Cooking time on HIGH in minutes		
	500W	**600W**	700W
heaped ½ cup	5-8	**5-8**	5-8

Cooking technique Place in a large bowl and add 3¾ cups boiling water. Cover and cook, stirring once. Leave to stand for 10-30 mins. Avoid doing more than 1 cup at one time as they swell during cooking.

Nuts and seeds

The microwave can help you to toast nuts and seeds in a few minutes. They can then be used for toppings, fillings and to garnish other dishes. Adding spices and seasonings to the nuts will make them into tasty snacks.

Dried chestnuts

Fresh chestnut

Sunflower seeds

Sesame seeds

DRIED CHESTNUTS

Quantity	Cooking time on HIGH and MEDIUM DEFROST in minutes		
	500W	**600W**	700W
⅓ cup	6/22	**5/15**	4/12

Cooking technique Steep the chestnuts in boiling water for 1 hour. Cover and cook on HIGH for 5 mins. then reduce power and simmer for 15 mins. or until soft.

FRESH CHESTNUTS

Quantity	Cooking time on HIGH in minutes		
	500W	**600W**	700W
⅓ cup (shelled)	1-2	**1-2**	½-1

Cooking technique To shell fresh chestnuts, score the outer case of each nut (or they might explode). Place on a flat dish and shake halfway through. If they don't peel easily, cook for a further 10-15 secs.

NUTS (GENERAL)

Quantity	Cooking time on HIGH in minutes		
	500W	**600W**	700W
⅔ cup	3-5	**2-3**	2-3

Cooking technique To roast nuts for garnishes and toppings, simply shell, chop and spread out on a small plate. Cook uncovered and shake or stir the nuts 2 or 3 times to prevent any scorching. Whole nuts and large pieces will take a little longer; try doubling the times. To make savory nuts, roast as described then add 1-2 tablespoons soy sauce. Stir well, then cook for another minute. Cool and serve as a snack or as an addition to salads.

HAZELNUTS (FILBERTS) AND PEANUTS

Quantity	Cooking time on HIGH in minutes		
	500W	**600W**	700W
scant ⅓ cup	6-10	**5-8**	3-6

Cooking technique To toast and skin, shell the nuts and put on a small plate. Cook uncovered and stir 3 or 4 times during the cooking period. Leave to cool, then place the nuts in a clean dishtowel and rub off the skins.

SEEDS (GENERAL)

Quantity	Cooking time on HIGH in minutes		
	500W	**600W**	700W
scant ⅓ cup	2-4	**2-3**	1-2

Cooking technique Sunflower and pumpkin seeds are delicious plainly toasted or mixed with 1 tablespoon soy sauce and cooked for a further minute to make a tangy snack. Stir frequently during the cooking period to avoid scorching. You can make gomasio (a nutty condiment from the Far East) by toasting sesame seeds and then grinding them with sea salt in a ratio of 10:1. Sprinkle over foods as a seasoning. Try toasting other seeds too when required in recipes as it always brings out their flavor. Cumin and coriander are particularly good toasted, then mixed with yogurt and served as an accompaniment to rice dishes.

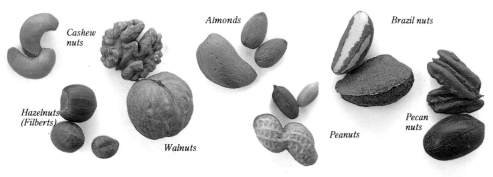

Cashew nuts

Almonds

Brazil nuts

Hazelnuts (Filberts)

Walnuts

Peanuts

Pecan nuts

Dried beans

All dried beans, except for split peas and lentils, need to be soaked for 8 hours and then rinsed before being cooked in the microwave. Always use a large container as the beans will swell and often need more water during cooking.

WHOLE LENTILS

Quantity	Cooking time on HIGH in minutes		
	500W	**600W**	700W
1 ¼ cups	15-20	**15-20**	15-20

Cooking technique Sift through for grit and stones, rinse and place in a bowl. Cover with fresh boiling water. Cook covered, stirring 2 or 3 times. Leave to stand for 10-15 mins. If they are still hard, cook for a further 5 mins. and test again.

Adzuki beans

ADZUKI BEANS

Quantity	Cooking time on HIGH in minutes		
	500W	**600W**	700W
heaped 1 cup	25-30	**25-30**	25-30

Cooking technique After soaking, rinse the beans and place them in a bowl. Fill with fresh boiling water and then cook covered. Stir 2 or 3 times during cooking then leave to stand for 15-20 mins. If they are not completely soft, cook for a further 5 mins. and test again.

WHOLE GREEN PEAS

Quantity	Cooking time on HIGH in minutes		
	500W	**600W**	700W
heaped 1 cup	25-30	**25-30**	25-30

Cooking technique Presoak then rinse and drain. Put in a bowl and cover with fresh boiling water. Cook covered, stirring 2 or 3 times. Leave to stand for 5-10 mins. Test, and extend the cooking time by a further 5 mins. if still hard, then test again.

Mung beans

MUNG BEANS

Quantity	Cooking time on HIGH in minutes		
	500W	**600W**	700W
heaped 1 cup	20-25	**20-25**	20-25

Cooking technique Soak the mung beans overnight. Rinse then drain. Put in a bowl and cover with fresh boiling water. Cook covered, stirring 2 or 3 times. Leave to stand for about 10 mins.

SPLIT PEAS AND RED LENTILS

Quantity	Cooking time on HIGH in minutes		
	500W	**600W**	700W
heaped 1 cup	12-15	**10-12**	8-10

Cooking technique Put in a bowl and cover with boiling water. Stand the dish on a plate in case the liquid boils over. Cook covered then allow to stand for 5-10 mins.

Split red lentils

Split green peas

Split yellow peas

Black beans

Red kidney beans

These *must* boil for the first 10 mins.

Black-eyed peas

Chick peas

Pinto beans

ALL LARGER BEANS

Quantity	Cooking time on HIGH in minutes		
	500W	**600W**	700W
1 ¼ cups	20-30	**20-30**	20-30

Cooking technique Presoak, rinse and drain. Put in a large bowl and cover with fresh boiling water. Cook covered but ensure the beans are boiling hard for the first 10 mins. Stir 2 or 3 times. Leave to stand for 5-10 mins. Cook for a further 5-10 mins. if hard, then test again.

Mushrooms and seaweeds

Wakame

Dried mushrooms and seaweeds quickly reconstitute in the microwave, keeping their flavor and nutritional value. The mushrooms can add flavor to soups and vegetable dishes; the seaweed is best used as a seasoning.

Kombu

Fresh mushrooms

Shiitake (Dried Chinese mushrooms)

Fresh oyster mushrooms

SHIITAKE (DRIED CHINESE MUSHROOMS)

Quantity	Cooking time on HIGH in minutes		
	500W	600W	700W
1oz	2-4	**2-3**	1-2

Cooking technique Place in a bowl and cover with boiling water. Cook covered, then leave to stand for 10-15 mins. Chop and use in soups, stews and stocks. Save the rich soaking liquid as it provides extra flavor in stocks and sauces.

FRESH MUSHROOMS

Quantity	Cooking time on HIGH in minutes		
	500W	**600W**	700W
1 ½ cups	3-5	**3-5**	2-4

Cooking technique Select dry, firm mushrooms for use in the microwave and avoid any that are wet, shriveled or limp. Wipe carefully, then slice or leave whole. Place in a bowl, sprinkle with lemon juice, or dot with butter or margarine, and cook. To yield more juice for use in sauces and stocks, cover and cook for 1-2 mins. longer.

DRIED WAKAME, KOMBU AND ARAME

Quantity	Cooking time on HIGH in minutes		
	500W	**600W**	700W
½oz	1-2	**1-2**	1-2

Cooking technique To reconstitute the dry seaweed, rinse and then cook, covered, in about 7 fl oz boiling water. Drain and mix with vegetables or allow to cool for use in salads. Alternatively, add uncooked to soups, stews and stocks or use as a seasoning for sprinkling over dishes by toasting for 1 min., then grinding with toasted seasame seeds.

DULSE

Quantity	Cooking time on HIGH in minutes		
	500W	**600W**	700W
½oz	2-3	**2-3**	2-3

Cooking technique Rinse fresh seaweed. Cook, covered, in 7 fl oz water and 1 tablespoon soy sauce.

Arame

Dulse

Grains and cereals

Cooking grains in the microwave won't save
you time, but they will stay separate and have
a light, fluffy texture. Cook them in large
containers as they increase greatly in size.
Cover loosely to let steam escape.

Barley

BARLEY

Quantity	Cooking time on HIGH in minutes		
	500W	**600W**	700W
heaped 1 cup			
	20-25	**20-25**	20-25

Cooking technique Place in a bowl
and pour over 2½ cups boiling
water. Soak for 1 hour then cook as
above, stirring 2 or 3 times. Stand for
10 mins. then drain. For a stronger
flavor, roast the grains for 1-2 mins.
before adding the water.

BULGUR WHEAT

Quantity	Cooking time on HIGH in minutes		
	500W	**600W**	700W
heaped ½ cup			
	2-3	**2-3**	2-3

Cooking technique Place in a bowl
with 2½ cups boiling water, stir
well. Cover and cook, stirring once.
Allow to stand for 5 mins. then drain
and fork through. Season well. Use
the same method for COUSCOUS.

POLENTA (CORNMEAL)

Quantity	Cooking time on HIGH in minutes		
	500W	**600W**	700W
1 cup	12-15	**10-12**	8-10

Cooking technique Add 2½ cups
boiling water to the polenta in a bowl
and stir until smooth. Mix in 2
tablespoons margarine. Cover and
cook, stirring 4 times. Spoon into a
greased shallow bowl. Stand for 10-
15 mins.

BROWN RICE

Quantity	Cooking time on HIGH in minutes		
	500W	**600W**	700W
1 ¼ cups	16-20	**16-20**	16-20

Cooking technique Place in a large
bowl. Fill with double the quantity of
boiling water. Cover and stir the rice
halfway through. Allow to stand for
5-10 mins. then drain.

Brown rice (long grain)

Boiled oats

BOILED OATS

Quantity	Cooking time on HIGH in minutes		
	500W	**600W**	700W
½ cup	4-6	**3-5**	2-4

Cooking technique To make cereal
for 1 person and serve it in the same
container, put the oats into a bowl
and fill with 2-3 times their volume of
cold water or milk. Stir in well, then
cover and cook. Stir once or twice
during cooking. Leave to stand for 3
mins. Stir again, then serve. Follow
the same method to make cereal from
other flaked grains.

BUCKWHEAT (KASHA)

Quantity	Cooking time on HIGH in minutes		
	500W	**600W**	700W
heaped 1 cup			
	8-10	**8-10**	8-10

Cooking technique Place grains in a
large bowl. Add 3¾ cups boiling
water and stir well. Cover and cook,
stirring once or twice. Leave to stand
for 4-5 mins. Excess water should be
absorbed, but drain if necessary.

WHOLE-WHEAT

Quantity	Cooking time on HIGH in minutes		
	500W	**600W**	700W
scant 2 cups	25-30	**25-30**	25-30

Cooking technique Place in a bowl,
fill with boiling water and soak for 1
hour. Drain and add 3¾ cups boiling
water. Cover and cook, stirring
frequently. Stand for 15-20 mins.
then drain. If hard, cook for a further
5 mins. and test again.

MILLET

Quantity	Cooking time on HIGH in minutes		
	500W	**600W**	700W
⅓ cup	12-15	**12-15**	12-15

Cooking technique Place grains in a
bowl. Add 1¼ cups boiling water.
Cover and stir 2 or 3 times. Stand for
4 mins. to cook through and drain if
necessary.

Millet

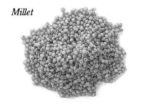

Pasta

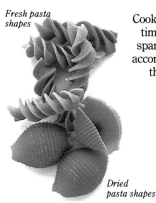

Fresh pasta shapes

Cooking pasta in the microwave will not save time from normal cooking, but you will be spared messy saucepans. You can also cook accompanying sauces in the microwave while the pasta is standing and still cooking.

Dried pasta shapes

Dried spaghetti

Fresh spaghetti

PASTA SHAPES

Dried

Quantity	Cooking time on HIGH in minutes		
	500W	**600W**	700W
½lb	6-8	**6-8**	6-8

Cooking technique Pour enough boiling water into a dish to immerse pasta completely. Add a little salt and 1 tablespoon oil. Stir to separate the pasta pieces. Cook uncovered. Allow to stand for 3 mins., then drain and toss well in some olive oil or butter.

Fresh

Quantity	Cooking time on HIGH in minutes		
	500W	**600W**	700W
½lb	1-3	**1-3**	1-3

Cooking technique Immerse in boiling water and stir. Cook uncovered. Allow to stand for 2 mins., then drain.

EGG AND SPINACH NOODLES

Dried

Quantity	Cooking time on HIGH in minutes		
	500W	**600W**	700W
½lb	2-5	**2-4**	2-4

Cooking technique Place in a bowl of boiling water and completely immerse. Stir, then cook. Stir once during cooking. Allow to stand for 3 mins., then drain.

ELBOW MACARONI

Dried

Quantity	Cooking time on HIGH in minutes		
	500W	**600W**	700W
½lb	6-8	**6-8**	6-8

Cooking technique Immerse in a bowl of boiling water. Stir, then cook and stir once during cooking. Allow to stand for 3 mins. Drain, then toss in some oil, margarine or butter.

LASAGNE

Dried

Quantity	Cooking time on HIGH in minutes		
	500W	**600W**	700W
½lb	8-10	**8-10**	8-10

Cooking technique Place lasagne in a large bowl of boiling water so it is completely immersed. Cook uncovered, stirring once to prevent pieces sticking together. Leave to stand for 5-10 mins., then drain. Fresh and precooked lasagne can be used as they are in pasta dishes as they will soften in the sauce.

Dried egg noodles

SPAGHETTI

Dried

Quantity	Cooking time on HIGH in minutes		
	500W	**600W**	700W
½lb	6-8	**6-8**	6-8

Cooking technique Immerse in boiling water, ensuring that every strand is covered. Add 1 tablespoon oil and stir. Cook, stirring once, then stand for 5 mins. Drain and toss in some olive oil, margarine or butter.

Fresh

Quantity	Cooking time on HIGH in minutes		
	500W	**600W**	700W
½lb	1-4	**1-3**	1-3

Cooking technique Immerse in boiling water, separate strands and ensure that none are protruding. Cook uncovered, then stand for 3 mins. Drain and then toss in some olive oil, margarine or butter before serving.

Fish

Fish cooks very fast by microwave. To stop
overcooking: score whole fish on both sides,
placing them head to tail in the dish; overlap
thin ends of fillets; arrange thin ends of steaks
towards the center.

STRIPED BASS

Fresh and defrosted

Quantity	Cooking time on HIGH in minutes		
	500W	**600W**	700W
2lb whole fish, head removed, dressed, with 1½ cups stuffing	11-12	**9-10**	7-8

Cooking technique Striped bass has a
sweet flavor when fresh and is well
suited to microwaving. Most
commonly sold whole, it can be left
whole, or dressed and stuffed. Cover.
Rotate dish one-half turn halfway
through cooking. Stand for 3-4 mins.

SEA BASS

Fresh and defrosted

Quantity	Cooking time on HIGH in minutes		
	500W	**600W**	700W
1lb	7-9	**5-6**	4-5
8oz	3½-4	**2½-3**	2-2½

Cooking technique Also known as
Black Sea Bass, it is sold as steaks or
fillets. It is tasty cooked on a bed of
chopped tomatos, garlic and herbs, or
oriental style in soy sauce, ginger
and scallions, or topped with butter,
parsely and bread crumbs. Cover.
Rotate dish one-half turn during
cooking. Stand for 3 mins. If using
bread crumbs cover with waxed
paper.

HAKE

Fresh and defrosted

Quantity	Cooking time on HIGH in minutes		
	500W	**600W**	700W
½lb	5-6	**3-4**	2-3

Cooking technique Hake is a member
of the cod family and usually sold as
cutlets. The flesh has little flavor so
is good cooked with lemon, garlic
and herbs. Place in a buttered dish
and cover. Turn during cooking.
Stand for 3 mins.

FLOUNDER

Fresh and defrosted

Quantity	Cooking time on HIGH in minutes		
	500W	**600W**	700W
per 1lb	5-7	**4-6**	3-4

Cooking technique This fish can be
cooked whole or as fillets. Place in a
greased dish with some lemon juice
and butter and cover. Stand for 3
mins. It is delicious served with a
well-flavored sauce such as
béarnaise.

Striped bass

Sea bass

Flounder

Hake

Halibut

Ocean Perch

Sole

HALIBUT

Fresh and defrosted

Quantity	Cooking time on HIGH in minutes		
	500W	**600W**	700W
per 1lb	5-7	**4-6**	3-4

Cooking technique This is a very large flat fish that is divided into steaks. The flesh is firm and white, but can be dry. To keep moist, wrap steaks individually in waxed paper with butter and herbs. Place the packages on a plate to cook. Stand for 3 mins. Top each steak with an extra pat of herb butter to serve.

BLUEFISH

Fresh and defrosted

Quantity	Cooking time on HIGH in minutes		
	500W	**600W**	700W
1lb	7-8	**5½-6**	4-5½
8oz	3½-4	**3-3½**	2½-3

Cooking technique Commonly sold as fillets, Bluefish has an oily dark flesh. Its mild flavor is enhanced by slightly acidic sauces such as lemon, mustard or tomato. Place in dish skin side down. Brush fillets with mixture of mustard with seeds, olive oil, lemon juice, dill, salt and pepper. Cover. Rotate dish one-half turn halfway through cooking. Stand for 3 mins.

OCEAN PERCH

Fresh and defrosted

Quantity	Cooking time on HIGH in minutes		
	500W	**600W**	700W
1lb	10-11	**9-10**	8-9

Cooking technique Ocean perch freezes well for long periods of time. It is the source of much of the frozen fish sold in the US. Fresh perch microwaves best when prepared in a sauce that just about covers the fish during cooking. A white wine sauce flavored with butter, garlic, and lemon juice is excellent. Cover.

CARP

Fresh and defrosted

Quantity	Cooking time on HIGH in minutes		
	500W	**600W**	700W
per 1lb, whole fish	5-7	**4-6**	3-4

Cooking technique Soak fishpond carp in vinegar-water to remove the muddy taste before cooking. Place in a greased dish, dot with butter and cover. Turn after half the cooking time, stand for 5 mins.

SOLE

Fresh and defrosted

Quantity	Cooking time on HIGH in minutes		
	500W	**600W**	700W
½lb	5-6	**3-4**	2-3

Cooking technique Sole fillets can be made into *paupiettes*. Make a moist stuffing from fresh bread crumbs, chopped mushrooms, butter and ground fish. Spread over the skinned side of the fish and roll up. Place in a circle in a greased dish with some white wine. Cover. Stand for 3 mins. Mix the juices with cream to make a delicious sauce.

Bluefish

RED MULLET

Fresh and defrosted

Quantity	Cooking time on HIGH in minutes		
	500W	**600W**	700W
2 × 6oz	7-9	**5-6**	4-5

Cooking technique Red mullet has a firm white flesh. Score and place on a buttered plate and tuck in a few sprigs of dill, cover. Turn over after half the cooking time. Stand for 5 mins.

Red mullet

Trout

STRIPED OR BLACK MULLET

Fresh and defrosted

Quantity	Cooking time on HIGH in minutes		
	500W	**600W**	700W
2 × 2lb	18-19	**16-17**	14-15

Cooking technique This fish is no relation to red mullet, has rather coarse fatty flesh, but is still good to eat. Place in a buttered dish with some white wine, lemon peel and chopped sage and cover. Turn over after half the cooking time. Stand for 5 mins.

TROUT

Fresh and defrosted

Quantity	Cooking time on HIGH in minutes		
	500W	**600W**	700W
2 × ½lb	10-12	**6-8**	5-6
4 × ½lb	11-15	**8-10**	6-7

Cooking technique The most common fish are rainbow trout, but river or brown trout have a superior flavor. Score and place in a buttered dish, add some lemon juice and cover. Turn over after half the cooking time and add ⅓ cup flaked almonds. Stand for 5 mins.

SALMON TROUT

Fresh and defrosted

Quantity	Cooking time on HIGH in minutes		
	500W	**600W**	700W
per 1lb, whole fish	5-7	**4-6**	3-4

Cooking technique A freshwater fish similar to salmon with a delicate flavor. Score and cut large fish in half crossways. Place in a dish with 5 tablespoons each of water and white wine, a few peppercorns and herbs, cover. Stand for 5 mins. Serve hot.

ATLANTIC SALMON

Fresh and defrosted

Quantity	Cooking time on HIGH in minutes		
	500W	**600W**	700W
Fillets:			
1lb	8-9	**6-7**	5-6
8oz	4-4½	**3-3½**	2½-3
Steaks:			
1¼lb	8-9	**6-7**	5-6
10oz	4-5	**3½-4**	3-3½

Cooking technique If the salmon is to be served cold, cook covered, with 1 tablespoon each of lemon juice and water. For a traditional flavor place in dish with melted butter, dill, lemon juice, and grated lemon peel. When cooking steaks, place the narrow ends towards the center of the dish. Rotate dish one-half turn halfway through cooking. Stand for 3 mins.

Salmon trout

Atlantic Salmon

COD

Fresh and defrosted

Quantity	Cooking time on HIGH in minutes		
	500W	**600W**	700W
½ lb	5-6	**3-4**	2-3

Cooking technique Cod has firm white flesh. Cook with a little butter, sliced mushrooms and crushed garlic. Arrange steaks with the thin ends toward the center and overlap thin parts of fillets, cover. Turn over after half the cooking time. Stand for 3 mins.

Cod

Pike

WALLEYED PIKE

Fresh and defrosted

Quantity	Cooking time on HIGH in minutes		
	500W	**600W**	700W
1 ½ lb whole fish, dressed, with 1 ½ cups bread stuffing	12-14	**10-11**	8-9

Cooking technique Pike has a mild sweet meat, a flaky texture and is low in fat. The most popular methods of preparation are curried or stuffed. It is also quite good served with beurre blanc. Cover. Rotate dish one-half turn halfway through cooking. Stand for 5-6 mins.

RED SNAPPER

Fresh and defrosted

Quantity	Cooking time on HIGH in minutes		
	500W	**600W**	700W
Fillets:			
1 lb	7-9	**5-6**	4-5
8 oz	3½-4	**2½-3**	2-2½

Cooking technique Red Snapper is among the most tasty warm water fish. It is usually sold as fillets but it is also delicious prepared whole or stuffed. For fillets, place in dish with melted butter, chopped dill or parsley, lemon juice and paprika, turning to coat each side. Cover. Rotate dish one-half turn during cooking. Stand for 2-3 mins.

SHAD

Fresh and defrosted

Quantity	Cooking time on HIGH in minutes		
	500W	**600W**	700W
1 lb	7-7½	**5-6**	4-5

Cooking technique Shad is a member of the herring family. This oily, bony, rich flavored fish is mouth-watering poached with fresh sorrel or with butter, shallots, and chopped parsley. Place fillets skin side down and sprinkle with butter, shallots and parsley. Cover. Rotate dish one-half turn halfway through cooking. Stand for 2-3 mins.

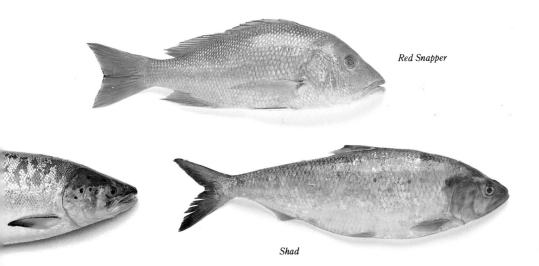

Red Snapper

Shad

Mackerel

MACKEREL

Fresh and defrosted

Quantity	Cooking time on HIGH in minutes		
	500W	**600W**	700W
2 × 1lb	18-19	**16-17**	14-15

Cooking technique This oily fish has rich pink flesh which needs to be cooked very fresh. Place in a greased dish with 2 tablespoons water and cover. Turn over after half the cooking time. Stand for 5 mins. Serve with a tangy tomato sauce.

CATFISH

Fresh and defrosted

Quantity	Cooking time on HIGH in minutes		
	500W	**600W**	700W
1lb	7-7½	**5-6**	4-5
8oz	4-4½	**3-3½**	2-2½

Cooking technique Catfish once a southern speciality is gaining popularity throughout the country. It has a mild tasting fresh water flavor with a firm texture that combines well with many sauces. It also freezes well without a loss of flavor. Place in dish with melted butter turning to coat each side. Sprinkle with commercially prepared Cajun fish spices. Cover.

HADDOCK

Fresh and defrosted

Quantity	Cooking time on HIGH in minutes		
	500W	**600W**	700W
½lb	5-6	**3-4**	2-3

Cooking technique Fillets of fresh haddock are cooked in the same way as cod. Smoked haddock has a lovely pale lemon color and delicate flavor. Place in a dish overlapping thin ends. Add 2-3 tablespoons milk and cover. Allow to stand for 5 mins.

PORGY

Fresh and defrosted

Quantity	Cooking time on HIGH in minutes		
	500W	**600W**	700W
per 1lb, whole fish	5-7	**4-6**	3-4

Cooking technique This is a fine fish that is best baked whole. Score and place in a dish with 5 tablespoons each olive oil and lemon juice, add chopped chives and marinate for half an hour. Cover. Turn after half the cooking time. Stand for 5 mins.

MONKFISH

Fresh and defrosted

Quantity	Cooking time on HIGH in minutes		
	500W	**600W**	700W
½lb	5-6	**3-4**	2-3

Cooking technique A large-headed ugly fish that is usually sold without the head. The tail has white, firm flesh similar to lobster and can be cut into steaks or even-size pieces for kebobs. Arrange on a plate, brush with butter and cover, turn during cooking. Stand for 5 mins.

Catfish

Haddock

Porgy

Shellfish

Large shellfish like crab and lobster must be cooked conventionally, but small shellfish, like mussels, work very well in the microwave. Watch timings carefully as they lose moisture easily.

Shrimp

Crayfish

SCALLOPS

Fresh and defrosted

Quantity	Cooking time on HIGH in minutes		
	500W	600W	700W
12	14-16	12-14	10-12

Cooking technique Scallops are normally sold open and cleaned. Place in a dish with lemon juice and herbs. Cover. Stir during cooking. Blend in (4-6 tablespoons) of cream if desired and stand for 3 mins.

CRAYFISH

Fresh

Quantity	Cooking time on HIGH in minutes		
	500W	600W	700W
per ½lb	1-1½	¾-1	½-¾

Cooking technique Crayfish is a freshwater shellfish. The salt water variety is also known as Dublin Bay prawn or langoustine. They are sold both cooked or raw, with or without heads. To heat up or cook, place in a dish and cover. Allow to stand for 3 mins.

Squid

MUSSELS

Fresh

Quantity	Cooking time on HIGH in minutes		
	500W	600W	700W
1½ lb	5-7	4-6	3-4

Cooking technique Cook mussels live on the day of buying, and wash under cold running water, scraping the shells clean. Pull off beards and discard mussels that are broken or open. Place in a bowl with some white wine. Cover. Stir once. Stand for 3 mins. Discard any closed mussels.

SQUID

Fresh

Quantity	Cooking time on HIGH in minutes		
	500W	600W	700W
1lb	9-11	8-10	6-7

Cooking technique Cleaned, prepared squid are available from supermarkets and fish stores. For microwave cooking, stuff with a mixture of cooked onion, bread crumbs and herbs. Close the ends with wooden cocktail sticks. Place in a dish with 1¼ cups fresh tomato sauce. Cover. Stand for 3 mins.

SHRIMP

Fresh and defrosted

Quantity	Cooking time on HIGH in minutes		
	500W	600W	700W
per 1lb	3-6	2-4	1-3

Cooking technique To heat cooked shrimp in a microwave, put on a plate and cover. Add some garlic butter and herbs before heating, if desired. To cook raw shrimps, place in a bowl and cover. Toss two or three times until they change color. Stand for 3 mins.

BABY SHRIMP

Fresh

Quantity	Cooking time on HIGH in minutes		
	500W	600W	700W
per 1lb	1½-2	1-1½	¾-1

Cooking technique These are often sold pre-cooked, but are available raw or frozen. To cook them, place in a dish and cover. Stand for 3 mins.

CLAMS

Fresh

Quantity	Cooking time on HIGH in minutes		
	500W	600W	700W
1½lb	5-7	4-6	3-4

Cooking technique Large clams are ideal for chowder, but can be cooked as mussels. Wash under cold water and place in a large bowl. Cover. Stir often during cooking. Stand for 3 mins. Remove top shell, serve with garlic butter.

Beef

Microwaved beef, when properly cooked, is tender and moist. Turn large pieces once, for even cooking. Test with a meat thermometer: 120°F for rare, 135°F for medium and 150°F for well done.

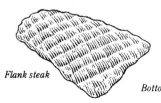

Flank steak

Bottom-round roast

Boneless rib roast

FLANK STEAK

Fresh and defrosted

Quantity	Cooking time on HIGH and LOW in minutes		
	500W	**600W**	700W
1½lb	75-80	**60-65**	50-55

Cooking technique Place meat in baking dish with ¼ cup soy sauce ¼ cup orange juice, 2 tablespoons sherry, 1 small sliced onion, 2 minced garlic cloves and ½ teaspoon peppercorns. Refrigerate 6-12 hours. Drain off marinade. Cover and cook on HIGH for 6-8 mins. then LOW, turning over once. Cut across grain into thin slices.

BOTTOM-ROUND ROAST

Fresh and defrosted

Quantity	Cooking time on HIGH and MEDIUM in minutes		
	500W	**600W**	700W
1lb	40-45	**35-40**	30-35

Cooking technique Pot-roast or slice and braise by placing in a baking dish with ⅔ cup beef broth, 1 tablespoon gravy granules, ⅔ cup sliced celery and 1 sliced onion. Cover and cook on HIGH for first 6-8 mins, then MEDIUM. Stir during cooking. Stand for 10 mins.

BONELESS RIB ROAST

Fresh and defrosted

Quantity	Cooking time on HIGH in minutes		
	500W	**600W**	700W
per 1lb, boned and rolled			
rare	9-11	**5-6**	5-5½
medium	11-12	**7-8**	6-6½
well done	14-15	**8-10**	7-8

Cooking technique Place fat side down on a roasting rack and baking dish and cook on HIGH. Drain off any liquid halfway through the cooking time. Cover and stand for 15 mins.

Sirloin steak

Porterhouse steak

Top round roast

SIRLOIN STEAK

Fresh and defrosted

Quantity	Cooking time on HIGH in minutes		
	500W	**600W**	700W
2 × 1lb			
rare	4	**2½-3**	2-2½
med-rare	5-5½	**3½-4**	2½-3
medium	6½	**5**	3½
well done	8-9	**7-7½**	4½-5

Cooking technique Cook as porterhouse steak. For a creamy pepper sauce, put 3 tablespoons sour cream, 1 tablespoon brandy, 1 teaspoon black pepper in a bowl with juices from steaks. Cook on HIGH for 1-1½ mins. Pour over steaks.

PORTERHOUSE STEAK

Fresh and defrosted

Quantity	Cooking time on HIGH in minutes		
	500W	**600W**	700W
4 × ½lb			
rare	4	**3**	2-2½
medium	6½	**5**	3½
well done	8-9	**6½-7**	4½-5

Cooking technique Also known as entrecote steak. Heat a browning dish on HIGH for 5 mins. Add 2 teaspoons oil, then the steaks, and press down well. Turn over after a third of cooking time. Cover and stand for 4 mins.

TOP ROUND ROAST

Fresh and defrosted

Quantity	Cooking time on HIGH and MEDIUM in minutes		
	500W	**600W**	700W
3lb	55-60	**50-55**	45-50

Cooking technique Place meat in a large bowl. Add ½ cup water, 3 tablespoons tomato paste, a bouquet garni and 1 tablespoon boullion powder. Cover and cook on HIGH for 6-8 mins. then MEDIUM. Stir sauce during cooking. Stand for 20 mins.

Tenderloin steaks   *Rib-eye roast*

TENDERLOIN STEAKS (FILET MIGNON)

Fresh and defrostded

Quantity	Cooking time on HIGH in minutes		
	500W	**600W**	700W
4 × 6oz			
rare	3½-4	**2½-3**	2-2½
med-rare	5-5½	**3½-4**	2½-3
medium	6-6½	**4-5**	3½
well done	8-9	**6½-7**	4½-5

Cooking technique Place on a greased baking dish, sprinkle with browning agent and cook on HIGH. Turn over and pour off any juices halfway through cooking time. Cover and stand for 3 mins.

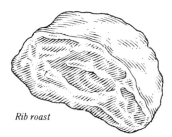

Rib roast

RIB ROAST

Fresh and defrosted

Quantity	Cooking time on HIGH and MEDIUM in minutes		
	500W	**600W**	700W
per 1lb			
rare	10	**7**	4-5
medium	11	**8**	5-5½
well done	12	**9**	6

Cooking technique Shield the bone ends with foil. Place fat side down on a roasting rack and dish to cook on HIGH for first 6-8 mins. then MEDIUM. Remove foil, turn over and drain off any liquid halfway through the cooking time. Cover and stand for 15 mins.

RIB-EYE ROAST

Fresh and defrosted

Quantity	Cooking time on HIGH and MEDIUM in minutes		
	500W	**600W**	700W
per 1lb, boned and rolled			
rare	13-16	**10-13**	7-10
medium	16-18	**12-14**	9-11
well done	19-22	**15-18**	10-12

Cooking technique Place fat side down on a roasting rack and baking dish and cook on HIGH for first 6-8 mins. then MEDIUM. Turn over, drain off cooking juices halfway through cooking time. Cover and stand for 15 mins.

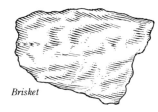

Brisket

BRISKET

Fresh and defrosted

Quantity	Cooking time on HIGH and MEDIUM in minutes		
	500W	**600W**	700W
3lb	55-60	**50-55**	45-50

Cooking technique Place brisket in a large dish with a sliced onion and celery stalk, a bouquet garni, ⅔ cup wine, and pepper. Marinate overnight. Cover and cook on HIGH for first 6-8 mins. then MEDIUM. Stand for 20 mins. If salted, soak overnight in cold water, then drain and cook covered with 2½ cups boiling water on MEDIUM for 25-35 mins. Drain, add 2½ cups boiling water, cover and cook for the remaining time. Stand for 15 mins.

HAMBURGERS

Fresh and defrosted

Quantity	Cooking time on HIGH in minutes		
	500W	**600W**	700W
¼lb	5½-6	**4**	3
½lb	9	**6**	5
1lb	15	**10**	8

Cooking technique Times refer to 2-oz or 4-oz hamburgers. Arrange on a greased baking dish and cook on HIGH. Halfway through the cooking time, turn over, rearrange and drain off accumulated cooking juices.

GROUND BEEF

Fresh and defrosted

Quantity	Cooking time on HIGH in minutes		
	500W	**600W**	700W
½lb	9-10	**6**	3
1lb	12-13	**9**	7

Cooking technique Put in a bowl and cook on HIGH. Stir two or three times during cooking time. Add any sauce ingredients, vegetables and herbs after half the cooking time. Cook for an extra 5 mins. or until the vegetables are tender.

Chuck steak

CHUCK STEAK

Fresh and defrosted

Quantity	Cooking time on HIGH in minutes		
	500W	**600W**	700W
1lb	60-65	**55-60**	50-55

Cooking technique To make a stew, cube and place in a bowl with sliced onions. Cover and cook on HIGH for 5 mins. Stir in 2 tablespoons flour, 1¼ cups boiling broth and herbs. Cover, cook on HIGH for 5 mins. then MEDIUM. Stir during cooking. Stand for 10 mins.

Pork

Pork is a meat that must be well cooked and not be pink in the center. Use a meat thermometer to make sure pork is cooked before leaving to stand – it should read 165°F rising to 170°F on standing.

Center-loin roast

Loin chops

Spareribs

CENTER-LOIN ROAST

Fresh and defrosted

Quantity	Cooking time on HIGH in minutes		
	500W	**600W**	700W
per 1lb			
bone-in	12-14	**10-12**	8-9
boned and rolled			
	14-15	**11-13**	9-10

Cooking technique Score the shin and rub in some salt to improve the flavor. Place on a roasting rack and dish, fat side down. Turn over halfway through cooking time. Cover and stand for 15-20 mins.

LOIN CHOPS

Fresh and defrosted

Quantity	Cooking time on HIGH in minutes		
	500W	**600W**	700W
2 × 6oz	5-6	**4-5**	3-4

Cooking technique Usually cut about ½-inch thick. Arrange on a baking dish with narrow ends toward the center. Turn over after half the cooking time. To add extra flavor, split the meaty part to make a pocket and fill with a moist mixture of chopped mushrooms and herbs; cook for 1-2 mins. longer. Cover and stand for 5 mins.

SPARERIBS

Fresh and defrosted

Quantity	Cooking time on HIGH and MEDIUM in minutes		
	500W	**600W**	700W
per 1lb	11-13	**10-11**	8-10

Cooking technique Cut into single rib pieces and place in a baking dish, add 6 tablespoons water. Cover and cook on HIGH, for first 5 mins., then MEDIUM. Halfway through, drain the ribs of fat, turn them over and brush with barbecue or sweet-and-sour-sauce. Stand for 5 mins.

Blade end roast

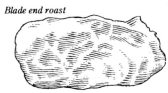

Blade chop

Boston shoulder

BLADE END ROAST

Fresh and defrosted

Quantity	Cooking time on HIGH and MEDIUM in minutes		
	500W	**600W**	700W
per 1lb	18-22	**15-17**	12-14

Cooking technique To braise, place in a dish with 8 tablespoons dry white wine and herbs. Cover and cook on HIGH for first 6-8 mins., then MEDIUM. Halfway through cooking turn meat over and add 2 sliced cooking apples for flavor. Stand for 20 mins.

BLADE CHOPS

Fresh and defrosted

Quantity	Cooking time on HIGH in minutes		
	500W	**600W**	700W
2 × 8oz	13-15	**9-11**	6-8

Cooking technique Usually about ¾-inch thick, these chops are less meaty than loin chops, but have a sweeter taste. Arrange in a baking dish with the thin parts toward the center. Turn after half the cooking time. Cover and stand for 5 mins.

BOSTON SHOULDER

Fresh and defrosted

Quantity	Cooking time on HIGH in minutes		
	500W	**600W**	700W
2lb			
bone-in	24-30	**20-24**	16-17
boned and stuffed			
	33-35	**26-28**	19-21

Cooking technique This may be cooked on the bone or boned, stuffed and rolled. Score the peel and rub in some salt and crushed garlic for flavor. Place fat side down on a roasting rack and baking dish. Turn after half the cooking time. Cover and stand for 15 mins.

Tenderloin

TENDERLOIN

Fresh and defrosted

Quantity	Cooking time on HIGH and MEDIUM in minutes		
	500W	**600W**	700W
per 1lb	20-25	**17-21**	14-18

Cooking technique Cut a pocket the length of the fillet and add herbs or a more substantial filling. Tie with string and shield thin ends with foil. Place on a roasting rack and dish, cook on HIGH for first 3-5 mins. then MEDIUM. Remove foil and turn over after half the cooking time. Cover and stand for 10 mins.

Leg

LEG

Fresh and defrosted

Quantity	Cooking time on HIGH in minutes		
	500W	**600W**	700W
per 1lb			
bone-in	12-14	**10-12**	8-9
boned	14-15	**11-13**	9-10

Cooking technique Rub some salt into the skin to improve flavor. Place on a roasting rack the baking dish fat side down, and shield bone ends with foil. Turn over halfway through cooking time. Cover and stand for 15-20 mins.

Slab bacon

SLAB BACON

Fresh and defrosted

Quantity	Cooking time on HIGH in minutes		
	500W	**600W**	700W
2 × 3oz	6-8	**4-5**	3-4
4 slices	3	**3**	2

Cooking technique Snip fat at ¾-inch intervals. Place on a roasting rack and baking dish with narrow ends toward the center and cover with a paper towel. Turn over after half the cooking time. Remove paper to stop it sticking. Cover and stand for 2-3 mins. Cook slices in the same way but do not stand.

SAUSAGES

Fresh and defrosted

Quantity	Cooking time on HIGH in minutes		
	500W	**600W**	700W
½lb	8	**6**	4
1lb	12	**8**	6

Cooking technique Arrange in a dish. Brush with a browning agent, if preferred. Cover and turn and rearrange two or three times during cooking time. Allow to stand for 3 mins.

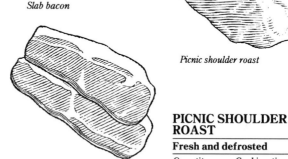

Picnic shoulder roast

PICNIC SHOULDER ROAST

Fresh and defrosted

Quantity	Cooking time on HIGH in minutes		
	500W	**600W**	700W
per 1lb			
boned and stuffed	14-15	**11-13**	9-10

Cooking technique A large economical piece if bought whole. Cut off the hock to make soup or broth. The lower part of the shoulder is delicious boned, stuffed and rolled. Cut off two or three steaks from the thin end and cook as for loin chops. To roast the rest of the meat, follow the cooking technique for loin. Cover and stand for 15 mins.

HAM

Fresh and defrosted

Quantity	Cooking time on HIGH in minutes		
	500W	**600W**	700W
per 1lb	15-20	**11-13**	9-10

Cooking technique Unsmoked roasts microwave best as smoked tends to shrink and dry up. Soak overnight in cold water to remove excess salt. Drain, dry and place fat side down on a roasting rack and baking dish. Turn over after half the cooking time. To glaze score then brush with honey and brown under a hot broiler. Cover and stand for 15 mins.

Lamb

Prime cuts from the loin, legs and shoulder can be microwave roasted, or the meat can be cubed for kebobs and casseroles. Cheaper cuts like neck need longer cooking, but are just as tasty.

Rib chops

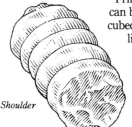

Shoulder

Shoulder-blade chops

SHOULDER

Fresh and defrosted

Quantity	Cooking time on HIGH in minutes		
	500W	**600W**	700W
per 1lb, boned and rolled			
med-rare	14	**10**	8
well done	16-17	**12**	9
1lb cubed	55-60	**35-40**	30-35

Cooking technique Place on a roasting rack and dish, stick slivers of garlic and fresh rosemary leaves into the fat for flavor. Turn after half the cooking time. Cover and stand for 15 mins. Cook a whole shoulder as for leg of lamb. This meat can also be diced and used in a casserole dish.

SHOULDER-BLADE CHOPS

Fresh and defrosted

Quantity	Cooking time on HIGH and LOW in minutes		
	500W	**600W**	700W
1½lb	78-82	**70**	55-60

Cooking technique These bony, fatty cuts, are best cut up and stewed. Layer in a greased casserole with 1-lb thickly sliced potatoes, a sliced onion, 1½ cups mushrooms and herbs. Add a 15-oz can crushed tomatoes and cover. Cook on HIGH, then LOW until tender. Stand for 10 mins.

RIB CHOPS

Fresh and defrosted

Quantity	Cooking time on HIGH in minutes		
	500W	**600W**	700W
4 × 2-3oz			
med-rare	7	**5**	4
well done	8	**6**	5

Cooking technique These small chops are cut from the rib roast. To cook, heat a browning dish for 5 mins. Add 2 teaspoons oil and place the chops in the dish with the bony ends toward the center; press down to seal. Turn over after a third of the cooking time. Cover and stand for 3 mins.

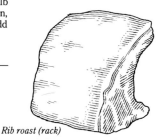

Rib roast (rack)

Riblets

RIBLETS

Fresh and defrosted

Quantity	Cooking time on HIGH and MEDIUM in minutes		
	500W	**600W**	700W
2lb	35-40	**30-35**	25-30

Cooking technique Braise these strips of breast meat on the bone to make them tender. Place in a dish, add 1 sliced onion, 1 cup broth and 1 tablespoon Worcestershire sauce. Cover and cook on HIGH for first 5-7 mins. then MEDIUM. Stand for 10 mins.

Loin chops

LOIN CHOPS

Fresh and defrosted

Quantity	Cooking time on HIGH in minutes		
	500W	**600W**	700W
per 1lb			
med-rare	10	**7**	5
well done	13	**10**	7

Cooking technique Place the chops in a single layer in a shallow baking dish with the narrow ends toward the center. Turn over and rearrange after half the cooking time. To cook in a preheated browning dish (see sirloin chops), reduce cooking time by about 1 min. Cover and stand for 5 mins.

RIB ROAST (RACK)

Fresh and defrosted

Quantity	Cooking time on HIGH in minutes		
	500W	**600W**	700W
per 1lb			
med-rare	12	**7½**	6-6½
well done	14-15	**9-10**	7½

Cooking technique This joint has 6 or 7 chops, cook two together to form a rack of lamb to serve 6 people. Cut away top 1½ inches of fat and meat from the rib bones. Interlock the rib bones of the two racks and tie with string. Rub with garlic and herbs to flavor. Cook on a roasting rack and dish. Cover and stand for 10-15 mins.

Boneless loin chops

Breast

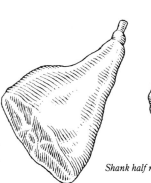

Shank half roast

BONELESS LOIN CHOPS

Fresh and defrosted

Quantity	Cooking time on HIGH in minutes		
	500W	**600W**	700W
8 × 2-3oz			
med-rare	7	**6**	5
well done	9-9½	**8**	6½-7

Cooking technique Small, round, thick slices cut from the loin or best end cook quickly and evenly by microwave. Heat a browning dish for 5 mins. Add 2 teaspoons oil. Arrange in a circle in the dish and press down. Turn and rearrange after a third of the cooking time. Cover and stand for 3 mins.

SHANK HALF ROAST

Fresh and defrosted

Quantity	Cooking time on HIGH in minutes		
	500W	**600W**	700W
per 1lb, bone-in			
med-rare	12-13	**9**	8
well done	15	**10**	7
1lb kebobs	10-13	**7-10**	5-7

Cooking technique Wrap the shanks narrow end with smooth foil and place on a roasting rack and dish. Remove foil and turn over after half the cooking time. Cover and stand for 15 mins. For boned and rolled pieces follow shoulder of lamb timings. This lean cut can also be cubed and used for kebobs.

BREAST

Fresh and defrosted

Quantity	Cooking time on MEDIUM in minutes		
	500W	**600W**	700W
1¾lb, boned and stuffed			
	45-50	**40**	30-35

Cooking technique Breast is a fatty cut, best boned, stuffed and slow roasted. A 1¾-lb breast needs about ¾lb savory stuffing. Spread over the lamb, fold in half crosswise and tie securely with string. Place in a dish with ½ cup meat broth. Turn over after half the cooking time. Cover and stand for 15 mins.

Loin roast

Sirloin chops

Neck

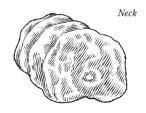

LOIN ROAST

Fresh and defrosted

Quantity	Cooking time on HIGH in minutes		
	500W	**600W**	700W
per 1lb, bone-in			
med-rare	12-13	**9**	8
well done	15	**10**	7
per lb, boned and rolled			
med-rare	14	**10**	8
well done	16-17	**12**	9

Cooking technique Loin roast is sold as a special cut, but can also be rolled around a homemade stuffing. Place on a roasting rack and dish, fat side down. Turn after half the cooking time. Cover and stand for 15 mins.

SIRLOIN CHOPS

Fresh and defrosted

Quantity	Cooking time on HIGH in minutes		
	500W	**600W**	700W
per 1lb			
med-rare	9-10	**6-7**	4-5
well done	12-13	**9-10**	6-7

Cooking technique These meaty chops are cut from between the leg and loin. Heat a browning dish for 5 mins., add 2 teaspoons oil, and press the chops down into the oil. Turn over and rearrange after half the cooking time. Cover and stand for 5 mins.

NECK

Fresh and defrosted

Quantity	Cooking time on HIGH and LOW in minutes		
	500W	**600W**	700W
1½lb	80-85	**70-75**	60-65

Cooking technique This bony cut is ideal for Irish stew. Layer slices of the meat in a dish with 3 sliced potatoes and 2 large sliced onions, topping with a potato layer. Add 1 cup water and cover. Cook on HIGH for first 5 mins. then LOW. Stand for 10 mins. Brown topping conventionally under a hot broiler.

Poultry and game

Poultry and game cook quickly and keep
moist in the microwave. Cook whole birds on
a roasting rack and small ones in a roasting
bag to promote browning. Cover wing tips
and breastbones with foil.

POULTRY

Fresh and defrosted

Quantity	Cooking time on HIGH in minutes		
	500W	**600W**	700W
rock Cornish game hen (1lb)			
	10-12	**8-10**	6-7
Broiler/fryer chicken			
3lb	26-28	**18-20**	14-16
capon			
6-8lb	60-75	**40-55**	30-40

Cooking technique Different sizes of
chickens are available, but they are
all cooked in the same way. Place
breast side down on a roasting rack
inside a pierced roasting bag. Turn
over after half the cooking time. Cook
a capon as the instructions for
turkey. Cover and stand for 10-15
mins.

*Rock Cornish
game hen*

1lb

Chicken

3-4 lbs

Duck

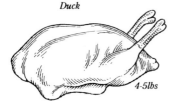

4-5lbs

CHICKEN PIECES

Fresh and defrosted

Quantity	Cooking time on HIGH in minutes		
	500W	**600W**	700W
2 × 2-3oz	5	**4**	3
2 × 8oz	12	**8**	6

Cooking technique Arrange portions
on a dish in a single layer with
thinner ends toward the center.
Brush with soy or barbecue sauce for
flavor. Rearrange and turn over after
half the cooking time. Cover and
stand for 5 mins.

BONELESS CHICKEN PIECES

Fresh and defrosted

Quantity	Cooking time on HIGH in minutes		
	500W	**600W**	700W
2 × 3-4oz	8	**5**	4

Cooking technique Skin breasts and
thighs, if necessary, and brush with
herb-and-garlic butter, if preferred.
Place in a dish and cover. Turn over
and rearrange halfway through
cooking time. Stand for 5 mins.

DUCK

Fresh and defrosted

Quantity	Cooking time on HIGH in minutes		
	500W	**600W**	700W
4lb	38-40	**26-30**	20-24

Cooking technique Prick duck all
over and rub skin with some salt to
improve the flavor. Place breast side
down on a roasting rack over a deep
dish. Drain off juices and turn duck
over after half the cooking time.
Cover and stand for 15 mins.

HARE PIECES

Fresh and defrosted

Quantity	Cooking time on MEDIUM in minutes		
	500W	**600W**	700W
per 1lb	20-24	**14-18**	11-14

Cooking technique Trim off fat and
place in a dish with 1½ cups sliced
vegetables, chopped herbs, 15-oz can
chopped tomatoes and ⅔ cup broth
and cover. Turn over, rearrange the
portions and stir after half the
cooking time. Stand for 5 mins.

RABBIT PIECES

Fresh and defrosted

Quantity	Cooking time on HIGH and MEDIUM in minutes		
	500W	**600W**	700W
1¼lb	25-29	**19-23**	16-19

Cooking technique Trim joints and
place in dish. In another dish, cook 2
cups sliced carrots, 1 chopped onion
in some oil on HIGH for 5 mins. Stir
in 2 teaspoons grated orange peel, 2
tablespoons flour and 1¼ cups hot
broth. Add to rabbit pieces, cover
and cook on MEDIUM for remaining
time. Stir once and stand for 5 mins.

Rabbit pieces

TURKEY

Fresh and defrosted

Quantity	Cooking time on HIGH in minutes		
	500W	600W	700W
6-8lb	60-75	40-55	30-40

Cooking technique Place on one side of the breast on a roasting rack and dish. Turn onto the other breast after a third of the cooking time and right over for final third. Shield any parts that are over-cooking with pieces of foil. Cover and stand for 20 mins.

TURKEY PIECES

Fresh and defrosted

Quantity	Cooking time on HIGH in minutes		
	500W	600W	700W
1lb	10-12	8-10	6-7
2lb	16-20	13-15	9-12

Cooking technique Place turkey pieces on a roasting rack and dish, meaty side down. Wrap bony parts with foil. Remove the foil and turn after half the cooking time. Cover and stand for 10 mins. Cook 4 duck quarters in the same way as 2lb of turkey pieces.

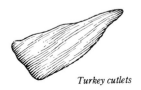

Turkey cutlets

TURKEY CUTLETS

Fresh and defrosted

Quantity	Cooking time on HIGH in minutes		
	500W	600W	700W
4 × 3oz	12	9	7

Cooking technique Cook these thin breast slices in a browning dish, preheated for 5 mins. Coat in egg and bread crumbs, if you like. Add 1 tablespoon oil to the hot dish, then the escalopes and press down. Turn after a third of cooking time. Cover and stand for 3 mins.

Saddle of venison

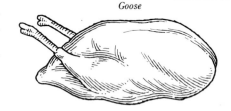

Goose

6-8lbs

GOOSE

Fresh and defrosted

Quantity	Cooking time on HIGH in minutes		
	500W	600W	700W
6-8lb	60-75	40-55	30-40

Cooking technique Goose has a slightly gamy flavor. It is very fatty so prick the skin before cooking. Place breast down on a roasting rack over a deep dish. Drain off juices and turn over after half the cooking time. Cover and stand for 20 mins.

GUINEA HENS

Fresh and defrosted

Quantity	Cooking time on HIGH in minutes		
	500W	600W	700W
per 1lb	12-15	8-10	6-8

Cooking technique Place breast down on a roasting rack and dish inside a pierced roasting bag. Turn over after half the cooking time. Cover and stand for 10 mins.

VENISON

Fresh and defrosted

Quantity	Cooking time on HIGH in minutes		
	500W	600W	700W
per 1lb	9-11	14-16	11-14

Cooking technique Marinate overnight in a bowl with ⅔ cup red wine, 1 sliced onion, 1 sliced carrot and herbs. Drain before cooking and place on a roasting rack and dish in a pierced roasting bag. Turn over after half the cooking time. Stand for 15 mins.

PHEASANT

Fresh and defrosted

Quantity	Cooking time on HIGH in minutes		
	500W	600W	700W
1 × 2lb	30	20	15

Cooking technique Pheasants dry out easily so cover the breasts with bacon. Place breast down on a roasting rack and dish in a pierced roasting bag. Turn over halfway through cooking time. Protect any parts that overcook with small pieces of foil. Cover and stand for 5 mins.

Pheasant

2½-3lbs

Guinea hen

2-2¼lbs

Variety Meats

Variety meats have always been much maligned but with careful cooking they can be tender and tasty as well as nutritious. The finer types of liver and kidneys especially will toughen if they are overcooked.

LIVER

Fresh and defrosted

Quantity	Cooking time on HIGH in minutes		
	500W	**600W**	700W
½lb	6-7	**4-5**	3-4
1lb	10-11	**7-8**	5-6

Cooking technique Peel skin and cut out any tough membranes. Soak pork and beef livers in milk for some hours to mellow. Cook pork and beef livers whole but slice calf's and lamb's liver. Cook in a browning dish preheated for 5 mins., add a little oil and press liver down. Turn after a third of the cooking time. Do not overcook, the liver should be slightly pink inside. Cover and stand for 3 mins. Cook pork and beef livers further in a broth for 25-30 mins. or until tender. Stand for 5 mins.

Calf kidney

Beef kidney

Lamb kidney

Pork kidney

Calf liver

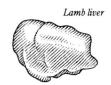
Lamb liver

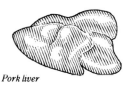
Pork liver

KIDNEYS

Fresh and defrosted

Quantity	Cooking time on HIGH in minutes		
	500W	**600W**	700W
½lb	9-10	**7-8**	5-6
1lb	13-14	**11-12**	8-9

Cooking technique Pork and beef kidneys are only used in slow cooked casseroles. For lamb's and pig's kidneys, remove outer membrane, halve lamb's kidneys and chop pig's kidneys and snip out the white cores. Cook in a browning dish preheated for 5 mins., add 1 tablespoon oil and press down. Stir once. To "devil" them, add some mustard, Worcestershire sauce and dry sherry after half the cooking time. Cover and stand for 3 mins.

HEARTS

Fresh and defrosted

Quantity	Cooking time on MEDIUM in minutes		
	500W	**600W**	700W
1lb	55-60	**45-50**	40-45

Cooking technique Beef and pork hearts are very tough and are best chopped and used in stews. Lamb's and calf's can be stuffed with an onion and sage mixture and braised. Allow 1 heart per person, snip out arteries and tendons before stuffing, and fasten with a wooden tooth pick. Place in a dish, add broth, chopped vegetables and cover. Turn and stir halfway through cooking time. Stand for 10 mins.

Beef heart

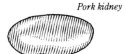
Pork heart *Lamb heart*

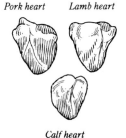
Calf heart

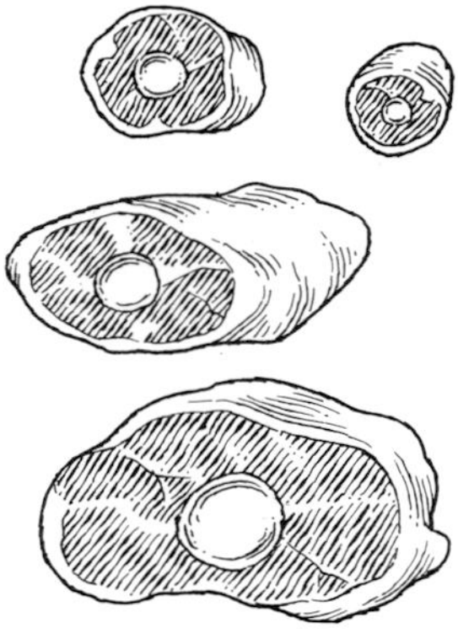

Oxtail

BRAINS

Fresh and defrosted

Quantity	*Cooking time on HIGH and MEDIUM in minutes*		
	500W	**600W**	700W
1lb	25	**22**	19

Cooking technique Brains are always sold in sets. Calf's have a more delicate flavor than lamb's. Place in a bowl and cover with broth. Cook on HIGH for 6-8 mins. then MEDIUM for 10-12 mins. Drain and slice, coat with egg and bread crumbs and cook on HIGH in a browning dish preheated for 5 mins., add 2 tablespoons butter, press down and cook for 3-5 mins. stirring once. Serve at once.

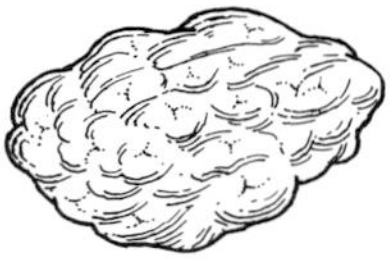

Calf brain

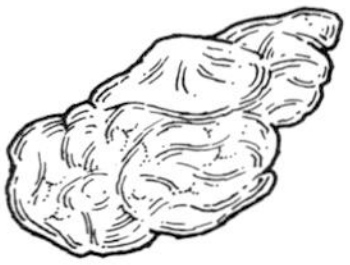

Lamb brain

OXTAIL

Fresh and defrosted

Quantity	*Cooking time on HIGH and MEDIUM in minutes*		
	500W	**600W**	700W
2lb	80-85	**70-75**	60-65

Cooking technique Oxtail is sold skinned and chopped into 2-inch pieces for stewing. Cook in browning dish preheated for 5 mins., add some oil, press down and cook for 6-8 mins. turning once. Add 2 sliced onions, 2 cups sliced carrots, 2 sliced celery stalks, 2 tablespoons flour and 1¼ cups hot broth. Cover and cook on HIGH for first 6-8 mins. then MEDIUM. Stir during cooking. Stand for 10 mins.

TONGUE

Fresh and defrosted

Quantity	*Cooking time on HIGH and MEDIUM in minutes*		
	500W	**600W**	700W
2¼lb	80-85	**70-75**	60-65

Cooking technique Fresh (not corned) tongues need slow cooking. Trim bones and gristle, then place in a large bowl with 1¼ cups boiling water, ½ teaspoon salt, some peppercorns and an onion. Cover and cook on HIGH until boiling, then MEDIUM. Remove skin when cool, slice and serve with parsley sauce.

Calf sweetbreads

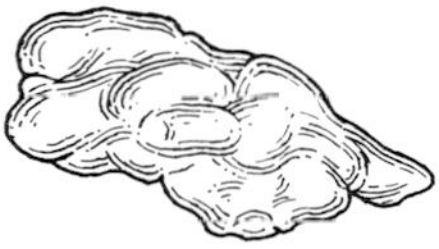

Lamb sweetbreads

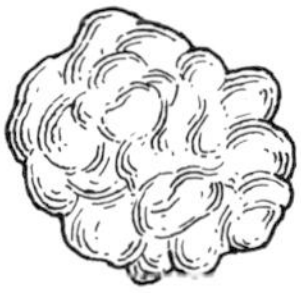

SWEETBREADS

Fresh and defrosted

Quantity	*Cooking time on HIGH and MEDIUM in minutes*		
	500W	**600W**	700W
1lb	17-20	**14-17**	11-14

Cooking technique Calf's and lamb's sweetbreads have a subtle flavor. Soak in a dish of cold water for a few hours to remove blood. Drain, cover with cold water and cook on HIGH until boiling. Drain, remove black veins and membrane. Add ⅔ cup broth and some butter. Cover and cook on HIGH for first 3-5 mins. then MEDIUM. Serve with a creamy sauce. Stand for 3 mins.

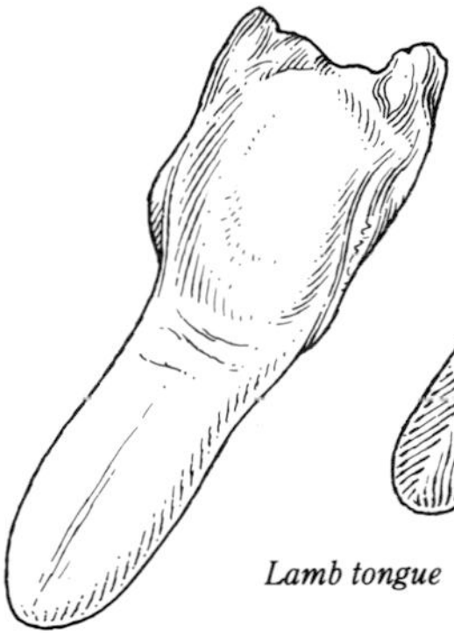

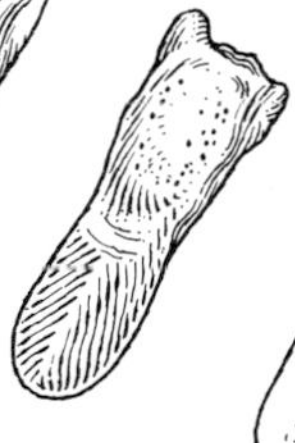

Lamb tongue

Beef tongue

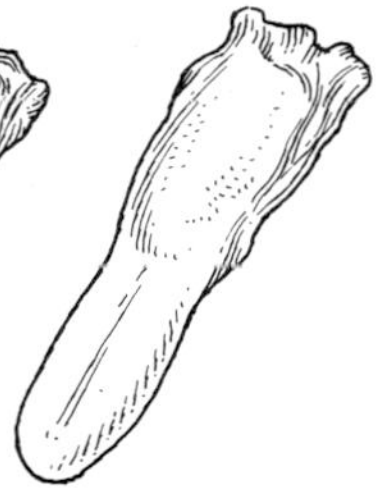

Pork tongue

Veal

Loin roast

Veal has a delicate flavor, but can dry out. Marinating large roasts then cooking them in a roasting bag, helps to keep the meat moist. Don't overcook chops and cutlets, let them finish cooking in the standing time.

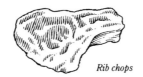

Rib chops

Shank

LOIN ROAST

Fresh and defrosted

Quantity	Cooking time on HIGH in minutes		
	500W	**600W**	700W
per 1lb, bone-in	12-14	**10-12**	8-9
per 1lb, boned and rolled	12-15	**10-13**	8-10

Cooking technique Marinate overnight in oil, wine, lemon peel and tarragon to flavor and tenderize. Drain and place on a roasting rack and baking dish, fat side down, inside a pierced roasting bag. Turn over after half the cooking time. Stand for 5 mins. Boneless shoulder roast can be cooked in the same way as boneless loin roast.

RIB CHOPS

Fresh and defrosted

Quantity	Cooking time on HIGH in minutes		
	500W	**600W**	700W
4 × 6oz	13-15	**12-13**	9-11

Cooking technique These chops contain rib-eye but not the tenderloin. Place with 2 teaspoons oil, narrow ends toward the center, in a browning dish preheated for 5 mins. Turn over after a third of the cooking time. Cover and stand for 5 mins.

SHANK

Fresh and defrosted

Quantity	Cooking time on HIGH and MEDIUM in minutes		
	500W	**600W**	700W
2½lb	38-40	**33-36**	28-30

Cooking technique This cut is ideal for Osso bucco. Place 1 tablespoon oil in a large dish with 1 sliced onion, 1 chopped carrot and some sliced celery stalks. Cover and cook for 3-5 mins., then stir in 2 tablespoons flour, add the veal and cover. Cook on HIGH, for first 10 mins., then MEDIUM. Stand for 10 mins.

Escalopes

Veal for stew

LOIN CHOPS

Fresh and defrosted

Quantity	Cooking time on HIGH in minutes		
	500W	**600W**	700W
2 × 8oz	10-13	**7-10**	5-7

Cooking technique Heat a browning dish for 5 mins. and add 2 teaspoons oil. Put in chops with the narrow ends toward the center and press down. Turn over after a third of the cooking time. Cover and stand for 5 mins.

Loin chops illustration

ESCALOPES (CUTLETS)

Fresh and defrosted

Quantity	Cooking time on HIGH and MEDIUM in minutes		
	500W	**600W**	700W
2 × 4oz	7	**6**	5

Cooking technique Beat out these veal slices thinly and coat with flour. Heat a browning dish for 5 mins., add 2 teaspoons oil and 1 tablespoon butter or margarine. Add the escalopes, press down and cook on HIGH for 1 minute both sides then MEDIUM. Cover and stand for 2 mins.

VEAL FOR STEW

Fresh and defrosted

Quantity	Cooking time on HIGH and MEDIUM in minutes		
	500W	**600W**	700W
1lb	50-55	**45-50**	40-45

Cooking technique Use for slow cooked stews. For a blanquette of veal, cook 1 sliced onion and garlic clove in some oil for 3-5 mins. in a dish. Add the veal, 2½ cups white sauce and 1½ cups chopped mushrooms. Cover, cook on HIGH for first 8-10 mins., then on MEDIUM. Stir during cooking. Stand for 5 mins.

RECIPES

The delight of using a microwave is that it will cook more quickly and efficiently many of the foods that you cook conventionally. Where foods do not brown very well, as with roasts of meat or poultry, a microwave browning dish can be used which will finish the dish off perfectly giving the desired golden-brown effect.

A wide variety of recipes has been included in this section so that you have a good selection to choose from when cooking for friends and family. If you are having a dinner party you can plan your menu from the range of soups and appetizers, main courses, vegetable accompaniments and desserts. If a vegetarian friend is coming to dinner, don't worry, as there are several vegetarian main courses to choose from. Appetizing sauce and preserve recipes are included to add that extra spice and flavor to the main dishes. Snacks are also featured, with several delicious cake and cookie recipes, plus some tasty and easy to make bread recipes.

All the recipes have been tested in 500W, 600W and 700W ovens so that you can see at a glance the correct cooking times for your own microwave. Adapt a recipe, where necessary, by increasing or decreasing the cooking time if you find that the food is not finished to your liking.

Recipe guidelines

Each recipe is supplied with a range of symbols so that you can see how much time you should allow for preparation and cooking, how many servings it will make, whether you can reheat it or freeze it, and whether you should make it in advance.

KEY TO THE SYMBOLS

⭐ The time allowed for preparing the ingredients: measuring, scrubbing, chopping, mixing, blending.

〰 The total cooking time required in a 600-650W microwave oven.

⊘ The power settings used.

〰 This dish reheats well.

❄ This dish freezes well.

▤ This dish should be made in advance to allow for chilling times or for the various flavors to blend.

◎ The approximate number of servings. These will depend upon size of appetite and whether the dish is being served as an appetizer, a side dish or a main course.

POINTS TO REMEMBER

● The times in the recipes are for the quantities of food stated. If you alter the amounts, you'll need to adjust the timing accordingly. As a rule, extend the cooking time by a third to a half again when doubling the amount, and reduce by the same amount when cooking less.

● Follow the recipe instructions for covering, piercing, stirring and rearranging. Never cover dishes so they are airtight.

● Follow any recipe instructions on the size and type of container. Use smaller ones when reducing amounts.

● Always leave the food to stand for the time specified as this is an essential part of the cooking process.

● Flour is assumed to be all-purpose.
● Let microwave-safe cookware stand on heat-safe surfaces.

● Use pot holders when removing containers from the microwave.

COMPARISON OF POWER OUTPUTS USED IN RECIPES

The wattage of your microwave oven determines how long different foods take to cook. All the recipes in this book give times for 600W (700W and 500W) ovens respectively. Occasionally, you'll see that times are the same for all powers either because they are so short or because of the food type. However, as microwave ovens vary appreciably from one manufacturer to another and even from one model to another, you may need to adapt some of the times slightly to suit your own oven.

The chart below shows the power settings employed to test the following recipes, as well as some of the descriptions used by different manufacturers.

Description on 700W and 600-650W oven	Keep warm	**Low**	Stew	**Medium**	Bake	**Medium-High**	**High**
500W oven	Warm	**Defrost**		Simmer	Roast	Reheat	**High**
% power output	20%	**25-30%**	40%	**50%**	60-70%	**75-80%**	100%
Approximate power output							
700W oven	140W	**170-210W**	280W	**350W**	420-450W	**525-550W**	**700W**
600-650W oven	100-150W	**150-200W**	250W	**300W**	370-400W	**435-470W**	**600-650W**
500W oven	100W	**125-175W**	200W	255W	300-350W	375-400W	**500W**

Figures in bold = *settings used in* RECIPES

SOUPS AND APPETIZERS

Chestnut and tomato soup

INGREDIENTS

⅓ cup dried chestnuts
2½ cups boiling water
1-2 teaspoons vegetable oil
1 medium onion, finely chopped
2 cups diced carrots
2 bay leaves
15-oz can tomatoes
1-2 tablespoons tomato paste
1-2 teaspoons soy sauce
salt and black pepper
Garnish
fresh parsley

The sweet flavor of the chestnuts blends well with the carrots, and together they balance any acidity in the tomatoes.

1 Put the chestnuts in a medium bowl and pour over the boiling water. Leave to soak for 1 hour, then cover and ▨ HIGH for 5 mins. 600W (*4 mins. 700W; 6 mins. 500W*) until boiling, then ▨ MEDIUM for 15 mins. 600W (*12-13 mins. 700W; ▨ DEFROST for 22 mins. 500W*) or until tender, stirring several times. Leave to stand for 5 mins., then drain, reserving the broth.

2 Put the oil in a medium dish and ▨ HIGH for 1 min. 600W (*30 secs. 700W; 1 min, 500W*). Add onion, then ▨ HIGH for 2 mins. 600W (*1½ mins. 700W; 2½ mins. 500W*).

3 Add the carrots, chestnuts and bay leaves. Cover and ▨ HIGH for 3 mins. 600W (*2½ mins. 700W; 3½ mins. 500W*).

4 Add the tomatoes, tomato paste and 1¼ cups of the chestnut broth. Re-cover and ▨ HIGH for 10 mins. 600W (*8½ mins. 700W; 12½ mins. 500W*), stirring several times.

5 Cool slightly, remove the bay leaves, then purée, adding a little more chestnut broth if necessary. Season well with soy, salt and pepper. To reheat, cover and ▨ HIGH for 1-2 mins., then garnish with parsley before serving.

★ **Preparation:**
15 minutes, plus 1 hour soaking

▨ **Cooking time:**
37 minutes

▨ **Power settings:**
HIGH and MEDIUM

▨ **Good reheated**

◎ **Serves 4-6**

★ If you don't have time to soak the chestnuts, you can cook them from dried. Cover with plenty of boiling water and ▨ HIGH for 10 mins. *(all powers).* Continue ▨ MEDIUM for 20-25 mins. 600W *(and 700W: ▨ HIGH for 20-25 mins. 500W*).

Illustrated on p. 53

Onion and cider soup

INGREDIENTS

1 tablespoon butter or margarine

3 medium onions, thinly sliced

2 garlic cloves, crushed

1 tablespoon flour

1 10½-ounce can beef broth

1 cup apple cider

1 teaspoon dry mustard

1 teaspoon chopped sage sprigs or ½ teaspoon ground sage

1-2 tablespoons soy sauce (optional)

For the topping

1 tablespoon olive oil

⅓ cup plain bread crumbs

½ teaspoon dry mustard

¼ cup walnuts or pecans, finely chopped

This tasty version of French onion soup has a delicious crunchy topping in place of the traditional toasted slice of French bread with Gruyère cheese. Alternatively, serve with some croutons.

1 Place butter or margarine, onions, and garlic in 3-quart casserole. Cover and ▨ HIGH for 4 mins. 600W (*3-3½ mins. 700W; 5 mins. 500W*) or until just tender, stirring halfway through cooking.

2 Stir in flour until blended; add broth, 1 can water, cider, mustard, sage and if you like, soy sauce. Cover and ▨ HIGH for 5 mins. 600W (*4 mins. 700W; 6 mins. 500W*), then ▨ MEDIUM 10 mins. 600W (*8 mins. 700W; ▨ MEDIUM-HIGH 8-10 mins. 500W*), stirring once or twice. Remove garlic.

3 For the topping, place the oil, bread crumbs and mustard in a small bowl, stir until crumbs are coated with oil. Add nuts, stir until evenly distributed. ▨ HIGH for 2-2½ mins. 600W (*1-1½ mins. 700W; 2½-3 mins. 500W*) or until crumbs are lightly browned, stirring halfway through cooking time. Sprinkle over soup. To reheat soup: ▨ HIGH 1-2 mins.

 Preparation: 20 minutes

 Cooking time: 20 minutes

▨ **Power settings:** HIGH and MEDIUM

 Serves 4

★ To make croutons, heat 1 tablespoon oil for 1 min. Add 1 cup small bread cubes and stir. ▨ HIGH for 2 mins. 600W (*1½ mins. 700W; 2½ mins. 500W*), stirring halfway through. Cover and allow to stand for 2 mins. before using.

Illustrated opposite

Top: **Onion and cider soup** (*see opposite*); Bottom: **Chestnut and tomato soup** (*see p. 51*)

Cream of lettuce soup

INGREDIENTS

2½ cups skim milk
½ medium onion
1 bay leaf
6 peppercorns
1 tablespoon vegetable oil
3 scallions, trimmed and chopped
1 clove garlic, crushed
½ teaspoon celery seeds
½ teaspoon grated nutmeg
1 large lettuce, shredded
Garnish
chopped scallion tops or chives

To make a good lettuce soup, you need a well-flavored milk base or broth. It's quick and easy to infuse milk in the microwave using a measuring cup, but make sure that it is large enough to allow for any liquid expansion.

1 Put the milk, onion, bay leaf and peppercorns in a large cup or bowl and ▨ HIGH for 4 mins. 600W (*3 mins. 700W; 5 mins. 500W*). Leave to stand for 3 mins., then strain.

2 Put the oil in a medium bowl and ▨ HIGH for 1 min. 600W (*30 secs. 700W; 1 min. 500W*). Stir in the onions, garlic, celery seeds and nutmeg. Cover and ▨ HIGH for 1½ mins. 600W (*1 min. 700W; 1 ½ mins. 500W*).

3 Stir in the shredded lettuce, re-cover and ▨ HIGH for 3 mins. 600W (*2 ½ mins. 700W; 3 ½ mins. 500W*).

4 Pour in the infused milk, then purée.

5 Return the soup to the bowl, cover and ▨ HIGH (*all powers*) for 1-2 mins. to reheat.

6 Garnish with the chopped scallion tops or chives.

 Preparation: 15 minutes

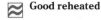 **Cooking time:** 10½ minutes

▨ **Power setting:** HIGH

≋ **Good reheated**

◎ **Serves 4**

⬒ Warmed dinner rolls are always delicious with soup. To heat them through, place in the oven and ▨ HIGH for about 30 secs.

Illustrated on p. 57

Cream of garlic soup

INGREDIENTS

1 tablespoon olive oil
1 head garlic (10-12 cloves), crushed
2 cups diced parsnips
2½ cups boiling broth
4 eggs
2-3 teaspoons vinegar
salt and black pepper

Despite the large amount of garlic, this creamy soup has a delicious, subtle flavor.

1 Put the oil in a medium dish and ▨ HIGH for 1 min. 600W (*30 secs. 700W; 1 min. 500W*). Add the garlic and ▨ MEDIUM for 2 mins. 600W (*1 ½ mins. 700W; ▨ DEFROST for 3 mins. 500W*).

2 Add parsnips and broth, cover and ▨ MEDIUM for 6 mins. 600W (*5 mins. 700W; ▨ DEFROST for 9 mins. 500W*), stir once.

3 In a separate bowl, beat the eggs with the vinegar, then add to the soup. Re-cover and ▨ MEDIUM for a further 2 mins. 600W (*1 ½ mins. 700W; ▨ DEFROST for 3 mins. 500W*), beating once. Season and serve hot.

 Preparation: 10 minutes

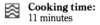 **Cooking time:** 11 minutes

▨ **Power settings:** HIGH and MEDIUM

≋ **Good reheated**

◎ **Serves 4**

 Reheat on LOW or DEFROST to prevent the mixture from separating.

Oriental mushroom soup

INGREDIENTS

8 dried shiitake mushrooms
1¼ cups boiling water
1 tablespoon vegetable oil
½ cup chopped shallots
½ teaspoon grated fresh ginger root or ground ginger
2½ cups button mushrooms wiped and thinly sliced
1 cup carrots, sliced into thin rings
¼ oz dried seaweed (optional)
2 cups boiling vegetable broth
1-2 tablespoons soy sauce
1 tablespoon sherry

Dried mushrooms are an invaluable ingredient for adding extra flavor and texture to soups. The microwave speeds up the process of reconstituting them, making this recipe quick to prepare.

1 Put the mushrooms in a medium dish and pour over the boiling water. Cover and ▓ HIGH for about 2 mins. (*all powers*). Leave to soak for 10-15 mins., then slice the mushrooms and reserve the water.

2 Put the oil in a medium dish and ▓ HIGH for 1 min. 600W (*30 secs. 700W; 1 min. 500W*). Add the shallots and grated ginger root, stir well, then ▓ HIGH for 2 mins. 600W (*1 ½ mins. 700W; 2 ½ mins. 500W*).

3 Add the dried and button mushrooms and the carrots. Cover and ▓ HIGH for 2 mins. 600W (*1 ½ mins. 700W; 2 ½ mins. 500W*), stirring once or twice.

4 Add the seaweed if desired, broth, mushroom water, soy sauce and sherry. Re-cover and ▓ HIGH for 3-4 mins. 600W (*2-3 mins. 700W; 4-5 mins. 500W*).

5 Leave to stand for 5 mins., then season to taste and serve.

 Preparation: 20 minutes

 Cooking time: 10 minutes

 Power setting: HIGH

▓ **Good reheated**

◎ **Serves 4**

Illustrated on p. 57

Borscht

INGREDIENTS

1 tablespoon vegetable oil

1 small onion, finely chopped

2 stalks celery, diced

1 medium carrot, diced

1 medium parsnip, diced

1 ⅔ cups diced uncooked beets

8-oz can tomato sauce

2 teaspoons caraway seeds

1 tablespoon dill weed

3 tablespoons fresh parsley

1 ¼ cups boiling meat broth

juice of ½ lemon

salt and black pepper

½ teaspoon sugar

For serving

sour cream

chopped chives (optional)

This microwave version of borscht is quick to make, and the flavor retains all the freshness of raw vegetables.

1 Put the oil in a large bowl and ▨ HIGH for 1 min. 600W (*30 secs. 700W; 1 min. 500W*).

2 Stir in the chopped onion and celery, then ▨ HIGH for 2 mins. 600W (*1 ½ mins. 700W; 2 ½ mins. 500W*), stirring once during cooking.

3 Add the carrot, parsnip, beets, tomato sauce, caraway seeds, chopped herbs and boiling broth. Cover and ▨ HIGH for 7 mins. 600W (*6 mins. 700W; 8 ½ mins. 500W*).

4 Cool slightly, then purée to make either a textured or smooth consistency.

5 Add lemon juice and sugar to taste, then season well with salt and pepper. Chill thoroughly.

6 Add a swirl of sour cream and chopped chives, if using, to the soup just before serving it.

 Preparation:
20 minutes, plus chilling

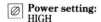 **Cooking time:**
10 minutes

 Power setting:
HIGH

 Make in advance

◎ **Serves 4**

Illustrated opposite

Split pea and parsnip soup

INGREDIENTS

1 tablespoon vegetable oil

1 medium onion, finely chopped

1 clove garlic, crushed

2 cups diced parsnips

2 stalks celery, diced

2 tablespoons chopped fresh parsley

1 teaspoon fresh thyme or ½ teaspoon dry thyme

½ cup split peas

2 cups boiling vegetable or meat broth

1 teaspoon soy sauce

salt and black pepper

A warming soup for cold winter evenings.

1 Put the oil in a medium dish and ▨ HIGH for 1 min. 600W (*30 secs. 700W; 1 min. 500W*). Stir in the onion and garlic and ▨ HIGH for 1 min. 600W (*30 secs. 700W; 1 min. 500W*).

2 Add the parsnips, celery and herbs, cover and ▨ HIGH for 3 mins. 600W (*2 ½ mins. 700W; 3 ½ mins. 500W*).

3 Add the split peas and broth, re-cover and ▨ HIGH for 30 mins. 600W (*25 mins. 700W; 37 mins. 500W*), while stirring.

4 Cool slightly, then purée. Stir in the soy sauce, dissolved in a little water, and season.

5 Return the soup to the dish, cover and ▨ HIGH for 1-2 mins. to reheat.

★ **Preparation:**
25 minutes

〰 **Cooking time:**
36 minutes

⊘ **Power setting:**
HIGH

〰 **Good reheated**

❉ **Freezes well**

◎ **Serves 4**

Top: Borscht (*see opposite*); Center: **Oriental mushroom soup** (*see p. 55*); Bottom: **Cream of lettuce soup** (*see p. 54*)

Chunky chowder

INGREDIENTS

1 tablespoon vegetable oil
1 medium onion, finely sliced
1½ cups quartered baby mushrooms
1 medium red pepper, quartered and finely sliced
2 tablespoons flour
2½ cups milk
pinch of saffron threads (optional)
¾ lb smoked haddock, skinned, boned and cubed
1¾ cups corn kernels, drained or frozen
salt and black pepper

Saffron is expensive, but it gives the soup a delicate flavor. Don't be tempted to use ground turmeric – the flavor is too strong and quite different.

1 Put the oil and onion in a large bowl and cover. ▨ HIGH for 5 mins. 600W (*4 mins. 700W; 6 mins. 500W*), stirring once.

2 Add the mushrooms and pepper and re-cover. ▨ HIGH for 2 mins. 600W (*1 ½ mins. 700W; 2 ½ mins. 500W*), stirring once.

3 Stir in the flour, then gradually add the milk. Cover and ▨ HIGH for 5 mins. 600W (*4 mins. 700W; 6 mins. 500W*), or until thickened, stirring two or three times.

4 Stir in the saffron, haddock and corn, cover and ▨ HIGH for 12 mins. 600W (*10 mins. 700W; 15 mins. 500W*) until the fish is cooked, stirring once. Season to taste with salt and pepper (if the fish is salty, you may only need to add pepper).

5 Leave to stand for 5 mins., then serve while still hot.

★ **Preparation:** 5 minutes

≋ **Cooking time:** 24 minutes

⊘ **Power setting:** HIGH

≋ **Good reheated**

◎ **Serves 4**

★ You can substitute other firm white or smoked fish like halibut or cod in the chowder.

Illustrated on p. 60

Beef and bean soup

INGREDIENTS

½ lb lean ground beef
1 stalk celery, sliced
1 small onion, sliced
1 clove garlic, crushed
1 cup sliced mushrooms
1½ cups green beans, cut into 1-inch pieces
15-oz can black-eyed peas drained
8-oz can crushed tomatoes
3¾ cups boiling beef broth
1 tablespoon soy sauce
salt and black pepper
1 tablespoon cornstarch

A colorful, hearty soup with a dash of soy sauce added for extra flavor. Serve with some crusty, whole-wheat rolls for a really filling winter lunch.

1 Put the meat in a large bowl and ▨ HIGH for 1 min. 600W (*30 secs. 700W; 1 min. 500W*). Stir well, breaking up the meat thoroughly, then ▨ HIGH for 2½-3 mins. 600W (*2-2½ mins. 700W; 3-3½ mins. 500W*), stirring two or three times, until the meat has lost its pink color. Drain off the excess fat.

2 Stir in the celery, onion, garlic and mushrooms. Cover and ▨ HIGH for 4 mins. 600W (*3 mins. 700W; 5 mins. 500W*), stirring once.

3 Stir in the green and black-eyed peas, tomatoes, broth and soy sauce. Re-cover and ▨ HIGH for 15 mins. 600W (*12½ mins. 700W; 18 mins. 500W*), until the green beans are tender, stirring two or three times. Season to taste.

4 Blend the cornstarch with a little water and stir into the soup, ▨ HIGH for 2 mins. 600W (*1½ mins. 700W; 2½ mins. 500W*), stirring two or three times until thickened slightly. Serve hot.

 Preparation: 10 minutes

 Cooking time: 24½ minutes

▨ **Power setting:** HIGH

▨ **Good reheated**

◎ **Serves 6**

★ You can substitute cut frozen green beans for the fresh ones. ▨ HIGH for 2-3 mins. (*all powers*) extra, or until tender.

Illustrated on p. 60

Top: **Beef and bean soup** (*see p. 59*); Bottom: **Chunky chowder** (*see p. 58*).

Mushrooms
stuffed with garlic vegetables

INGREDIENTS

4 large mushrooms	
For the filling	
1 tablespoon olive oil	
3 scallions, trimmed and diced	
2 cloves garlic, crushed	
1 zucchini, diced	
1 teaspoon dried oregano	
2 tablespoons tomato paste	
1 teaspoon soy sauce	
salt and black pepper	

Choose large mushrooms as their broad caps make shallow shells and are easy to stuff. Chop the filling ingredients finely, so they bind together with the tomato paste.

1 Wipe the mushrooms carefully. Remove the stems and some of the center to form a shell. Chop the stems finely.

2 Put the oil in a medium dish and ⊠ HIGH for 1 min. 600W (*30 secs. 700W; 1 min. 500W*). Stir in the scallions and garlic and ⊠ HIGH for 2 mins. 600W (*1 ½ mins. 700W; 2 ½ mins. 500W*), stirring halfway through.

3 Add the chopped mushroom stems and all the remaining ingredients, except the whole mushrooms and seasoning. Cover and ⊠ HIGH for 4 mins. 600W (*3 mins. 700W; 5 mins. 500W*), stirring once.

4 Season the filling to taste with salt and pepper, then pile it into the mushroom caps. Place in a shallow dish, cover and ⊠ HIGH for 4 mins. 600W (*3 mins. 600W; 5 mins. 500W*), rearranging halfway through.

5 Leave to stand for 2-3 mins. before serving.

 Preparation:
15 minutes

 Cooking time:
11 minutes

 Power setting:
HIGH

◎ **Serves 4**

Illustrated on p. 65

Lentil and coconut pâté

INGREDIENTS

½ cup split red lentils

1¾ cups boiling water

2 oz canned coconut milk

juice of ½ lemon

4-5 drops Tabasco sauce

¼ teaspoon grated nutmeg

salt and black pepper

This makes a delicious creamy pâté with a subtle flavor. Red lentils are particularly quick to cook in the microwave, but be sure to put them in a large bowl or the cooking liquid will froth over the top. Serve the pâté with crudités or Melba toast.

1 Place the red lentils in a deep bowl and pour over the boiling water. Cover and ▓ HIGH for 10 mins. (*all powers*), stirring several times. Drain well, if necessary, reserving any liquid.

2 Stir in the creamed coconut, lemon juice, Tabasco sauce and nutmeg. Purée until smooth, adding a little of the reserved lentil broth, or water, if necessary.

3 Season to taste with salt and pepper, then chill thoroughly before serving.

★ **Preparation:** 10 minutes, plus chilling

🌊 **Cooking time:** 10 minutes

⊘ **Power setting:** HIGH

▤ **Make in advance**

◎ **Serves 4**

Illustrated on p. 65

Coriander ramekins

INGREDIENTS

3 eggs

⅔ cup yogurt

3 tablespoons chopped fresh coriander or flat-leaf parsley

salt and black pepper

If fresh coriander is unavailable, try using flat-leaf parsley or mixtures of other fresh herbs, such as chives, parsley or tarragon, or chopped spinach, sorrel or cooked leeks.

1 Beat the eggs thoroughly, then add in the yogurt. Fold in the coriander, and season to taste with salt and pepper.

2 Spoon the mixture into four ramekin dishes. Cover, then arrange the baking dishes in a circle in the microwave and ▓ HIGH for 3 mins. 600W (*2½ mins. 700W; 3 mins. 500W*), rearranging halfway through.

3 Leave to stand for 3 mins. before serving.

★ **Preparation:** 5 minutes

🌊 **Cooking time:** 3 minutes

⊘ **Power setting:** HIGH

◎ **Serves 4**

🌊 These should be quite soft when served; if overcooked they can become rubbery in texture.

Illustrated on p. 65

Stuffed avocados

INGREDIENTS

2 tablespoons raisins
juice of 1 orange
¼ cup short-grain brown rice
1¼ cups boiling water
⅓ cup sunflower seeds
3 scallions, finely chopped
1 teaspoon soy sauce
1 teaspoon grated fresh ginger or ground ginger
2 avocados

Hot, stuffed avocados make an unusual alternative to the more usual avocado vinaigrette. The microwave heats up the avocado halves without drying them out or making them bitter.

2 Put the raisins in a small bowl, pour over the orange juice and ▩ HIGH for 1 min. 600W *(30 secs. 700W; 1 min. 500W)* to plump them up.

2 Put the rice in a medium bowl with the boiling water. Cover and ▩ HIGH for 18 mins. *(all powers)*, stirring 2-3 times. Leave to stand for 5 minutes.

3 Spread out the sunflower seeds on a small plate and ▩ HIGH for 2 mins. 600W *(1 ½ mins. 700W; 2 ½ mins. 500W)*, shaking halfway through.

4 Mix the raisins, cooked rice, roasted seeds, onions, soy sauce and ginger root or ground ginger together.

5 Halve the avocados, scoop out the flesh and dice. Mix the flesh with the other ingredients, then spoon back into each of the avocado halves.

6 Arrange the halves in a large round dish with the thicker ends outward. Cover and ▩ HIGH for 2 mins. 600W *(1 ½ mins. 700W; 2 ½ mins. 500W)*. Serve at once.

 Preparation:
20 minutes

 Cooking time:
23 minutes

Power setting:
HIGH

Serves 4

To get more juice from oranges and lemons, microwave individually for 30 secs. before squeezing.

Eggplant dip

INGREDIENTS

1 large eggplant
2 teaspoons sesame seeds
2 teaspoons sunflower seeds
2 tablespoons olive oil
2 cloves garlic, crushed
juice of ½ lemon
½ teaspoon ground coriander
salt and black pepper

Eggplants cook very quickly in the microwave, saving time and the need to heat an entire oven simply to make this tasty dip. Choose an eggplant that feels heavy for its size and has a smooth, glossy skin.

1 Trim the eggplant, then pierce the skin. Wrap in a paper towel and ▧ HIGH for 5 mins. 600W (*4 mins. 700W; 6 mins. 500W*), turning once. Leave to stand for 4 mins.

2 Spread out the seeds on a small plate and ▧ HIGH for 3 mins. 600W (*2 ½ mins. 700W; 3 ½ mins. 500W*), shaking halfway through. Crush lightly.

3 Scoop out the eggplant flesh, mash well and mix with the oil, garlic, lemon juice and coriander. Season well with salt and pepper, then stir in the crushed, toasted seeds. Serve warm as a dip with crudités or strips of toast, or serve as a spread.

Preparation:
10 minutes

Cooking time:
8 minutes

Power setting:
HIGH

Make in advance

Serves 4

Wrapping eggplants in paper towels prevents them from collapsing during cooking.

Illustrated opposite

Leeks vinaigrette

INGREDIENTS

1 lb young leeks, trimmed weight
6 tablespoons olive oil
2 tablespoons lemon juice
1 tablespoon cider vinegar
2 teaspoons capers
1 teaspoon coarse-grained mustard
1 clove garlic, crushed
salt and black pepper

Vegetables cooked in the microwave retain a crisp, fresh flavor and are excellent served chilled in a vinaigrette dressing. The same recipe can be used for artichoke hearts, mushrooms or green beans.

1 Chop the leeks into 1 inch pieces and wash thoroughly.

2 Arrange in a dish with 2 tablespoons water. Cover and ▧ HIGH for 4 mins. 600W (*3 mins. 700W; 5 mins. 500W*), shaking the dish once or twice during cooking. Drain well.

3 Combine all the remaining ingredients, except the seasoning, and add to the cooked leeks. Cover and ▧ HIGH for 1 min. 600W (*30 secs. 700W; 1 min. 500W*).

4 Leave to cool completely. Season well with salt and pepper, then chill thoroughly. Serve with whole-wheat bread or with a crisp green salad.

Preparation:
15 minutes, plus chilling

Cooking time:
5 minutes

Power setting:
HIGH

Make in advance

Serves 4

Clockwise from top left: **Lentil and coconut spread** (*see p. 62*); **Eggplant dip** (*see opposite*); **Mushrooms stuffed with garlic vegetables** (*see p. 61*); **Coriander ramekins** (*see p. 62*)

Seafood shells

INGREDIENTS

8 fresh sea scallops
½ lb cod steaks
1 cup sliced mushrooms
2 tablespoons butter
2 tablespoons flour
about ⅔ cup milk
1 tablespoon dry sherry
2 tablespoons heavy cream
salt and black pepper
3 tablespoons grated Parmesan cheese
3 tablespoons dried bread crumbs

For the potato border

3 cups potatoes cut into chunks
1 tablespoon butter
2 tablespoons heavy cream
2 tablespoons chopped fresh parsley
4 scallop half-shells (optional)

Make a few sea scallops go further when serving four people, by combining with cod in a creamy sauce, topped with cheesy bread crumbs. The potato border won't brown in the microwave but looks and tastes good, speckled with chopped fresh parsley instead.

1 To make the potato border, put the potatoes in a large bowl with ¼ cup water. Cover and ☒ HIGH for 12 mins. 600W (*10 mins. 700W; 15 mins. 500W*), stirring once.

2 Leave to stand for 5 mins., then drain and mash with the butter and cream. Stir in the parsley and spoon into a large pastry bag fitted with a star tip. Pipe a border around the edge of four scallop shells or small plates.

3 Put the scallops on a plate and cover. ☒ MEDIUM for 2½-3 mins. 600W (*2-2½ mins. 700W; 3-3½ mins. 500W*) or until just cooked, stirring once. Leave to stand for 5 mins., then drain and reserve the liquid. Thickly slice into 4-6 pieces.

4 Put the cod steaks on a plate, top with the mushrooms and ☒ HIGH for 3 mins. 600W (*2½ mins. 700W; 3½ mins. 500W*) until just cooked, turning over once. Leave to stand for 5 mins., drain and reserve liquid.

5 Put the butter in a medium bowl and ☒ HIGH for 1 min. 600W (*30 secs. 700W; 1 min. 500W*). Stir in the flour. Combine the fish cooking liquids and make up to 1¼ cups with the milk and stir into the flour mixture. ☒ HIGH for 3-4 mins. (*all powers*), until thickened, stirring twice.

6 Add the sherry and cream and season to taste. Flake the cod, removing any skin and bones, and add to the sauce with the mushrooms and scallops. Spoon into the prepared scallop shells or plates.

7 Combine the cheese and crumbs and sprinkle over the sauce. ☒ HIGH for 5 mins. 600W (*4 mins. 700W; 6 mins. 500W*). Leave to stand for 3 mins., then serve at once.

 Preparation:
10 minutes

 Cooking time:
26½ minutes

Power settings:
HIGH and MEDIUM

◎ **Serves 4**

 The deep shells from sea scallops make good individual dishes. Scrub them thoroughly before use.

Crab and shrimp salad

INGREDIENTS

1 tablespoon vegetable oil
½ small onion, finely chopped
1 small garlic clove, crushed
½ lb cooked, shelled shrimp
6 oz canned crabmeat, drained
grated peel and juice of ½ orange
1 mango, peeled, pitted and thinly sliced
1 orange, peeled and cut into segments
12 small lettuce leaves
For the dressing
6 tablespoons mayonnaise
grated peel and juice of ½ orange
salt and black pepper
Garnish
4 whole shrimp

This salad has a fresh, tropical taste. You can make it up to 24 hours in advance, but don't add the sliced mango until the last minute or its strong taste will overpower all the other flavors.

1 Put the oil, onion and garlic in a medium bowl, cover and ▨ HIGH for 3 mins. 600W (*2½ mins. 700W; 3½ mins. 500W*), stirring once. Leave to cool, then add the shrimp, crab, orange peel and juice and stir well.

2 To make the dressing, mix the mayonnaise with the orange peel and juice and season to taste. Stir into the shrimp and crab mixture and chill until ready to serve.

3 Reserve four pieces of mango and orange for the garnish and mix the remainder into the shrimp mixture until well coated in the dressing.

4 Arrange the lettuce leaves on four individual plates and spoon the shrimp mixture on top, dividing it into equal portions.

5 Garnish each salad with a whole shrimp a slice of mango and a segment of orange. Serve at once, with whole-wheat bread.

Preparation: 10 minutes, plus chilling

Cooking time: 3 minutes

Power setting: HIGH

Make in advance

Serves 4

To thaw frozen shrimp, spread in a shallow dish and ▨ LOW for 4 mins. 600W (*3 mins. 700W; 5 mins. 500W*), stirring once. Leave to stand for 5 minutes before serving.

Illustrated on p. 69

Chicken liver pâté

INGREDIENTS

½ cup butter
1 small onion, finely chopped
½ lb chicken livers, chopped
⅔ cup chopped mushrooms
1 clove garlic, crushed
1 tablespoon dry sherry
1 tablespoon chopped fresh parsley
salt and black pepper

Garnish

a few lettuce leaves, and tomato wedges (optional)

A rich butter-topped pâté that is very quick and easy to make in the microwave. For a dinner party, garnish with a few red-tipped, curly lettuce leaves.

1 Put ¼ cup of the butter and onion in a medium bowl and cover. ▦ HIGH for 4 mins. 600W (*3 mins. 700W; 5 mins. 500W*) until softened, stirring once.

2 Stir in the livers, mushrooms and garlic, re-cover and ▦ MEDIUM-HIGH for 4 mins. 600W (*3 mins. 600W; 5 mins. 500W*), or until the livers are no longer pink, stirring twice.

3 Purée the liver mixture in a blender or food processor until smooth. Add the sherry, parsley and seasoning to taste and mix together until well blended.

4 Spoon either into four individual dishes or one large dish and smooth the surface. Put the remaining butter in a small bowl and ▦ HIGH for 1½ mins. 600W (*1 min. 700W; 1 ½-2 mins. 500W*) to melt.

5 Spoon the melted butter over the pâté and leave to set, then chill for 6-8 hours or overnight. Serve with toast and garnish with lettuce leaves, if desired.

 Preparation: 20 minutes, plus chilling

 Cooking time: 9½ minutes

 Power settings: HIGH and MEDIUM-HIGH

Make in advance

Serves 4

 Check over the livers carefully and cut away any green-tinged parts, which would give the pâté a bitter taste.

Illustrated opposite

Top: **Chicken liver pâté** (*see opposite*); **Crab and shrimp salad** (*see p. 67*).

Fruity spareribs

INGREDIENTS

1½ lb pork spareribs
3 tablespoons undiluted grape juice
1 teaspoon lemon juice
1 tablespoon honey
3 tablespoons tomato ketchup
1 tablespoon soy sauce

Garnish

lemon slices

These ribs have a delicious sweet-and-sour taste. The only way to eat them is with your fingers, so provide lots of napkins and finger bowls so your guests can easily clean up afterward.

1 Cut the spareribs into single rib pieces and place in a large shallow dish in a single layer. Add 6 tablespoons water and cover. ▨ HIGH for 3½ mins. 600W *(3 mins. 700W; 4 mins. 500W).* Rearrange and turn over the ribs and drain off the cooking liquid.

2 Re-cover and ▨ HIGH for 3½ mins. 600W *(3 mins. 700W; 4 mins. 500W).* Leave to stand for 4 mins., then drain off the cooking juices.

3 Mix together the grape juice, lemon juice, honey, tomato ketchup, soy sauce and 1 tablespoon water. Brush the sauce over the ribs to coat completely.

4 Arrange the ribs on a microwave roasting rack over a shallow dish and cover with waxed paper. ▨ MEDIUM for 8-10 mins. 600W *(6½-8½ mins. 700W; 10-12½ mins. 500W),* rearranging ribs and basting with the sauce two or three times.

5 Cover and leave to stand for 5 mins. Garnish with lemon slices and serve at once with any remaining sauce poured over.

 Preparation:
5 minutes

 Cooking time:
15 minutes

Power settings:
HIGH and MEDIUM

Serves 4

Cover the ribs with a firm lid for the first part of cooking, then loosely with waxed paper (which lets the steam escape, but prevents splashing) for the second part.

MAIN DISHES
FISH AND SHELLFISH

Sole Véronique

INGREDIENTS

1 tablespoon butter
1 lb sole fillets, skinned
salt and black pepper
¼ cup dry white wine
¼ cup fish broth
few sprigs of parsley
bay leaf
¼ cup heavy cream
1 ½ teaspoons cornstarch
1 cup seedless green grapes

Rolled fillets of sole can be coated with a variety of sauces. Cooked in the microwave, they keep moist and tender. This light wine-and-cream sauce includes seedless grapes which add a delicious sweetness to the dish.

1 Dot the butter on to the skinned side of each of the fillets, season with salt and pepper and roll up from the tail end. Arrange the fish rolls in a greased dish.

2 Pour in the wine and broth, and add the parsley and bay leaf. Cover and ▒ HIGH for 4 mins. 600W (*3 mins. 700W; 5 mins. 500W*) until the fish is opaque and flaky, rearranging once.

3 Drain off the cooking liquid from the fish and discard the herbs. Cover the fish and keep warm while you make the sauce. Pour the liquid into a cup measure and ▒ HIGH for 2 mins. 600W (*1 ½ mins. 700W; 2 ½ mins. 500W*) until reduced by about half.

4 Blend the cream with the cornstarch, stir into the reduced broth and mix until smooth. ▒ HIGH for 1-1 ½ mins. 600W (*1 min. 700W; 1 ½-2 mins. 500W*), stirring twice until hot.

5 Season to taste, add the grapes and ▒ HIGH for 1 min. 600W (*30 secs. 700W; 1 min. 500W*) to heat through. Pour over the fish and serve at once.

 Preparation:
5 minutes

 Cooking time:
8 minutes

 Power setting:
HIGH

Serves 4

Moules marinière

INGREDIENTS

3 lb fresh mussels
1 small onion, finely chopped
6 tablespoons dry white wine
2 tablespoons butter
1 teaspoon flour
2 teaspoons tomato paste

Garnish

1 tablespoon chopped fresh parsley

This classic dish cooks very well in the microwave. Mussels, however, are very bulky so if you increase the quantities, cook the extra mussels in another batch so they have a chance to cook evenly. This quantity will also serve four as an appetizer.

1 Discard any mussels with broken shells. Scrub the rest under cold running water, scraping off any barnacles. Use a sharp knife to pull away the beards. Shake the mussels in several changes of water to remove any traces of sand.

2 Put the onion and wine in a large bowl. Cover and ▨ HIGH for 3 mins. 600W *(2½ mins. 700W; 3½ mins. 500W)*, to soften.

3 Add the mussels, re-cover and ▨ HIGH for 4-5 mins. 600W *(3-4 mins. 700W; 5-6 mins. 500W)*, or until they are almost all open, stirring two or three times.

4 Spoon the mussels into a warm serving dish, cover and leave to stand for 3 mins., then discard any that remain closed.

5 Mix the butter and flour together and whisk a little at a time into the cooking liquid. Add the tomato paste and ▨ HIGH for 3 mins. 600W *(2½ mins. 700W; 3½ mins. 500W)* until boiling and thickened, stirring two or three times.

6 Pour all of the sauce over the mussels and garnish with the chopped parsley. Serve immediately.

Preparation: 15 minutes

Cooking time: 10 minutes

Power setting: HIGH

Serves 2-3

There is always a chance that some sand will escape the washing process, so it is a good idea to strain the sauce into the serving dish.

Illustrated opposite

Top: **Salmon with tarragon sauce** (*see p. 74*); Bottom **Moules marinière** (*see opposite*).

Salmon with tarragon sauce

INGREDIENTS

4 salmon steaks, 4-6 ounces cach
juice of 1 lemon

For the sauce

2 tablespoons butter
grated peel of 1 lemon
2 tablespoons flour
⅔ cup milk
⅔ cup fish broth
1 egg yolk
2 tablespoons heavy cream
2 tablespoons chopped fresh tarragon
salt and black pepper

Garnish

four sprigs of tarragon and 9 lemon slices

Salmon steaks cook so quickly in the microwave that you need to make the sauce first. Reheat the sauce while the fish is standing for a short time.

1 To make the sauce: Put the butter and lemon peel in a small bowl and 🔲 HIGH for 1 min. 600W (*30 secs. 700W; 1 min. 500W*) to melt.

2 Stir in the flour, then the milk and fish broth. 🔲 HIGH for 4 mins. 600W (*3 mins. 700W; 5 mins. 500W*) until boiling and thickened, stirring every minute.

3 Beat the yolk and cream together, then blend in a little of the hot sauce. Beat back into the rest of the sauce and 🔲 HIGH for 30 secs. (*all powers*).

4 Stir in the tarragon and leave to stand while you cook the fish. Place the fish in a dish with the narrow ends toward the center. Sprinkle with the lemon juice and cover. 🔲 HIGH or 6-8 mins. 600W (*5-6 ½ mins. 700W; 7-10 mins. 500W*), turning over halfway through cooking.

5 Leave to stand for 3 mins. and reheat the sauce, 🔲 HIGH for 2 mins. 600W (*1 ½ mins. 700W; 2 ½ mins. 500W*). Season to taste, pour over the fish and garnish with the tarragon sprigs and the lemon slices.

Preparation: 10 minutes

Cooking time: 13½ minutes

Power setting: HIGH

Serves 4

⭐ It's not worth using dried tarragon for this delicately flavored sauce – if you can't get fresh tarragon, use a mixture of fresh parsley and chives instead.

Illustrated on p. 73

Fish lasagne

INGREDIENTS

6 spinach lasagne noodles
5 cups boiling water
1 tablespoon vegetable oil
¾ lb white fish fillets
¾ lb trout fillets
1 cup grated mozzarella cheese
1 cup grated Cheddar cheese
salt and black pepper

For the tomato sauce

15-oz can chopped tomatoes
2 tablespoons tomato paste
1 teaspoon chopped fresh oregano or ½ teaspoon dried oregano
1 teaspoon dried thyme
1 bay leaf
pinch of garlic salt
black pepper

For the white sauce

2 tablespoon butter
2 tablespoons flour
about 1 cup milk

This filling main course dish is full of rich flavors – it is easy to make, but time consuming because there are four different parts to microwave. To save time, you can cook the lasagne conventionally while the fish and sauces are microwaving.

1 Put the lasagne, water and oil into a large baking dish and ☷ HIGH for 6-8 mins. (*all powers*) until just tender, stirring two or three times. Leave to stand for 5 mins.

2 Arrange the fish fillets in a dish and cover. ☷ HIGH for 4-6 mins. 600W (*3-5 mins. 700W; 5-7 mins. 500W*), until flaking easily. Leave to stand for 3 mins. Drain off the juices and make up to 1¼ cups with the milk for the white sauce. Flake the fish, removing any skin and bones.

3 To make the tomato sauce: Put the tomatoes, tomato paste, oregano, thyme, bay leaf, garlic salt and pepper in a bowl and cover. ☷ HIGH for 10 mins. 600W (*8½ mins. 700W; 12½ mins. 500W*), stirring once. Set aside and remove bay leaf.

4 To make the white sauce: Put the butter in a large bowl and ☷ HIGH for 1 min. 600W (*30 secs. 700W; 1 min. 500W*) to melt. Stir in the flour and flavored milk and ☷ HIGH for 3-4 mins. 600W (*2½-3 mins. 700W; 3½-5 mins. 500W*), until boiling and thickened, stirring twice.

5 Mix the cheeses together and stir half into the white sauce with the fish. Season to taste. Grease a large baking dish and spread one third of the tomato sauce in the bottom, add two sheets of lasagne in a single layer and cover with one-third of the white sauce. Repeat these layers twice more, then sprinkle with the rest of the cheese.

6 ☷ MEDIUM for 15-20 mins. 600W (*12-17 mins. 700W; 18-25 mins. 500W*) until hot, rotating the dish twice. Leave to stand for 5 mins., then serve hot with a crisp salad and whole-wheat bread.

 Preparation: 10 mins

 Cooking time: 39 mins

 Power settings: HIGH and MEDIUM

 Good reheated

 Freezes well

◎ **Serves 4**

Illustrated on p. 76

Top right: **Shrimp and coconut curry** (*see opposite*); Center: **Fish lasagne** (*see p. 75*). Bottom: **Seafood paella** (*see p. 78*).

Shrimp and coconut curry

INGREDIENTS

1 pound large shrimp or 1 16-ounce bag frozen shelled and deveined shrimp, thawed and drained
2 tablespoons butter
1 medium onion, thinly sliced
1 garlic clove, minced
1 ½ tablespoons curry powder
1 teaspoon fresh grated ginger or ¼ teaspoon ground ginger
¼ teaspoon ground cardamom (optional)
2 medium zucchini, diced
1 medium red pepper, diced (about 1 cup)
1 tablespoon flour
1 cup heavy cream
¼ cup cream of coconut
1 tablespoon flaked coconut, toasted (optional)

This curry sauce makes a delicious base for shrimp or chicken. The flavor of the sauce improves if it is made in advance. Directions for reheating are given below. Serve over hot cooked rice.

1 If using fresh shrimp, shell and devein; pat dry.

2 Place butter in 2-quart casserole and ✽ HIGH 30 secs.-1 min. or until melted. Stir in onions, garlic, curry powder, ginger and cardamom. Cover and ✽ HIGH for 4 mins. 600W (*3 mins. 700W; 5 mins. 500W*).

3 Add zucchini and red pepper. Cover and ✽ HIGH for 6 mins. 600W (*5 mins. 700W; 7-8 mins. 500W*) or until just tender, stirring halfway through cooking time.

4 Stir in flour, add milk and cream of coconut, stir until well blended. Cover and ✽ HIGH for 5 mins. 600W (*4 mins. 700W; 6 mins. 500W*) or until mixture begins to boil and thicken, stirring halfway through the cooking time.

5 Add shrimp. Cover and ✽ HIGH for 2-2½ mins. 600W (*1 ½-2 mins. 700W; 3-3 ½ mins. 500W*). Let stand 2 minutes before serving. If you like, sprinkle with toasted flaked coconut.

 Preparation:
17 minutes

 Cooking time:
1 ½ minutes

 Power setting:
HIGH

 Good reheated

 Serves 4

★ To prepare sauce in advance follow recipe up to and including Step 4. Allow to cool, cover and refrigerate. To reheat, keep covered, ✽ HIGH for 6½-9 minutes, stirring 2-3 times during cooking. Add uncooked shrimp; follow cooking times in Step 5.

Illustrated opposite

Seafood paella

INGREDIENTS

½ lb fresh mussels, cleaned (see page 37)
2 tablespoons vegetable oil
1 medium onion, sliced
1 clove garlic, crushed
1 heaping cup long-grain rice
¼ teaspoon saffron threads or ground saffron
3 cups boiling fish broth
½ lb white fish, cut into large chunks
1 red pepper, sliced
1 yellow pepper, sliced
½ cup frozen peas
¼ lb shelled cooked shrimp
2 teaspoons chopped fresh basil or 1 teaspoon dried basil
salt and black pepper
Garnish
sprigs of basil

Paella is a colorful dish that combines many different flavors and textures. This version takes almost as long to make in a microwave as it does the conventional way, but in the microwave the dish needs less attention and cooks to perfection without any sticking problems.

1 Put the mussels in a bowl and cover. ▨ HIGH for about 1½ mins. 600W (*1 min. 700W; 2 mins. 500W*), until the shells open. Discard any mussels that remain closed. Leave to stand for 5 mins., then remove the mussels from their shells and set aside.

2 Put the oil, onion and garlic in a large bowl and cover. ▨ HIGH for 4 mins. 600W (*3 mins. 700W; 5 mins. 500W*) to soften.

3 Stir in the rice, saffron and broth and cover. ▨ HIGH for 5 mins. 600W (*4 mins. 700W; 6 mins. 500W*), or until boiling, stirring once.

4 Add the fish and peppers, stir gently and re-cover. ▨ HIGH for 4 mins. 600W (*3 mins. 700W; 5 mins. 500W*), stir in the peas, shrimp, mussels, basil and seasoning and ▨ HIGH for 3-5 mins. 600W (*2½-4 mins. 700W; 3½-6 mins. 500W*), until cooked, and almost all the liquid has been absorbed, stirring two or three times.

5 Leave to stand for 5 mins., then serve at once, garnished with the basil.

★ **Preparation:** 15 mins

▧ **Cooking time:** 17½ minutes

⊘ **Power setting:** HIGH

◎ **Serves 4**

★ Paella should be moist but not wet, so if there is any broth left in the bottom of the dish after standing, uncover and ▨ HIGH for a further 2-3 mins. (*all powers*), stirring once.

Illustrated on p. 76

Stuffed trout with fennel sauce

INGREDIENTS

4 trout, about ½ lb each, scored both sides

For the stuffing

¼ cup butter
1 small onion, finely chopped
⅔ cup chopped button mushrooms
grated peel and juice of 1 lemon
1 tablespoon chopped fresh fennel or 1 teaspoon dried fennel
1 cup fresh bread crumbs
1 egg yolk
salt and black pepper

For the sauce

6 tablespoons butter
3 egg yolks
1 tablespoon lemon juice
1 tablespoon chopped fresh fennel or 1 teaspoon dried fennel

Garnish

fresh fennel leaves

The mild aniseed flavor of fennel goes very well with trout, and the feathery leaves also make a very pretty garnish.

1 To make the stuffing: Put the butter in a bowl and ❄ HIGH for 1½ mins. 600W (*1 min. 700W; 1½-2 mins. 500W*) to melt. Stir in the onion, mushrooms, lemon peel and juice and half of the fennel. Cover and ❄ HIGH for 6 mins. 600W (*5 mins. 700W; 7 mins. 500W*), stirring the mixture once.

2 Leave to cool slightly, then stir in the bread crumbs and egg yolk and mix well. Season to taste. Divide the stuffing between the trout. Arrange the fish in a shallow dish and cover.

3 ❄ HIGH for 7-9 mins. 600W (*6-7 mins. 700W; 11-13 mins. 500W*), turning over halfway through cooking. Leave to stand for 5 mins.

4 Meanwhile, make the sauce: Put the butter in a medium bowl and ❄ HIGH for 2 mins. 600W (*1½ mins. 700W; 2½ mins. 500W*) to melt. Beat the egg yolks and lemon juice until frothy, then gradually beat into the butter. ❄ HIGH for 45 secs. 600W (*30 secs. 700W; 1 min. 500W*), beating every 15 seconds, until thickened slightly.

5 Stir the remaining fennel into the sauce and season to taste. Serve the trout at once with a little of the sauce poured over each of them. Garnish with the fennel leaves.

⭐ **Preparation:**
10 minutes

〰 **Cooking time:**
17¼ minutes

▨ **Power setting:**
HIGH

◎ **Serves 4**

⭐ Arrange the trout head to tail in the dish, turning once for even cooking.

Illustrated on p. 81

Lemony sea bass

INGREDIENTS

1 ¾ lb sea bass

1 lemon

1 bay leaf

For the stuffing

½ cup fresh bread crumbs

2 tablespoons chopped fresh parsley

grated peel of 1 lemon

salt and black pepper

a little beaten egg

Sea bass is considered to be as fine a fish as salmon – cook it simply with herbs and seasonings "en papillote." Keep the accompanying sauce very light; just stir a little light cream and chopped herbs in the cooking juices.

1 To make the stuffing: Mix together the bread crumbs, parsley, lemon peel and salt and pepper with enough beaten egg to bind.

2 Cut four very thin slices from the lemon and squeeze the juice from the rest. Sprinkle the juice into the cavity of the fish and season to taste. Spoon the stuffing into the cavity, then score each side of the fish carefully with a sharp knife.

3 Place the fish on a large sheet of waxed paper and tuck the lemon slices and bay leaf underneath. Fold the edges of the paper together to make a package, completely enclosing the fish. Place the package in a large shallow dish.

4 HIGH for 7-10½ mins. 600W *(6-8½ mins. 700W; 8½-12½ mins. 500W)* until the fish flakes easily, turning over once during cooking. Leave to stand for 5 mins. Serve hot.

 Preparation:
8 minutes

 Cooking time:
7 minutes

 Power setting:
HIGH

 Serves 4

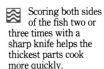 Scoring both sides of the fish two or three times with a sharp knife helps the thickest parts cook more quickly.

Top left: **Cod steaks Niçoise** (*see p. 83*); Center: **Orange and parsley monkfish kebobs** (*see p. 82*); Bottom: **Stuffed trout with fennel sauce** (*see p. 79*).

Orange and parsley monkfish kebobs

INGREDIENTS

1 lb monkfish fillet
grated peel and juice of ½ orange
1 tablespoon butter
1 scallion, finely chopped
1 tablespoon flour
½ cup milk
2 teaspoons chopped fresh parsley
2 tablespoons heavy cream
salt and black pepper

Garnish

orange slices and parsley sprigs

The firm white flesh of monkfish becomes tender and moist during microwaving, but doesn't fall apart once it's cooked so is very suitable for kebobs. Marinate the fish in orange juice for extra flavor.

1 Cut the fish into twelve 1 × 4-in strips and thread onto 12 small wooden skewers. Place in a single layer in a shallow baking dish and sprinkle with the orange juice. Cover and leave to marinate for up to 2 hours.

2 Put the butter and scallion in a small bowl and ▓ HIGH for 2 mins. 600W (*1 ½ mins. 700W;2 ½ mins. 500W*). Stir in the flour, milk, orange peel and parsley and ▓ HIGH for 2 mins. 600W (*1 ½ mins. 700W; 2 ½ mins. 500W*), until boiling and thickened, stirring twice. Cover and set aside.

3 Baste the kebobs with the orange juice, re-cover and ▓ HIGH for 2½-3 mins. 600W (*2-2 ½ mins. 700W; 3-3 ½ mins. 500W*), until the fish goes white, rearranging once. Drain the cooking juices into the sauce, then leave the kebobs to stand for 2-3 mins.

4 Stir the cream and seasoning into the sauce and ▓ HIGH for 1 min. 600W (*30 secs. 700W; 1 min. 500W*). Pour the sauce over the kebobs, garnish with the orange slices and parsley sprigs and serve at once.

★ **Preparation:**
15 minutes

〰 **Cooking time:**
7½ minutes

▱ **Power setting:**
HIGH

▤ **Make in advance**

◎ **Serves 4**

★ Always use wooden or bamboo skewers for microwaving – they can be bought in Oriental supermarkets.

Illustrated on p. 81

Cod steaks Niçoise

INGREDIENTS

4 cod steaks, about ½ lb each
juice of ½ lemon
For the sauce
1 tablespoon vegetable oil
1 medium onion, sliced
1 clove garlic, crushed
2 teaspoons chopped fresh basil or 1 teaspoon dried basil
1 medium green pepper, sliced
1 medium red pepper, sliced
15-oz can chopped tomatoes
2 tablespoons tomato paste
¼ cup sliced pitted ripe olives
salt and black pepper

In this dish, the colorful blend of vegetables complements the cod perfectly. But the versatile sauce is also good with hamburgers, pork chops and chicken.

1 To make the sauce: Put the oil and onion in a medium bowl and cover. 🕸 HIGH for 5 mins. 600W (*4 mins. 700W; 6 mins. 500W*). Add the garlic, basil and peppers and 🕸 HIGH for 2 mins. 600W (*1 ½ mins. 700W; 2 ½ mins. 500W*).

2 Stir in the tomatoes, tomato paste, olives and seasoning to taste. 🕸 HIGH for 4 mins. 600W (*3 mins. 700W; 5 mins. 500W*), stirring twice. Cover and leave to stand for 5 mins.

3 Arrange the cod steaks in a large shallow dish with the narrow ends towards the center. Sprinkle with the lemon juice and cover. 🕸 HIGH for 8 mins. 600W (*6 ½ mins. 700W; 10 mins. 500W*).

4 Drain off the cooking juices and spoon the tomato sauce over the cod steaks. Re-cover and 🕸 HIGH for 3-4 mins. 600W (*2 ½-3 mins. 700W; 3 ½-5 mins. 500W*) until the fish flakes easily. Leave to stand for 3 mins., then serve hot.

⭐ **Preparation:** 10 minutes

〰 **Cooking time:** 22 minutes

⊘ **Power setting:** HIGH

◎ **Serves 4**

⭐ The bones in cod steaks sometimes "pop" during microwaving; this is just the sound of little bursts of steam escaping.

Illustrated on p. 81

MEAT, POULTRY AND GAME

Chili con carne

INGREDIENTS

2 tablespoons flour
1-2 teaspoons chili powder
2 teaspoons ground cumin
2 teaspoons dried oregano
1 lb chuck steak, cubed
15-oz can chopped tomatoes
2 tablespoons tomato paste
⅔ cup boiling beef broth
15- to 19-oz can kidney beans, drained and rinsed
2 cloves garlic, crushed
salt and black pepper

You can make this dish as mild or hot as you like, depending on whether you like really spicy food. The rich tomato-flavored sauce is enhanced with cumin and oregano, which give it a rounded taste. Serve with brown rice and a green salad tossed in a vinaigrette dressing.

1 Mix together the flour, chili powder to taste, ground cumin and oregano. Add the cubed beef and toss well to coat with all the spices.

2 Place in a large bowl, add the tomatoes, tomato paste, broth, kidney beans and garlic. Stir the mixture thoroughly.

3 Cover and ▨ HIGH for 10 mins. 600W (*8½ mins. 700W; 12½ mins. 500W*) or until boiling, stirring twice. ▨ MEDIUM for 30-35 mins. 600W (*25-30 mins. 700W; 35-40 mins. 500W*) or until tender, stirring once.

4 Leave to stand for 5 mins. Serve with the rice and the salad.

 Preparation:
15 minutes

 Cooking time:
40 minutes

 Power settings:
HIGH and MEDIUM

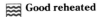 **Good reheated**

 Serves 4

 Cut the beef into small, neat cubes to ensure that it cooks evenly.

Illustrated opposite

Top: **Chili con carne** (*see opposite*); Bottom: **Veal stew with artichokes in sour cream sauce** (*see p. 87*).

Steak and kidney pie

INGREDIENTS

2 tablespoons vegetable oil
2 medium onions, sliced
1 lb chuck steak, cubed
½ lb beef kidney, chopped
3 tablespoons seasoned flour
⅔ cup beer

For the pastry

1¾ cups self-rising flour
¼ lb shredded suet, or ½ cup vegetable shortening
about ⅔ cup cold water

The flavor of this rich meat filling benefits from the double cooking – once on its own and once inside the pastry crust. Eat the pie as soon as it is cooked because the pastry will start to harden as it cools.

1 Put the oil and the onions in a large bowl and cover. ☒ HIGH for 5 mins. 600W (*4 mins. 700W; 6 mins. 500W*) to soften. Toss the steak and kidney in the seasoned flour, then stir into the onions. Re-cover and ☒ HIGH for 10 mins. 600W (*8½ mins. 700W; 12½ mins. 500W*), stirring two or three times.

2 · Stir in the ale, re-cover and ☒ MEDIUM for 40 mins. 600W (*34 mins. 700W; 50 mins. 500W*), or until tender, stirring two or three times. Leave to cool.

3 To make the pastry: Sift the flour into a mixing bowl, tipping in the bran from the sifter. Add the suet and enough of the water to mix to a soft dough, but make sure it is not sticky. Knead lightly and roll out on a floured board to a 10-inch circle. Cut out a quarter and set aside for the lid.

4 Line a 3¾-cup pudding bowl or heatproof bowl with the dough, brush the seam with water and press to seal. Roll out the reserved dough to a circle to fit the top of the bowl.

5 Spoon the steak-and-kidney mixture into the bowl. Brush the edge with water and press on the lid, pinching the edges together to seal firmly. Cover loosely with plastic wrap.

6 ☒ HIGH for 8-10 mins. 600W (*6½-8½ mins. 700W; 10-12½ mins. 500W*). Leave to stand for 5 mins., then invert onto a serving dish and serve at once.

 Preparation: 10 minutes, plus cooling

 Cooking time: 63 minutes

 Power setting: HIGH

 Make in advance

◎ **Serves 4**

★ Leave the meaty filling to cool completely before assembling the pudding, otherwise the pastry will be soggy.

Veal with artichokes in sour cream sauce

INGREDIENTS
1 9-ounce package frozen artichoke hearts
2 tablespoons butter or margarine
2 tablespoons flour
¼ teaspoon white pepper
1½ pounds veal for stew, cut into 1½-inch chunks
2 tablespoons cornstarch
3 tablespoons sherry
2 teaspoons Dijon-type mustard
1 10¾-ounce can chicken broth
½ lb small mushrooms
½ lb small white onions
1 8-ounce container sour cream
dash salt
1 tablespoon chopped parsley or dill for garnish (optional)

Cooking with lower power settings keeps the meat tender and enhances the flavor of the sauce. The delicately flavored stew is delicious served over noodles or a combination of white and wild rice.

1 Thaw artichoke hearts in colander under cool running water.

2 Combine flour and white pepper in a medium bowl or plastic bag; add veal stew meat; toss until coated with flour. Place butter or margarine in 3-quart casserole. ▧ HIGH for 30 secs.-1 min, or until melted. Add veal stew meat; stir to coat chunks with butter. Cover and ▧ MEDIUM-HIGH for 12 mins. 600W (*10 mins. 700W.* ▧ *HIGH 12 mins. 500W*), stirring halfway through the cooking time.

3 In the meantime, stir sherry and cornstarch in 2-cup glass measuring cup until blended. Add mustard; stir until mixture is smooth; gradually stir in chicken broth.

4 Pour chicken broth mixture over veal stew meat; stir in mushrooms, and onions. Cover and ▧ MEDIUM for 18 mins. 600W (*15 mins. 700W.* ▧ *HIGH 20 mins. 500W*). Stir in artichoke hearts and continue to cook on the same power setting and for the same amount of time as given above, or until meat is fork tender.

5 Stir in sour cream until blended; salt to taste. Cover and ▧ MEDIUM for 5 mins. 600W (*4 mins. 700W; 6 mins. 500W*). Serve over noodles or rice. Sprinkle with chopped parsley or dill.

Preparation:
20 minutes

Cooking time:
53 minutes

Power setting:
MEDIUM-HIGH and MEDIUM 600 and 700W
HIGH 500W

Serves 4-6

Illustrated on p. 85

Top: **Sweet-and-sour pork** (*see p. 91*); Center: **Lemony lamb kebobs** (*see p. 90*); Bottom: **Ham steaks with orange and raisin sauce** (*see opposite*).

Ham steaks with orange and raisin sauce

INGREDIENTS

4 slices ham steak,
about 3 oz

1 tablespoon vegetable oil

For the sauce

½ cup soft light brown
sugar, packed

1 tablespoon cornstarch

¼ teaspoon ground
cinnamon

¼ teaspoon dry mustard

¼ cup orange juice

½ cup raisins

1 tablespoon butter

Ham steaks can be cooked either on a microwave roasting rack or on a browning dish. With the latter, the steaks brown a little more and keep very moist. Serve with a sweet tangy sauce to complement the savory taste of the ham steaks.

1 Preheat a browning dish, ▨ HIGH for 5 mins. 600W (*4 mins. 700W; 6 mins. 500W*), or according to the manufacturer's directions. Snip the fat off the steaks at inch intervals to prevent it curling.

2 Pour the oil into the hot dish and swirl to coat the bottom. Add the steaks and press them down well. Cover and ▨ HIGH for 8-9 mins. 600W (*6 ½-7 ½ mins. 700W; 10-11 ½ mins. 500W*), turning over and rearranging once. Leave to stand for 3 mins.

3 Meanwhile, to make the sauce: Put the sugar, cornstarch, cinnamon and mustard into a medium bowl and mix well. Stir in the orange juice, raisins and butter and ▨ HIGH for 3 mins. 600W (*2 ½ mins. 700W; 3 ½ mins. 500W*), or until boiling, stirring twice. Serve hot, poured over the steaks.

 Preparation:
10 minutes

 Cooking time:
11 minutes

Power setting:
HIGH

Serves 4

Illustrated opposite

Lemony lamb kebobs

INGREDIENTS

1 lb boned leg of lamb
2 small onions, quartered
2 zucchini, each cut into 8 chunks
2 tablespoons olive oil
1 teaspoon chopped fresh thyme or ½ teaspoon dried thyme
grated peel and juice of 1 lemon
½ teaspoon cornstarch

Lamb cubes threaded onto skewers cook quickly and stay tender when cooked in the microwave. To keep them really moist, stop cooking when the cubes are still slightly pink and leave to stand in a warm place while microwaving the sauce.

1 Cut the lamb into 24 even-sized chunks. Thread the lamb onto eight short wooden skewers, alternately with the onion and zucchini chunks. Place in a shallow baking dish.

2 Mix together the olive oil, thyme, lemon peel and juice and spoon over the kebobs. Leave them in a cool place to marinate for about 30 mins., basting with the marinade occasionally.

3 Drain the kebobs and reserve the marinade. Place on a microwave roasting rack over a shallow dish and 🌊 HIGH for 12-14 mins. 600W (*10-11 mins. 700W; 15-17 mins. 500W*) until just cooked, basting with the marinade and turning and rearranging two or three times. Drain the cooking juices into a bowl, then cover the kebobs and leave to stand for 3 mins.

4 Mix the cornstarch with a little water to form a paste and stir into the juices, then add any remaining marinade and mix well. 🌊 HIGH for 1-1½ mins. 600W (*½-1 min. 700W; 1-2 mins. 500W*), until boiling and thickened, stirring every 30 secs. Pour over the kebobs and serve at once with a salad.

 Preparation: 15 minutes, plus marinating

 Cooking time: 13 minutes

Power setting: HIGH

Make in advance

 Serves 4

★ Thread the smaller-sized chunks of lamb onto the centers of the skewers, keeping any slightly larger chunks at the ends, where they will cook more quickly.

Illustrated on p. 88

Sweet-and-sour pork

INGREDIENTS

1 tablespoon vegetable oil

1 lb pork tenderloin, cut into thin strips

2 carrots, thinly sliced

4 scallions, cut into 1-inch pieces

1 medium green pepper, quartered and sliced

2 tablespoons light brown sugar

1 tablespoon cornstarch

pinch of garlic salt

1 tablespoon white-wine vinegar

2 tablespoons soy sauce

1 tablespoon tomato ketchup

7 1/2-oz can pineapple chunks

Garnish

1/3 cup roasted cashew nuts

By first cooking the pork and vegetables separately, then quickly heating them through in the sweet-and-sour sauce, everything keeps its individual flavor. The pork remains very tender and the vegetables stay pleasantly crisp.

1 Preheat a browning dish, ▓ HIGH for 5 mins. 600W (*4 mins. 700W; 6 mins. 500W*), or according to the manufacturer's directions. Add the oil and swirl to coat the bottom. Spread the pork in an even layer in the hot dish and press down well for a few seconds, then stir and press down again until the sizzling stops.

2 Cover and ▓ HIGH for 4 mins. 600W (*3 mins. 700W; 5 mins. 500W*), stirring once, until the pork is no longer pink. Remove the pork from the dish with a slotted spoon and set aside.

3 Add the carrots, onions and green pepper to the juices in the dish and cover. ▓ HIGH for 4-5 mins. 600W (*3-4 mins. 700W; 5-6 mins. 500W*), until just tender, stirring once.

4 Mix the sugar, cornstarch and garlic salt with the vinegar, soy sauce and tomato ketchup. Pour onto the vegetables, add the pineapple and its juice and stir well.

5 Stir in the pork and ▓ HIGH for 4-6 mins. 600W (*3-5 mins. 700W; 5-7 mins. 500W*), until the sauce is boiling and thickened. Stir twice during cooking. Serve hot garnished with the cashew nuts, accompanied by rice.

 Preparation:
15 minutes

 Cooking time:
12 minutes

 Power setting:
HIGH

 Serves 4

Illustrated on p. 88

Duck with cherry sauce

INGREDIENTS

1 5lb duckling, quartered

For the sauce

16 oz can pitted black cherries

grated peel and juice of 1 orange

1 teaspoon chopped fresh mint or ½ teaspoon dried mint

3 tablespoons port

2 tablespoons black cherry jam

2 teaspoons cornstarch

Garnish

sprigs of mint

Balance the rich flavor of duck with a sharp sauce. This quick, colorful cherry sauce can be made while the duck is standing and still cooking through.

1 Put the duck portions (with the thinner parts to the center) in a shallow baking dish and ▧ HIGH for 13-15 mins. 600W (*10-12½ mins. 700W; 16-18 mins. 500W*), rearranging and turning over after halfway through cooking. Cover and leave to stand for 5 mins.

2 To make the cherry sauce: Drain the cherries and reserve the juice. Put the cherries, orange peel and juice, mint, port and cherry jam in a small bowl. Mix the cornstarch with ¼ cup of the cherry juice and stir into the cherry mixture.

3 ▧ HIGH for 2-3 mins. 600W (*1½-2½ mins. 700W; 2½-3½ mins. 500W*) until boiling and thickened, stirring twice. Serve hot, poured over the duck and garnish with the mint sprigs.

⊡ **Preparation:** 10 minutes

≋ **Cooking time:** 15 minutes

⊘ **Power setting:** HIGH

◎ **Serves 4**

⊡ Skim the fat from the cooking juices and add the juices to the sauce for extra flavor.

Illustrated opposite

Top: **Duck with cherry sauce** (*see opposite*); Bottom: **Roast chicken with red currants** (*see p. 94*).

Roast chicken with red currants

INGREDIENTS

chicken, about 3 lb

microwave browning

For the stuffing

scant ½ cup red currant jelly

grated peel and juice of 1 lemon

3 tablespoons butter

½ cup bread crumbs

⅓ cup chopped toasted hazelnuts (filberts)

salt and black pepper

Stuffing the chicken under the skin rather than in the cavity ensures that it cooks thoroughly and has the added advantage of making the breast meat moist and full of flavor.

1 To make the stuffing: put the red currant jelly and lemon peel and juice in a bowl and ▨ HIGH for 2 mins. 600W (*1 ½ mins. 700W; 2 ½ mins. 500W*), then stir to melt. Put the butter in a separate bowl and ▨ HIGH for 1 min. 600W (*30 secs. 700W; 1 min. 500W*) to melt.

2 Reserve one-third of the butter for basting the chicken and pour the rest into a mixing bowl. Stir in the bread crumbs, hazelnuts, seasoning to taste and three-quarters of the red currant jelly mixture and mix well.

3 Loosen the skin over the breast of the chicken, then stuff the neck end, pushing the stuffing in an even layer, over the breast, under the skin. Secure the neck flap with a wooden skewer.

4 Brush the chicken with the reserved butter and sprinkle with the microwave browning. Place the prepared chicken on a microwave roasting rack and dish, breast-side down and ▨ HIGH for 9 mins. 600W (*7 mins. 700W; 13 mins. 500W*).

5 Turn the chicken over and drain off the cooking juices. Sprinkle with a little more microwave browning and ▨ HIGH for 9-11 mins. 600W (*7½-9 mins. 700W; 11½-13½ mins. 500W*) until the juices run clear. Cover and leave to stand for 10 minutes.

6 Just before serving, pour the remaining red currant jelly mixture into a small bowl and ▨ HIGH for 1 min. 600W (*30 secs. 700W; 1 min. 500W*). Serve hot with the sliced chicken and stuffing.

★ **Preparation:**
25 minutes

≋ **Cooking time:**
22 minutes

⌀ **Power setting:**
HIGH

◎ **Serves 4**

Illustrated on p. 93

Chicken curry

INGREDIENTS

1 medium onion, chopped
2 tablespoons vegetable oil
½ cup plain yogurt
8 chicken legs
1 tablespoon chopped fresh coriander or flat-leaf parsley
1 tablespoon lemon juice

For the curry sauce

⅓ cup unsalted cashew nuts
1-inch piece fresh ginger, finely grated, or 1 teaspoon ground ginger
1 teaspoon chili powder
1 teaspoon ground cinnamon
¼ teaspoon cardamom seeds
¼ teaspoon ground cloves
1 tablespoon poppy seeds
1 tablespoon ground coriander
2 teaspoons ground cumin
½ teaspoon saffron threads (optional)
2 tablespoons boiling water

Garnish

slices of lemon
sprigs of fresh coriander or flat-leaf parsley

This mild curry with its wonderful blend of spices cooks quickly, but it really needs to be left for a few hours after cooking to allow the flavors to develop properly. It's ideal for a dinner party as it can be made the day before.

1 To make the curry sauce: Put the cashew nuts, ginger and all the spices except the saffron in a blender with ⅔ cup water and blend until smooth. Add the saffron to the boiling water and leave to soak (optional).

2 Put the onion and oil in a large bowl and cover. ▓ HIGH for 4 mins. 600W (*3 mins. 700W; 5 mins. 500W*) to soften. Stir in the sauce and yogurt and ▓ HIGH for 3 mins. 600W (*2½ mins. 700W; 3½ mins. 500W*).

3 Add the chicken legs, placing the narrow parts toward the center, and spoon over the sauce to cover. Add the soaked saffron, if desired, and the fresh coriander or flat-leaf parsley.

4 Cover and ▓ HIGH for 5 mins. 600W (*4 mins. 700W; 6 mins. 500W*). Stir, re-cover and ▓ MEDIUM for 20-25 mins. 600W (*17-21 mins. 700W; 25-30 mins. 500W*), until the chicken is tender, stirring once.

5 Uncover and leave to cool, then cover and keep in a cool place for at least 2 hours (overnight if possible). To serve, ▓ HIGH for 10-12 mins. 600W (*8½-10 mins. 700W; 12½-15 mins. 500W*), stirring once until heated through. Leave to stand for 5 mins., then serve at once, garnished with the coriander or parsley sprigs and lemon slices.

Preparation:
10 minutes

Cooking time:
28 minutes

Power settings:
HIGH and MEDIUM

Make in advance

Good reheated

Serves 4

Top: **Turkey tetrazzini** (*see opposite*); Bottom: **Turkey breasts with port sauce** (*see p. 98*).

Turkey tetrazzini

INGREDIENTS

1 cup elbow macaroni
5 cups boiling salted water
1 lb turkey breast
2 tablespoons butter
3½ cups quartered button mushrooms
½ cup grated Cheddar cheese
2 tablespoons bread crumbs
For the sauce
3 tablespoons butter
3 tablespoons flour
⅔ cup turkey or chicken broth
2 tablespoons dry vermouth (optional)
⅓ cup heavy cream
salt and black pepper

This dish is based on the well-known chicken recipe. It was originally made with leftovers, and invented to honor a San Francisco singer.

1 Put the macaroni and water in a deep bowl. Cover and ▧ HIGH for 8 mins. (*all powers*), stirring two or three times. Leave to stand for 5 mins., then drain.

2 Put the turkey, butter and mushrooms in a shallow dish and ▧ HIGH for 8-10 mins. 600W (*6-8½ mins. 700W; 10-12½ mins. 500W*), turning the turkey over halfway through cooking. Leave to stand for 5 mins., then slice the turkey thickly.

3 To make the sauce: Put the butter in a medium bowl and ▧ HIGH for 1 min. 600W (*30 secs. 700W; 1 min. 500W*) to melt. Stir in the flour, then the broth and ▧ HIGH for 3-4 mins. 600W (*2½-3 mins. 700W; 3½-5 mins. 500W*) until boiling, stirring twice.

4 Stir in vermouth and the cream and seasoning to taste, then mix in the turkey, mushrooms and macaroni. Spoon into individual serving dishes and spread evenly.

5 Mix the cheese and crumbs together and sprinkle over the tops. ▧ HIGH for 4-6 mins. 600W (*3-5 mins. 700W; 5-7 mins. 500W*) until bubbling and hot, giving the dishes a half turn once. Leave to stand for 3 mins., then serve hot.

 Preparation:
10 minutes

 Cooking time:
24 minutes

 Power setting:
HIGH

 Good reheated

Serves 4

Illustrated opposite

Turkey breast with port sauce

INGREDIENTS

1 4½ to 5 pound fresh or frozen (thawed) turkey breast
1 teaspoon fresh thyme leaves
⅛ teaspoon white pepper
3 tablespoons butter, melted
2 teaspoons soy sauce
4 bacon slices, uncooked

For the sauce

2 teaspoons cornstarch
2 tablespoons cold water
½ cup port
¼ cup turkey drippings
2 teaspoons brown sugar
2 teaspoons chopped fresh thyme or ¼ teaspoon thyme leaves
2 teaspoons lemon juice

Turkey breast is especially easy to prepare in a microwave oven. The results are so moist and juicy you won't want to reserve this dish just for the holidays.

1 Rinse turkey with cold running water and pat dry. Rub cavity with thyme and white pepper.

2 Stir butter and soy sauce in small bowl until well blended, brush skin with mixture. Using toothpicks or string, secure bacon crosswise on breast. Brush bacon with butter mixture.

3 Place bird skin side down on microwave-safe rack. Cover with waxed paper, cook for half the time noted above. Turn bird skin side up, baste with remainder of butter mixture. Continue to cook, uncovered, for remainder of time or until turkey reaches 160°F when tested with microwave-safe meat thermometer. Cover turkey with aluminum foil let stand approximately 10 minutes. Turkey will continue to cook to reach 170°F. In the meantime, prepare sauce.

4 Blend the cornstarch and water in a 2-cup glass measuring cup until smooth. Stir in port, drippings, brown sugar, and fresh or dried thyme. ⊠ HIGH for 2-2½ mins. 600W *(1-1 ½ mins. 700W; 2 ½-3 mins. 500W)* or until boiling and thickened, stirring 2-3 times during cooking. Stir in lemon juice.

5 Slice the turkey breast and spoon over sauce. If you like, garnish with sprigs of thyme and serve at once.

 Preparation: 20 minutes

 Cooking time per pound:
700W 6-7 mins.
600W 8-9 mins.
500W 10-12 mins.

Power setting: HIGH

Serves 4

 It is possible to replace the turkey with chicken.

Illustrated on p. 96

VEGETABLE MAIN COURSES

Crunchy Chinese vegetables

INGREDIENTS

2 cups julienne strips of carrots
1 ⅔ cups diced turnips
1 ½ cups sliced snow peas
⅔ cup julienne strips daikon (white radish)
salt and black pepper
For the sauce
1 tablespoon vegetable oil
1 clove garlic, crushed
2 scallions, chopped
⅔ cup boiling vegetable broth
1 tablespoon wine vinegar
2 tablespoons honey
1 tablespoon soy sauce
1 tablespoon sherry
½ cup grated fresh pineapple
1 teaspoon aniseed
2 teaspoons cornstarch

This is a microwave version of a stir-fry where the vegetables are cooked very quickly. The difference is that here the sauce is made before they are cooked and is used as a marinade.

1 Prepare all the vegetables and arrange in a large dish.

2 For the sauce, put the oil in a medium dish and 🐟 HIGH for 1 min. 600W (*30 secs. 700W; 1 min. 500W*). Stir in the garlic and scallions and 🐟 HIGH for 30 secs.

3 Add the remaining ingredients, except the cornstarch, and 🐟 HIGH for 3 mins. 600W (*2 ½ mins. 700W; 3 ½ mins. 500W*), stirring once or twice.

4 Dissolve the cornstarch in a little water, then stir into the sauce. 🐟 HIGH for 2 mins 600W (*1 ½ mins. 700W; 2 ½ mins. 500W*), stirring once.

5 Pour the sauce over the vegetables, stir well, then cover and 🐟 HIGH for 5 mins. (*4 mins. 700W; 6 mins. 500W*), stirring once or twice.

6 Leaves to stand for 2 mins., then season to taste. Serve with noodles or rice.

⭐ **Preparation:**
25 minutes

〰 **Cooking time:**
11 ½ mintes

⊘ **Power setting:**
HIGH

〰 **Good reheated**

❄ **Freezes well**

◎ **Serves 4**

⭐ Vary the ingredients according to the seasons. Daikon (Japanese radish) is a spicy-flavored white radish which is available in Asian stores and large supermarkets.

Stuffed cabbage leaves

INGREDIENTS

½ cup pearl barley
2½ cups boiling water
scant ½ cup sunflower seeds
1 tablespoon vegetable oil
1 medium onion, finely chopped
2½ cups diced button mushrooms
1¼ cups shredded cabbage
1 apple, grated
1 teaspoon caraway seeds
1 cup grated carrots
1 tablespoon soy sauce
salt and black pepper
8-12 cabbage leaves

For the sauce

1⅓ cups carrots, cooked
2 tablespoons orange juice
¼ cup plain yogurt
½ teaspoon grated nutmeg
salt and black pepper

Garnish

some cumin seeds

Barley is an underrated grain all too often confined to soups. It has a delicate flavor and is ideal as a vegetable filling.

1 Put the barley in a deep bowl and pour over the boiling water. Leave to soak for 1 hour. Cover and ▓ HIGH for 20 mins. (*all powers*), stirring 2-3 times. Stand for 5 mins., then drain.

2 Spread out the sunflower seeds on a small plate and ▓ HIGH for 2 mins. 600W (*1 ½ mins. 700W; 2 ½ mins. 500W*).

3 Put the oil in a medium bowl and ▓ HIGH for 1 min. 600W (*30 sec. 700W; 1 min. 500W*). Add the onion and ▓ HIGH for 2 mins. 600W (*1 ½ mins. 700W; 2 ½ mins. 500W*). Stir in the mushrooms, shredded cabbage, apple and caraway seeds. Cover and ▓ HIGH for 4 mins. 600W (*3 mins. 700W; 5 mins. 500W*).

4 Mix the cooked vegetables and barley with the raw carrot, sunflower seeds and soy sauce. Season well with salt and pepper.

5 To soften the cabbage leaves, place in a large bowl with 2 tablespoons water. Cover and ▓ HIGH for 2 mins. 600W (*1 ½ mins. 700W; 2 ½ mins. 500W*). Spoon 1-2 tablespoons filling on to each cabbage leaf, then roll up to make packages. Arrange these in a shallow dish, cover and ▓ HIGH for 3 mins. 600W (*2 ½ mins. 700W; 3 ½ mins. 500W*) or until warmed.

6 Make the sauce. Purée the cooked carrots with the orange juice and yogurt, and season well. ▓ HIGH for 1 ½ mins. 600W (*1 min. 700W; 2 mins. 500W*), then serve garnished with cumin seeds.

 Preparation:
25 minutes

 Cooking time:
44 minutes

⌀ **Power setting:**
HIGH

◎ **Serves 4**

 Choose dark cabbage leaves such as the outer leaves of a Savoy for this recipe or the end result will look pale.

Illustrated opposite

Stuffed tomatoes

INGREDIENTS

4 large tomatoes
⅓ cup peanuts
1 tablespoon sesame seeds
1 teaspoon cumin seeds
1 teaspoon coriander seeds
1-1½ cups bread crumbs
scant ⅓ cup chopped pitted ripe olives
2 stalks celery, diced
4 scallions, diced
1 tablespoon tomato paste
2 teaspoons miso (optional) dissolved in a little broth or water (see note opposite)
salt and black pepper

The spicy flavor of the roasted nut and seed filling complements the sweet, moist tomatoes perfectly.

1 Slice a lid from the bottom of each tomato, then scoop out the flesh and chop well.

2 Mix the peanuts, seasame seeds and spices together, spread out on a small plate and ▓ HIGH for 3 mins. 600W (*2½ mins. 700W; 3½ mins. 500W*), shaking the plate once or twice. Grind quite finely.

3 Mix the ground nuts and seeds with about half of the tomato flesh and the remaining ingredients, seasoning well with salt and pepper. Fill the tomatoes with the mixture and cover each one with its lid.

4 Arrange the tomatoes in a baking dish, cover and ▓ HIGH for 7 mins. 600W (*6 mins. 700W; 8½ mins. 500W*), rearranging once or twice during cooking.

5 Serve hot with a spicy tomato sauce (*see page 147*) or sharp yogurt dressing.

★ **Preparation:** 25 minutes

▓ **Cooking time:** 10 minutes

⊘ **Power setting:** HIGH

◎ **Serves 4**

▓ Be careful not to overcook the tomato shells or they will collapse. Miso is a soybean paste which is available in health food stores and Japanese and Chinese stores.

Illustrated below

Left: **Stuffed tomatoes** (*see above*); Right: **Stuffed cabbage leaves** (*see opposite*)

Hazelnut loaf

INGREDIENTS

½ cup short-grain brown rice
2 cups boiling water
⅔ cup hazelnuts (filberts)
1 tablespoon vegetable oil
1 medium onion, finely chopped
2 cloves garlic, crushed
1 teaspoon celery seeds
1 cup diced carrots
1 tablespoon flour
⅔ cup dry red wine
2 tablespoons tomato paste
salt and black pepper

Using grains instead of bread crumbs in nut loaf makes the mixture chewy in texture, but lighter and more moist.

1 Put the rice in a 2-quart casserole and pour over the boiling water. Cover and ▨ HIGH for 18 mins. (*all powers*), stirring 2-3 times. After letting it stand for 5 mins, drain water remaining.

2 Spread the hazelnuts in a 9-inch pie plate and ▨ HIGH for 4 mins. 600W (*3 mins. 700W; 5 mins. 500W*), shaking the plate once or twice. (Toasting the nuts will enhance their flavor) cool and chop finely using a knife or a food processor.

3 Put the oil in a medium dish and ▨ HIGH for 1 min. 600W (*30 secs. 700W; 1 min 500W*). Stir in the onion, then ▨ HIGH for 1 min. 600W (*30 secs. 700W; 1 min. 500W*).

4 Add the garlic, celery seeds and carrots and ▨ HIGH for 4 mins. 600W (*3 mins. 700W; 5 mins. 500W*).

5 Mix the flour, wine, and tomato paste. Cover and ▨ HIGH for 2½ mins. 600W (*2 mins. 700W; 3 mins. 500W*).

6 Mix the chopped nuts and the rice into the sauce and season well with salt and pepper.

7 Line an 8½ × 4½-inch loaf pan with waxed paper and spoon in the mixture. Cover top with waxed paper and place pan on microwave – safe rack. ▨ HIGH for 10-12 mins. 600W (*8½-10 mins. 700W; 12½-15 mins. 500W*), giving the dish a quarter turn every 3 mins. Leave to stand for 4 mins. before removing from pan. Serve while still hot.

 Preparation: 20 minutes

 Cooking time: 40½ minutes

⊘ **Power setting:** HIGH

◎ **Serves 4**

Nut roasts are best when slightly undercooked and then left to stand. If overcooked, the outside becomes dry and hard.

Spicy layered mango pilaf

INGREDIENTS

1 tablespoon vegetable oil	
3 scallions, finely chopped	
1-2 cloves garlic, crushed	
1 teaspoon curry powder	
1 teaspoon cumin seeds	
½ teaspoon turmeric	
⅓ cup pine nuts	
scant 1 cup long-grain brown rice	
3¼ cups boiling water	
1 mango, peeled and diced	
juice of ½ lemon	
salt and black pepper	

For the filling

1 tablespoon vegetable oil	
3¼ cups diced mushrooms	
1 clove garlic, chopped	
1 cup diced French-style green beans	
1 tablespoon soy sauce	

The filling for this pilaf consists of a simple mixture of fresh vegetables which can be varied according to availability.

1 Put the oil in a medium dish and ▨ HIGH for 1 min. 600W (*30 secs. 700W; 1 min. 500W*). Stir in the onion and garlic and ▨ HIGH for 30 secs.

2 Mix the spices with a little water. Add to the onions with the pine nuts and ▨ HIGH for 30 secs.

3 Add the rice and boiling water. Cover and ▨ HIGH for about 18 mins. (*all powers*), stirring 2-3 times. Leave to stand for 5 mins. Then add the mango and the lemon juice. Season well.

4 For the filling, put the oil in a medium dish and ▨ HIGH for 1 min. 600W (*30 secs. 700W; 1 min. 500W*). Stir in the diced mushrooms and garlic, cover and ▨ HIGH for 3 mins. 600W (*2½ mins. 700W; 3½ mins. 500W*).

5 Add the beans, soy sauce and 1 tablespoon water. Re-cover and ▨ HIGH for 4 mins. 600W (*3 mins. 700W; 5 mins. 500W*). Season well.

6 Put half the rice into a large dish and cover with the mushroom and bean mixture. Spoon over the remaining rice, cover and ▨ HIGH for 3 mins. 600W (*2½ mins. 700W; 3½ mins. 500W*).

Preparation: 25 minutes

Cooking time: 31 minutes

Power setting: HIGH

Freezes well

Serves 4

The cooking time for rice will vary according to the age and variety of the grain. If it's not quite tender at the end of the time recommended here, cook for a little longer, adding more boiling water, if necessary.

Illustrated on p. 105

Leek and cauliflower bake

INGREDIENTS

2 teaspoons vegetable oil
1 medium leek, diced
4½ cups cauliflower flowerets
For the sauce
1 tablespoon margarine
1 tablespoon flour
1¼ cups skim milk
1 bay leaf
½ teaspoon grated nutmeg
1 teaspoon dry mustard
For the topping
⅔ cup flour
⅔ cup cornmeal
1½ teaspoons baking powder
½ teaspoon salt
1 teaspoon caraway seeds
½ teaspoon dry mustard
1 egg
⅔ cup milk
1 tablespoon olive oil
½ cup grated Cheddar cheese

In this dish, the lightly cooked vegetables retain a good crisp texture, the sauce is easy to prepare, and the biscuit topping provides a tasty and wholesome finish.

1 Put the oil in a medium bowl and ▨ HIGH for 1 min. 600W (*30 secs. 700W; 1 min. 500W*). Add the leek and cauliflower, cover and ▨ HIGH for 4 mins. 600W (*3 mins. 700W; 5 mins. 500W*). Leave to stand.

2 For the sauce, put the margarine in a 2½ cup bowl and ▨ HIGH for 1 min. 600W (*30 secs. 700W; 1 min. 500W*). Add the flour and ▨ HIGH for 30 secs. Pour in the milk, stirring well. Add the bay leaf and spices, then ▨ HIGH for 2 mins. 600W (*1 ½ mins. 700W: 2½ mins. 500W*), stirring every 30 secs. Season well, then mix into the vegetables.

3 For the topping, mix the flour, cornmeal, baking powder, salt and spices together.

4 In a separate bowl, beat the egg thoroughly, then add the milk and olive oil. Pour the mixture over the dry ingredients and mix to a stiff dough. Add the cheese. Roll out the dough and cut into 1-inch circle about ½ inch deep.

5 Put the vegetables and sauce in a baking dish and cover with the dough circles. ▨ HIGH for 5 mins. 600W (*4 mins. 700W; 6 mins. 500W*), then brown under a preheated microwave browning element or conventional broiler.

 Preparation: 30 minutes

Cooking time: 13½ minutes

Power setting: HIGH

Service 4

 If wished, top with a little more grated cheese before browning using a microwave browning element or conventional broiler.

Illustrated opposite

Top: **Spicy layered mango pilaf** (*see p. 103*); Bottom: **Leek and cauliflower bake** (*see opposite*)

Exotic rice with snow peas

INGREDIENTS

1 teaspoon vegetable oil
1 medium onion, chopped
1 clove garlic, crushed
½-inch piece fresh ginger, grated, or 1 teaspoon ground ginger
1 teaspoon ground coriander
8-oz can crushed tomatoes
1 teaspoon ground saffron (optional)
scant 1 cup brown rice
3¼ cups boiling water
½ lb snow peas
1 medium green pepper, seeded and diced
¾ cup mung bean sprouts
½ cucumber, diced
For the sauce
juice of 1 orange
juice of ½ lemon
1 tablespoon soy sauce
1 tablespoon sherry
1 teaspoon cornstarch

Grain dishes topped with mixtures of lightly cooked vegetables are really easy to cook in the microwave. Here, saffron, ginger and coriander add an exotic flavor to the rice while the vegetables give a fresh, crisp texture.

1 Put the oil in a baking dish and ▨ HIGH for 1 min. 600W (*30 secs. 700W; 1 min. 500W*). Stir in the onion and garlic and ▨ HIGH for 30 secs. (*all powers*). Stir well.

2 Add the ginger, coriander, tomatoes, saffron and rice. Pour over the boiling water, cover and ▨ HIGH for 18 mins. (*all powers*), stirring 2-3 times.

3 Add the vegetables, re-cover and ▨ HIGH for 4 mins. 600W (*3 mins. 700W; 5 mins. 500W*). Leave to stand for 4 mins.

4 For the sauce, mix the fruit juices, soy sauce and sherry together in a small bowl, then ▨ HIGH for 2 mins. 600W (*1 ½ mins. 700W; 2 ½ mins. 500W*).

5 Dissolve the cornstarch in a little water, then stir into the sauce. ▨ HIGH for 2 mins. 600W (*1 ½ mins. 700W; 2 ½ mins. 500W*), stirring twice.

6 Pour the sauce over the rice and vegetables and serve immediately.

Preparation: 20 minutes

Cooking time: 27½ minutes

Power setting: HIGH

Serves 4

Bean casserole

INGREDIENTS

heaping 1 cup pinto or borlotti beans, soaked overnight
5 cups boiling water
1 tablespoon olive oil
1 onion, finely chopped
1 clove garlic, crushed
1¾ cups diced zucchini
1 medium green pepper, seeded and diced
15-oz can crushed tomatoes
1 bay leaf
1 tablespoon tomato paste
salt and black pepper
For the pesto
2 tablespoons pine nuts
1 tablespoon grated Parmesan cheese
4 tablespoons chopped fresh basil or 4 teaspoons dried basil
1 tablespoon olive oil
1-2 cloves garlic
salt and black pepper

Pesto sauce adds a wonderful flavor to many dishes. It is particularly good in microwaved stews where the quick cooking means the flavors of the ingredients do not have much time to blend.

1 To make the pesto, grind the pine nuts using a mortar and pestle or food processor then work in the other ingredients to form a smooth paste. Set aside.

2 Drain the beans, put in a deep dish and pour over the boiling water. Cover and ▨ HIGH for 22 mins. (*all powers*), stirring 2-3 times and adding more boiling water if necessary. Leave to stand for 10 mins., then drain.

3 Put the oil in a medium bowl and ▨ HIGH for 1 min. 600W (*30 secs. 700W; 1 min. 500W*). Stir in the onion and garlic and ▨ HIGH for 2 mins. 600W (*1½ mins. 700W; 2½ mins. 500W*).

4 Add the zucchini, pepper and cooked beans, stir well and ▨ HIGH for 5 mins. 600W (*4 mins. 700W; 6 mins. 500W*), stirring once or twice.

5 Add the tomatoes, bay leaf and tomato paste. Cover and ▨ HIGH for 5 mins. 600W (*4 mins. 700W; 6 mins. 500W*).

6 Add the pesto sauce and ▨ HIGH for 5 mins. 600W (*4 mins. 700W; 6 mins. 500W*). Leave to stand for 5 mins., then season to taste. Serve hot, accompanied by rice, noodles, pasta or baked potatoes.

 Preparation: 20 minutes, plus overnight soaking

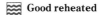 **Cooking time:** 40 minutes

 Power setting: HIGH

▨ **Good reheated**

◎ **Serves 4**

Illustrated on p. 108

Top **Bean casserole** (*see p. 107*); Bottom right: **Lentil and vegetable loaf** (*see opposite*); Bottom left: **Eggplant layer** (*see p. 110*)

Lentil and vegetable loaf

INGREDIENTS

½ cup brown lentils
2½ cups boiling water
1 potato, about 6 oz
1 tablespoon vegetable oil
1¾ cups trimmed and diced leeks
1 medium carrot, diced
1½ cups chopped mushrooms
2 teaspoons chopped fresh or dried sage
2 teaspoons miso (optional) (see p. 101)
¼ cup bean broth or dark vegetable broth
1 tablespoon tomato paste
⅔ cup quick-cooking oats
½ cup bread crumbs
1 tablespoon margarine
1 tablespoon flour
1 tablespoon soy sauce
1 teaspoon yeast extract (available from health food stores)
black pepper

This hearty loaf is full of rich flavors and moist vegetables. It is a good dish to serve for family supper with baked potatoes and green vegetables.

1 Put the lentils in a deep bowl and pour over the boiling water. Cover and ▩ HIGH for 12 mins. (*all powers*), stirring 2-3 times. Leave to stand for 5 mins., then drain.

2 Pierce the potato and wrap in paper towels. ▩ HIGH for 6 mins. 600W (*5 mins. 700W; 7½ mins. 500W*), turning over halfway through. Leave to cool slightly, then dice.

3 Put the oil in a medium bowl and ▩ HIGH for 1 min. 600W (*30 secs. 700W; 1 min. 500W*). Stir in the leeks and ▩ HIGH for 3 mins. 600W (*2½ mins. 700W; 3½ mins. 500W*).

4 Add the carrot, mushrooms, potato, sage and the miso dissolved in a little of the broth. Cover and ▩ HIGH for 5 mins. (*4 mins. 700W; 6 mins. 50W*), stirring once or twice. Stir in the tomato paste, oats, bread crumbs and lentils.

5 Put the margarine in a separate dish and ▩ HIGH for 30 secs (*all powers*). Stir in the flour and ▩ HIGH for 30 secs. Add the remaining bean broth, soy sauce and yeast extract. ▩ HIGH for 1-1½ mins., stirring once.

6 Stir the sauce into the lentil and vegetable mixture. Season to taste. Spoon into 9 × 5-inch loaf pan and ▩ HIGH for 10 mins. 600W (*8½ mins. 700W; 12½ mins. 500W*). Leave to stand for 5 mins. before removing from pan and serving.

 Preparation: 20 minutes

 Cooking time: 39 minutes

 Power setting: HIGH

 Good reheated

❄ **Freezes well**

◎ **Serves 4**

≋ This loaf also cooks well in a tube pan as the microwaves can easily penetrate the food from all sides.

Illustrated opposite

Eggplant layer

INGREDIENTS

2 large potatoes (about 8-ounces each)
1 tablespoon olive or salad oil
1 medium onion, chopped (about ¾ cup)
2 garlic cloves, minced
1 cup diced celery
1 medium green pepper, diced (about 1 cup)
1 medium red pepper, diced (about 1 cup)
3 8-ounce cans tomato sauce
2 tablespoons chopped fresh basil, or 1 teaspoon dried basil
salt and pepper
1 small eggplant (about 1 pound)
1 8-ounce package mozzarella cheese, shredded (about 2 cups)
¼ cup grated Parmesan cheese

This delicious vegetable and cheese packed dish is easier to prepare in the microwave. Because there is no need to bread and fry the eggplant it is much lower in calories and cholesterol than the traditional preparation.

1 Pierce the potatoes; place on paper towel in microwave oven. ▧ HIGH for 9-10 mins. 600W (*7-8 mins. 700W; 12-13 mins. 500W*) or until tender when pierced with fork. Remove from oven; allow to cool.

2 Place oil, onion, garlic, celery, and peppers in 1-quart casserole. Cover and ▧ HIGH for 9-10 mins. 600W (*8-8½ mins. 700W; 12-14 mins. 500W*), stirring occasionally. Stir in tomato sauce, and basil; add salt and pepper to taste. Cover and ▧ HIGH for 6 mins. 600W (*5 mins. 700W; 7 mins. 500W*), stirring halfway through cooking time. Discard liquid from vegetables.

3 Slice cooked potatoes about ⅛-inch thick. Peel and cut eggplant crosswise into ¼-inch thick slices. Spoon ⅔ cup tomato mixture onto bottom of 8 × 8-inch baking dish. Cover mixture with one-half of potato slices, then one-half of eggplant slices, and one-half of mozzarella and Parmesan cheeses. Spoon one-half of remaining tomato mixture on top of cheese; follow with a layer of the remaining potato slices and a layer of the remaining eggplant slices. Top with the remainder of the tomato mixture. ▧ HIGH for 26-28 mins. 600W (*24-26 mins. 700W; 30-35 mins. 500W*), or until eggplant is fork tender, rotating dish one-half turn halfway through cooking time. Sprinkle with the remaining cheese. ▧ HIGH until cheese melts. Let stand 5 mins. before serving.

Preparation:
25 minutes

Cooking time:
50 minutes

Power setting:
HIGH

Good reheated

Freezes well

Serves 4

Illustrated on p. 108

Marinated tofu with vegetables

INGREDIENTS

½ lb firm tofu, cut into 1-inch squares

For the marinade

6 tablespoons red wine
2 tablespoons soy sauce
1 tablespoon honey
1 tablespoon dry mustard
½ teaspoon chopped fresh or dried rosemary
½ teaspoon chopped fresh or dried sage
1 clove garlic, crushed

For the vegetable accompaniment

1 tablespoon vegetable oil
2 cups chopped leeks
1½ cups broccoli flowerets
⅔ cup julienne strips of turnips
1 cup julienne strips of carrots
salt and black pepper

The microwave is ideal for making quick marinades. Tofu benefits greatly from being marinated as it acts like a blotter, soaking up all the flavors of the marinade ingredients. Use firm tofu which slices easily and does not fall apart during cooking.

1 Mix the marinade ingredients together in a shallow dish. Add the tofu, baste well, cover and ▒ HIGH for 3 mins. 600W (*2½ mins. 700W; 3½ mins. 500W*), stirring once. Leave to stand for 10-15 mins.

2 For the vegetables, put the oil in a medium bowl and ▒ HIGH for 1 min. 600W (*30 secs. 700W; 1 min. 500W*). Stir in the chopped leeks and ▒ HIGH for 2 mins. 600W (*1½ mins. 700W; 2½ mins. 500W*).

3 Add the broccoli, turnips and carrots. Cover and ▒ HIGH for 2 mins. 600W (*1½ mins. 700W; 2½ mins. 500W*).

4 Add 2 tablespoons of the marinade, re-cover and ▒ HIGH for 4-5 mins. 600W (*3-4 mins. 700W; 5-6 mins. 600W*), stirring once. Leave to stand for 2 mins., then season to taste with salt and pepper.

5 Meanwhile, reheat the tofu mixture, cover and ▒ HIGH for 2 mins. 600W (*1½ mins. 700W; 2½ mins. 500W*).

6 Serve with the vegetables and some brown rice, either mixing the tofu with the vegetables or keeping them separate.

  Preparation: 25 minutes

Cooking time: 14 minutes

 Power setting: HIGH

Good reheated

Serves 4

The cooking time given in this recipe produces crisp vegetables; cook longer if a softer texture is preferred.

Illustrated on p. 113

Vegetable gado gado

INGREDIENTS

⅔ cup peanuts
2 tablespoons vegetable oil
1 medium onion, finely chopped
1 clove garlic, crushed
1 bay leaf
1 teaspoon grated fresh ginger or ground ginger
1 green chili, diced
juice of 1 lemon
1 tablespoon honey
1¼ cups boiling broth
1 tablespoon soy sauce
For the vegetables
4 scallions, diced
1½ cups sliced snow peas
⅔ cup diced Daikon (Japanese radish) (see p. 99)
2 red peppers, diced
¾ lb green beans, trimmed and cut in half
Garnish
Chopped scallion

The rich peanut sauce is quick and easy to make in the microwave. The vegetables should be crunchy but hot, so serve them as soon as they are cooked.

1 Spread out the peanuts in a shallow dish and ▓ HIGH for 3 mins. 600W (*2½ mins. 700W; 3½ mins. 500W*), shaking the dish halfway through. Grind to a fine powder.

2 Put the oil in a medium bowl and ▓ HIGH for 1½ mins. 600W (*1 min. 700W; 1½ mins. 500W*). Stir in the onion and garlic and ▓ HIGH for 1 min. 600W (*30 secs. 700W; 1 min. 500W*).

3 Add the remaining ingredients, including the peanuts. Season to taste with salt and pepper, and ▓ HIGH for 8 mins. 600W (*6½ mins. 700W; 10 mins. 500W*), stirring 3-4 times.

4 Mix together in a large bowl and add 2 tablespoons water. Cover and ▓ HIGH for 4 mins. 600W (*3 mins. 700W; 5 mins. 500W*), stirring once or twice.

5 Pour the sauce over the vegetables and garnish with the scallion. Serve with brown rice, barley or whole-wheat noodles.

 Preparation: 25 minutes

 Cooking time: 17½ minutes

 Power setting: HIGH

Good reheated

Serves 4

Illustrated opposite

Top: **Vegetable gado gado** (*see opposite*); Bottom: **Marinated tofu with vegetables** (*see p. 111*)

Creamy onion tart

INGREDIENTS

heaped ¾ cup flour
pinch of salt
¼ cup margarine or shortening and butter mixed
1 egg, beaten, plus a little milk or 2-3 tablespoons milk
For the filling
1 tablespoon vegetable oil
2 cups finely chopped onions
1 egg
2 tablespoons sour cream or cream cheese
2 tablespoons chopped fresh parsley
pinch of grated nutmeg
salt and black pepper

Pastry made with egg or milk as the binding agent gives the best result in the microwave. Covering the dough with a paper towel and a plate ensures that all the moisture is absorbed and the finished pastry stays crisp.

1 Mix the flour and salt together in a bowl, then cut in the margarine or vegetable shortening and butter until the mixture resembles fine bread crumbs. Mix in the egg to form a smooth dough, adding a little milk if necessary. Cover and leave to rest in a cool place for 15 mins.

2 Roll out the dough and line an 8-inch quiche dish. Prick the sides and bottom with a fork. Cover with a paper towel and a plate and ▨ HIGH for 5 mins. 600W (*4 mins. 700W; 6 mins. 500W*), giving the dish a quarter turn every 1½ mins. Uncover and leave to cool.

3 For the filling, put the oil in a medium bowl and ▨ HIGH for 1 min. 600W (*30 secs. 700W; 1 min. 500W*). Stir in the onions and ▨ HIGH for 3 mins. 600W (*2½ mins. 700W; 3½ mins. 500W*), stirring once or twice.

4 Cool slightly, then beat in the egg, sour cream, parsley and nutmeg. Season to taste with salt and pepper.

5 Pour the filling into the pie shell and ▨ HIGH for 2½ mins. 600W (*2 mins. 700W; 3 mins. 500W*) until just set.

 Preparation: 30 minutes

 Cooking time: 11½ minutes

 Power setting: HIGH

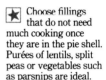 **Good reheated**

◎ **Serves 4**

★ Choose fillings that do not need much cooking once they are in the pie shell. Purées of lentils, split peas or vegetables such as parsnips are ideal.

VEGETABLE ACCOMPANIMENTS

Hungarian zucchini

INGREDIENTS

1-1 ½ lb zucchini
1 tablespoon vegetable oil
1 clove garlic, crushed
1 teaspoon paprika
2 tablespoons white wine
1 teaspoon dill weed
pinch of cayenne
salt and black pepper
Garnish
sprigs of dill

There is no need to add any extra water when cooking this zucchini recipe as its texture will remain firm and crisp, and it will easily absorb the full flavors of the ingredients.

1 Cut zucchini into ½-inch chunks.

2 Put the oil and garlic in a medium bowl and ▓ HIGH for 2 mins. 600W (*1 ½ mins. 700W; 2 ½ mins. 500W*). Add the zucchini and paprika and ▓ HIGH for 2 mins. 600W (*1 ½ mins. 700W; 2 ½ mins. 500W*).

3 Add the wine, dill weed and cayenne. Stir well, cover and ▓ HIGH for 3 mins. 600W (*2 ½ mins. 700W; 3 ½ mins. 500W*), stirring halfway through.

4 Season to taste with salt and pepper. Serve hot or cold, garnished with dill.

Preparation: 15 minutes

Cooking time: 7 minutes

Power setting: HIGH

Serves 4

Substitute yellow squash.

Illustrated on p. 117

Green bean, mushroom and artichoke medley

INGREDIENTS

3 cups trimmed and halved green beans
1½ cups quartered button mushrooms
½ 9-oz package frozen artichoke hearts, thawed and halved
1 medium tomato, skinned
1 tablespoon tomato paste
1 small onion, finely chopped
1 clove garlic, crushed
1 tablespoon soy sauce
2 tablespoons broth
salt and black pepper

Liven up different assortments of cooked vegetables with tasty sauces like this tomato-based one, which can be heated up in seconds. The speed of the cooking means that the sauce is not absorbed by the vegetables, it simply highlights their individual flavors.

1 Put the beans in a large bowl with 2 tablespoons water, cover and ▨ HIGH for 5 mins. 600W (*4 mins. 700W; 6 mins. 500W*), stirring once.

2 Add the mushrooms and artichoke hearts. Re-cover and ▨ HIGH for 3 mins. 600W (*2½ mins. 700W; 3½ mins. 500W*). Drain, reserving all the liquid to be used as broth.

3 Purée the tomato, tomato paste, onion, garlic, soy sauce and broth until smooth.

4 Stir the sauce into the vegetables. Cover and ▨ HIGH for 1 min., then season well with salt and pepper. Serve hot or cold.

 Preparation: 15 minutes

 Cooking time: 9 minutes

 Power setting: HIGH

 Serves 4

Illustrated opposite

Top: **Hungarian zucchini** (*see p. 115*); Center: **Green bean, mushroom and artichoke medley** (*see opposite*);
Bottom: **Spiced cauliflower** (*see p. 118*)

Spiced cauliflower

INGREDIENTS

1½ teaspoons sesame seeds
1½ teaspoons cumin seeds
1½ teaspoons mustard seeds
1 tablespoon vegetable oil
1 medium onion, finely chopped
1 clove garlic, crushed
1 small cauliflower, divided into small, even-sized flowerets
⅔ cup plain yogurt
salt and black pepper

Garnish

sprigs of coriander or flat-leaf parsley

Cauliflower cooked by this method in the microwave retains the crisp texture and nutty flavor of the raw vegetable. The mixture of aromatic spices gives extra flavor and transforms it into an unusual and tasty dish.

1 Put all the seeds on a small plate and ▒ HIGH for 1 min. 600W (*30 secs. 700W; 1 min. 500W*) to develop their flavors. Grind to a powder.

2 Put the oil in a medium bowl and ▒ HIGH for 1 min. 600W (*30 secs. 700W; 1 min. 500W*). Stir in the chopped onion and the garlic and ▒ HIGH for 2 mins. 600W (*1 ½ mins. 700W; 2 ½ mins. 500W*).

3 Add the cauliflower flowerets, seeds and 1 tablespoon water, stir well, then cover and ▒ HIGH for 2 mins. 600W (*1 ½ mins. 700W; 2 ½ mins. 500W*).

4 Stir in the yogurt, then re-cover and ▒ LOW for 2 mins. 600W (*1 ½ mins. 700W; ▒ DEFROST for 2 mins. 500W*). It is important that the yogurt doesn't boil or it will separate.

5 Season well with salt and pepper and serve hot or cold, garnish with coriander or flat-leaf parsley.

 Preparation: 15 minutes

 Cooking time: 7½ minutes

 Power settings: HIGH and LOW

 Serves 4

 Chop the cauliflower stalk into small pieces and use to make up a vegetable broth or soup.

Illustrated on p. 117

Italian-style beans with walnut sauce

INGREDIENTS

4 cups Italian-style (flat) green beans, cut into 1-inch pieces

For the sauce

1 tablespoon margarine

1 tablespoon flour

⅔ cup skim milk

⅓ cup chopped walnuts

salt and black pepper

Garnish

walnut half

Fresh beans are a true sign of summer. Their strong flavor goes particularly well with this creamy sauce enriched with crunchy walnut pieces.

1 Put the beans in a large bowl with 3 tablespoons water. Cover and ☒ HIGH for 5 mins. 600W (*4 mins. 700W; 6 mins. 500W*). Strain, reserving the liquid. Make up the liquid to ⅔ cup with water.

2 Put the margarine in a medium bowl and ☒ HIGH for 30 secs. Stir in the flour and ☒ HIGH for 30 secs.

3 Stir in the milk and the bean cooking water. Cover and ☒ HIGH for 4 mins. 600W (*3 mins. 700W; 5 mins. 500W*), stirring several times.

4 Stir in the chopped walnuts and season well. Pour the sauce over the beans and ☒ HIGH for 30 secs. to reheat. Serve hot, garnished with the walnut half.

★ **Preparation:**
15 minutes

≋ **Cooking time:**
10½ minutes

⊘ **Power setting:**
HIGH

◎ **Serves 4**

★ Any variety of green bean can be used instead of Italian-style beans, if preferred.

Illustrated on p. 120

Spinach creams

INGREDIENTS

1 lb fresh spinach

½ cup cottage cheese

¼ cup cream cheese

1 egg

½ teaspoon grated nutmeg

salt and black pepper

Garnish

slices of lemon

sprigs of dill

This dish can also make a delicious appetizer, or a light meal when served with a tomato salad and whole-wheat rolls. Use ¾ cup ricotta cheese in place of the cottage cheese and cream cheese mixture if you prefer.

1 Wash the spinach and shred finely. Place in a baking dish, cover and ☒ HIGH for 2 mins. 600W (*1 ½ mins. 700W; 2 ½ mins. 500W*).

2 Drain the spinach, then purée until smooth. Add the cheeses and blend until smooth. Beat in the egg and the nutmeg. Season well with salt and pepper.

3 Divide the mixture between four ramekin dishes, then ☒ HIGH for 3 mins. 600W (*2 ½ mins. 700W; 3 ½ mins. 500W*). The cream should still be soft at this stage – do not let it become rubbery. Serve hot, garnished with lemon and dill.

★ **Preparation:**
15 minutes

≋ **Cooking time:**
5 minutes

⊘ **Power setting:**
HIGH

◎ **Serves 4**

★ Spinach cooks very well in a microwave, especially if you buy young tender leaves which can be cooked in seconds. The water that clings to the leaves after washing is sufficient to cook all the spinach.

Illustrated on p. 120

Clockwise from the top: **Italian-style beans with walnut sauce** (*see p. 119*); **Baby beets with orange sauce** (*see opposite*); **Spinach creams** (*see p. 119*); **Ratatouille** (*see opposite*)

Baby beets with orange sauce

INGREDIENTS

¾ lb uncooked small beets, scrubbed

For the sauce

⅔ cup orange juice

juice of ½ lemon

1 tablespoon honey

½-inch piece fresh ginger, grated

¼ teaspoon celery seeds

1½ teaspoon cornstarch

parsley sprigs, to garnish

Hot beets are just as delicious cold, but they need a sauce to balance the slightly dry texture, and the sweetness of orange juice is ideal.

1 Pierce each beet once or twice, then arrange around the edge of a baking dish. Cover and ≋ HIGH for 8 mins. 600W *(6½ mins. 700W; 10 mins. 500W)*, rearranging twice during the cooking time. Leave to stand for 3 mins., then peel, if wished.

2 Meanwhile, mix all the sauce ingredients together, except the cornstarch, in a medium bowl. ≋ HIGH for 2 mins. 600W *(1½ mins. 700W; 2½ mins. 500W)*, stirring several times.

3 Dissolve the cornstarch in a little water, then stir into the sauce. ≋ HIGH for 2 mins. 600W *(1½ mins. 700W; 2½ mins. 500W)* until the liquid boils and clears.

4 Pour the sauce over the beets and serve hot. Garnish with parsley or color.

 Preparation: 15 minutes

 Cooking time: 12 minutes

 Power setting: HIGH

≋ **Good reheated**

◎ **Serves 4**

Illustrated opposite

Ratatouille

INGREDIENTS

1 tablespoon olive oil

1 medium onion, finely chopped

1 clove garlic, crushed

1 heaping cup of diced eggplant

1¾ cups diced zucchini

1 medium green or red pepper, seeded and diced

15-oz can tomatoes

1 tablespoon tomato paste

2 teaspoons chopped fresh thyme or 1 teaspoon dried thyme

1 teaspoon chopped fresh marjoram or ½ teaspoon dried marjoram

1 bay leaf

salt and pepper

Vegetable stews such as ratatouille work very well in the microwave. They are simple to prepare, the texture remains good and the flavors blend well into the sauce.

1 Put the oil in a bowl and ≋ HIGH for 1 min. 600W *(30 secs. 700W; 1 min. 500W)*.

2 Stir in the chopped onion and the garlic and ≋ HIGH for 2 mins. 600W *(1½ mins. 700W; 2½ mins. 500W)*.

3 Add the diced eggplant, zucchini, and pepper. ≋ HIGH for 3 mins. 600W *(2½ mins. 700W; 3½ mins. 500W)*.

4 Add the remaining ingredients, except the seasoning, stir well, then cover and ≋ HIGH for 8 mins. 600W *(6½ mins. 700W; 10 mins. 500W)*, stirring once or twice.

5 Season to taste with salt and pepper and serve hot.

 Preparation: 20 minutes

Cooking time: 14 minutes

Power setting: HIGH

Good reheated

◎ **Serves 4**

⬛ Different combinations of vegetables can be used in this recipe – try fresh lima beans, green beans and mushrooms.

Illustrated opposite

Marinated tomatoes

INGREDIENTS

1 tablespoon olive oil
3 scallions, finely chopped
1 clove garlic, crushed
1/3 cup chopped fennel or 1 teaspoon fennel seeds
3 tablespoons red wine
2 tablespoons tomato paste
1 teaspoon soy sauce
1 teaspoon chopped fresh tarragon or 1/2 teaspoon dried tarragon
1 lb large tomatoes
2 tablespoons chopped fresh parsley
salt and black pepper

These large ripe tomatoes make a delicious side vegetable. Their flavor is enhanced with this simple marinade, which is easy and quick to make using the microwave.

1 Put the oil in a medium bowl and HIGH for 1 min. 600W (*30 secs. 700W; 1 min. 500W*).

2 Stir in the onions, garlic and fennel or fennel seeds and HIGH for 30 secs.

3 Mix in the wine, tomato paste, soy sauce and tarragon. Add a little more olive oil if the dressing is too sharp.

4 Slice the tomatoes and lay them in the dressing, basting well. Sprinkle with parsley, cover and HIGH for 5 mins. 600W (*4 mins. 700W; 6 mins. 500W*).

5 Season with salt and pepper and serve hot or chilled.

★ **Preparation:** 10 minutes

≋ **Cooking time:** 6 1/2 minutes

⊘ **Power setting:** HIGH

◎ **Serves 4**

Cheese and potato layer

INGREDIENTS

1 1/2 cups grated Cheddar cheese
4 1/2 cups scrubbed and thinly sliced potatoes
2 cups onions cut into thin rings
1 teaspoon chopped fresh or 1/2 teaspoon dried sage
1 teaspoon chopped fresh thyme or 1/2 teaspoon dried thyme
2/3 cup skim milk
1/4 teaspoon grated nutmeg
salt and black pepper

This dish could be served as a side vegetable with a rich stew or on its own as an easy, light supper. It is best finished off under a conventional broiler so that the cheese is golden and bubbling.

1 Set aside 1/4 cup of the cheese for the topping. Layer the potatoes, onions and cheese in a baking dish, sprinkling the herbs over each of the layers. Finish with a layer of cheese.

3 Mix the milk and nutmeg together and season well with salt and pepper.

3 Pour the milk over the vegetables and cheese, cover and HIGH for 15 mins. 600W (*12 1/2 mins. 700W; 17-18 mins. 500W*), giving the dish a quarter turn every 5 mins.

4 Leave to stand for 4 mins. Sprinkle with the reserved cheese and melt under a preheated microwave browning element or conventional broiler. Serve hot.

★ **Preparation:** 30 minutes

≋ **Cooking time:** 15 minutes

⊘ **Power setting:** HIGH

≋ **Good reheated**

❉ **Freezes well**

◎ **Serves 4**

★ Add other vegetables or cooked beans to make a more substantial, filling dish. Increase the cooking time slightly.

Braised fennel
in tomato and apricot sauce

INGREDIENTS

1 ½ lb fennel bulbs, trimmed

For the sauce

7 tablespoon olive oil

1 medium onion, finely chopped

1 clove garlic, crushed

heaping ¼ cup slivered dried apricots

15-oz can crushed tomatoes

1 tablespoon tomato paste

½ teaspoon fennel seeds

salt and black pepper

Fennel cooked in the microwave retains its delicate flavor, and the texture remains crunchy. To make a more substantial dish, cover with grated cheese and brown under a conventional broiler, or serve with pasta and Parmesan cheese or chopped nuts.

1 For the sauce, put the oil in a medium bowl and ▨ HIGH for 1 min. 600W (*30 secs. 700W; 1 min. 500W*). Stir in the chopped onion and garlic and ▨ HIGH for 1 min. 600W (*30 secs. 700W; 1 min. 500W*).

2 Add the apricots, tomatoes, tomato paste and fennel seeds. Cover and ▨ HIGH for 10 mins. 600W (*8 ½ mins. 700W; 12 ½ mins. 500W*), stirring several times.

3 Slice the fennel into four chunks, or if using two bulbs, slice each one into four.

4 Arrange the fennel in a baking dish, add 2 tablespoons water, cover and ▨ HIGH for 6 mins. 600W (*5 mins. 700W; 7 ½ mins. 500W*), turning once or twice. Cook for longer if a softer vegetable is preferred. Drain, reserving the liquid.

5 Add the cooking liquid to the tomato sauce, then purée until smooth. Season well with salt and pepper.

6 Pour the sauce over the fennel in the dish and ▨ HIGH for 1 min. to reheat. Serve hot.

 Preparation:
20 minutes

 Cooking time:
19 minutes

 Power setting:
HIGH

 Serves 4

Barbecue-style baked potatoes

INGREDIENTS

½ cup pinto beans, soaked overnight
3¾ cups boiling water
4 large potatoes
For the sauce
1 cup tomato juice
3 tablespoons red wine
¼ cup lemon juice
2 tablespoons wine vinegar
2 tablespoons honey
½ cup diced mushrooms
2 stalks celery
2 tablespoons chopped fresh parsley
1 teaspoon chopped fresh thyme or ½ teaspoon dried thyme
salt and black pepper

It's easy to make a wholesome meal out of a baked potato by mixing the flesh with a selection of ingredients. On this page and p.126 are four tasty fillings, all of which cook very well in the microwave. You can easily speed up this recipe by using pre-cooked beans.

1 Drain the beans and place in a deep bowl. Pour over the boiling water. Ensure that it covers the beans by 1-2 inches. Add more if necessary. Cover and ▨ HIGH for 25 mins. 600W (*21 mins. 700W; 30 mins. 500W*) until just soft. Drain.

2 Pierce each potato, wrap in a paper towel and ▨ HIGH for 15 mins. 600W (*12½ mins. 700W; 18 mins. 500W*), turning over and rearranging halfway through. Stand for 5 mins.

3 For the sauce, mix all the ingredients together, then stir into the cooked beans.

4 Slice the potatoes in half and scoop out the flesh. Mix with the beans and sauce. Fill the potato halves with the mixture, piling it up into a mound.

5 Arrange the potato halves on a plate and ▨ HIGH for 3 mins. 600W (*2½ mins. 700W; 3½ mins. 500W*) or until heated through, rearranging once.

 Preparation: 15 minutes

 Cooking time: 43 minutes

 Power setting: HIGH

▨ **Good reheated**

◎ **Serves 4**

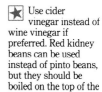 Use cider vinegar instead of wine vinegar if preferred. Red kidney beans can be used instead of pinto beans, but they should be boiled on the top of the stove for 10 minutes before cooking in the microwave.

Illustrated opposite

Clockwise from top right: **Barbecue-style baked potatoes** (*see opposite*); **Leek and horseradish filling** (*see p. 126*); **Peanut and yogurt filling** (*see p. 126*); **Cheese filling** (*see p. 126*)

Baked potato fillings
VARIATIONS

Leek and horseradish filling

INGREDIENTS

1 ⅓ cups finely chopped leeks
2-3 tablespoons water
1 teaspoon horseradish sauce
2 tablespoons plain yogurt
salt and black pepper
2 baked potatoes
Garnish
sprigs of flat-leaf parsley

1 Put the leeks in a medium bowl with the water. Cover and ▧ HIGH for 3 mins. 600W (*2 ½ mins. 700W; 3 ½ mins. 500W*), stirring once. Drain well.

2 Purée the leeks with the horseradish and yogurt. Season to taste with salt and pepper.

3 Scoop out a little of the potato flesh, add to the purée, then spoon back into the potatoes. ▧ HIGH for 2 mins. 600W (*1 ½ mins. 700W; 2 ½ mins. 500W*) or until hot. Serve, garnished with coriander or flat-leaf parsley.

◉ **Fills 2 potatoes**

★ To bake 2 potatoes, follow the same method as on p. 124 but bake for 8 mins. 600W (*7 mins. 700W; 10 mins. 500W*), remembering to turn over and rearrange halfway through. Leave for 3-4 mins. to soften.

Illustrated on p. 125

Peanut and yogurt filling

INGREDIENTS

1 tablespoon peanut butter
1 tablespoon plain yogurt
1 teaspoon soy sauce
2 baked potatoes
Garnish
sprigs of rosemary

1 Cream all the ingredients together.

2 Halve the baked potatoes and scoop out some of the flesh. Combine with the sauce and spoon back into the potato cases.

3 ▧ HIGH for 3 mins. 600W (*2 ½ mins. 700W; 3 ½ mins. 500W*). Serve, garnished with rosemary.

 Fills 2 potatoes

Illustrated on p. 125

Cheese filling

INGREDIENTS

½ cup grated cheese
2 tablespoons margarine
½ teaspoon caraway seeds
½ teaspoon mustard seeds
black pepper
2 baked potatoes
Garnish
some cumin seeds

1 Beat the cheese and margarine together in a small bowl, then add the remaining ingredients.

2 Scoop out a little of the potato flesh, and add to the cheese mixture. Spoon the filling into the hot potatoes, then ▧ HIGH for 2 mins. 600W (*1 ½ mins. 700W; 2 ½ mins. 500W*). Serve, garnished with cumin.

 Fills 2 potatoes

Illustrated on p. 125

Broccoli with olives and garlic

INGREDIENTS

1 tablespoon olive oil
1 small onion, finely chopped
2¼ cups broccoli flowerets
8-12 large olives, pitted
1 medium tomato, skinned
1 tablespoon red-wine vinegar
1 clove garlic
½ teaspoon curry powder
salt and black pepper

The pungent olive and tomato sauce with garlic and spices gives the broccoli an exotic flavor.

1 Put the oil in a medium bowl and ▨ HIGH for 1 min. 600W *(30 secs. 700W; 1 min. 500W)*. Stir in the onion and ▨ HIGH for 2 mins. 600W *(1 ½ mins. 700W; 2 ½ mins. 500W)*.

2 Stir in the broccoli, then add 2 tablespoons water. Cover and ▨ HIGH for 5 mins. 600W *(4 mins. 700W; 6 mins. 500W)*, stirring once. Leave to stand for 2-3 mins.

3 Meanwhile, purée the olives, tomato, vinegar, garlic and curry powder to make a coarse-textured sauce.

4 Drain the vegetables, then toss in the sauce. Cover and ▨ HIGH for 1 min. to reheat. Season well with salt and pepper. Serve hot or chilled.

 Preparation: 20 minutes

Cooking time: 8 minutes

Power setting: HIGH

Serves 4

Illustrated on p. 129

Creamy carrot and parsnip bake

INGREDIENTS

½ lb carrots, cut into 1-inch pieces
½ lb parsnips, cut into 1-inch pieces
1 3-ounce package cream cheese, softened
1-2 tablespoons butter or margarine
2 eggs
salt and pepper
1-2 tablespoons sesame seeds, toasted (optional)

Mixtures of root vegetables are an easy way of serving something just a little bit different. Using cream cheese gives this dish a subtle, creamy flavor

1 Place carrots, parsnips and 2 tablespoons water in 1-quart casserole. Cover and ▨ HIGH for 10 mins. 600W *(8-9 mins. 700W; 12 mins. 500W)*, or until fork tender. Let stand for 5 mins.; drain liquid.

2 Place cooked vegetables, cream cheese and butter or margarine in food processor. Blend until a smooth purée is formed. Add eggs and process until well blended; add salt and pepper to taste.

3 Spread vegetable purée in 9-inch pie plate. Cover and ▨ HIGH 6-7 mins. 600W *(5-6 mins. 700W; 8-9 mins. 500W)* or until center is set. Sprinkle with toasted sesame seeds. Cut into wedges.

Preparation: 15 minutes

Cooking time: 16 minutes

Power level: HIGH

Serves 6

If you prefer, substitute rutabaga cut into 1-inch pieces for the parsnips.

Illustrated on p. 129

Braised red cabbage

INGREDIENTS

1 tablespoon vegetable oil
1 medium onion, sliced into rings
1 clove garlic, crushed
1½ cups diced celery or fennel
1 teaspoon fennel or caraway seeds
5 cups shredded red cabbage
⅓ cup raisins
3 tablespoons red wine
1 tablespoon honey
salt and black pepper

Using the microwave is a marvelously quick way to make this delicious vegetable side dish. Try adding nuts like walnuts or extra fruit, such as fresh apple or dried apricots.

1 Put the oil in a medium bowl and ▨ HIGH for 1 min. 600W *(30 secs. 700W; 1 min. 500W)*. Stir in the sliced onion and the garlic and ▨ HIGH for 2 mins. 600W *(1½ mins. 700W; 2½ mins. 500W)*.

2 Add the celery or fennel, the seeds and 1 tablespoon water. Cover and ▨ HIGH for 4 mins. 600W *(3 mins. 700W; 5 mins. 500W)*, stirring once.

3 Stir in the remaining ingredients, except the seasoning, re-cover and ▨ HIGH for 10 mins. 600W *(8½ mins. 700W; 12½ mins. 500W)*, stirring 3 times.

4 Leave to stand for 3 mins., then season well with salt and pepper. Serve hot or cold.

 Preparation: 20 minutes

 Cooking time: 17 minutes

 Power setting: HIGH

Good reheated

 Serves 4

To produce cabbage with a slightly softer texture, cook for a few minutes longer than the time given in this recipe.

Illustrated opposite

Marinated peppers

INGREDIENTS

4 medium peppers
salt
For the marinade
6 tablespoons olive oil
2 tablespoons red-wine vinegar
1 teaspoon whole grain mustard
2 teaspoons chopped capers
1 tablespoon finely chopped fresh parsley
1 teaspoon chopped fresh thyme or ½ teaspoon dried thyme
1-2 cloves garlic, crushed
salt and black pepper
Garnish
1 tablespoon finely chopped fresh parsley

This is a rich, tasty idea for an interesting appetizer or a salad accompaniment. The salad can be made with eggplant instead of peppers.

1 Slit the skin of the peppers, then arrange on a plate and ▨ HIGH for 15 mins. 600W *(12½ mins. 700W; 19 mins. 500W)*, turning over and rearranging halfway through. Drop the peppers into a bowl of cold water, leave for 5 mins., then remove the skin and deseed.

2 Cut each pepper into four or six pieces and place in a small, deep bowl.

3 Mix all the marinade ingredients together, except the seasoning, and pour over the peppers. Cover and ▨ HIGH for 2 mins. 600W *(1½ mins. 700W; 2½ mins. 500W)*.

4 Leave until cold, then season to taste with salt and pepper. Serve straight from the dish or drain the peppers and place on individual plates. Garnish with parsley.

 Preparation: 20 minutes

 Cooking time: 18 minutes

 Power setting: HIGH

 Serves 4

 It doesn't matter if the peppers collapse a little during the microwaving, they need to be well cooked in order to remove the skins.

Top: **Broccoli with olives and garlic** (*see p. 127*); Center: **Braised red cabbage** (*see opposite*); Bottom: **Creamy carrot and parsnip bake** (*see p. 127*).

Hot green salad

INGREDIENTS

1 tablespoon olive oil
4 scallions, trimmed and chopped
4 stalks celery, diced
½ avocado, peeled and diced
1 medium green pepper, seeded and diced
1 Romaine lettuce, chopped
½ cucumber, diced

For the dressing

1 teaspoon mustard powder
1 tablespoon white-wine vinegar
2 tablespoons olive oil
2 teaspoons chopped fresh herbs, such as chives and basil or 1 teaspoon dried herbs
salt and black pepper

An unusual idea for a side salad that is only possible with a microwave. The salad ingredients remain crisp, but the avocado melts to give an extra buttery flavor to the dressing. This dish also makes a delicious appetizer.

1 Put the oil in a medium bowl and ▒ HIGH for 1 min. 600W (*30 secs. 700W; 1 min. 500W*).

2 Stir in the scallions and ▒ HIGH for 1 min. 600W (*30 secs. 700W; 1 min. 500W*).

3 Add all the salad ingredients.

4 Mix all the dressing ingredients together and toss into the salad. Cover and ▒ HIGH for 3 mins. 600W (*2½ mins. 700W; 3½ mins. 500W*).

5 Toss the salad, then leave to stand for 2 mins. Serve hot.

 Preparation:
20 minutes

 Cooking time:
5 minutes

 Power setting:
HIGH

 Serves 4

DESSERTS

Apricot petit pots

INGREDIENTS

¾ cup large dried apricots

2½ cups boiling water

2 eggs

¼ cup cornmeal

⅔ cup skim milk

¼ teaspoon ground cardamon

1-2 tablespoons honey
(optional)

Decoration

1 tablespoon slivered almonds,
chopped

*Custards work extremely well in the microwave
and can be flavored with different fruit purées
or a variety of spices and sweeteners.*

1 Cover the apricots with boiling water.
Cover and ▨ HIGH for 5 mins. 600W (*4 mins.
700W; 6 mins. 500W*). Leave until cool and
plump. Drain, then purée.

2 Beat all the remaining ingredients together,
sweetening to taste with honey if wished. Mix
in the apricot purée.

3 Divide the mixture between four ramekin
dishes. ▨ HIGH for 5 mins. 600W (*4 mins.
700W; 6 mins. 500W*), rearranging the
dishes halfway through.

4 Arrange the almonds on a small plate and
toast on ▨ HIGH for about 3 mins. 600W (*2
mins. 700W; 4 mins. 500W*), stirring at least
once a minute to prevent scorching.

5 Decorate with the almonds.

Preparation:
15 minutes, plus
cooling

Cooking time:
10 minutes

Power setting:
HIGH

Serves 4

*Illustrated on
pp. 132-133*

Plum and banana crumble

INGREDIENTS

2⅔ cups pitted and chopped plums

2 bananas, sliced

2 tablespoons honey

For the topping

⅓ heaping cup flour

⅔ cup quick-cooking oatmeal

¼ cup margarine

2 tablespoons sunflower seeds

2 tablespoons granulated brown sugar

Choose mixtures of dried and fresh fruits for natural sweetness and a better flavor.

1 Mix the fruit and honey in a medium bowl. Cover and ▓ HIGH for 4 mins. 600W (*3 mins. 700W: 5 mins. 500W*).

2 Mix flour and oatmeal together. Cut in margarine and add seeds and sugar.

3 Add the crumble to the fruit, then ▓ HIGH for 3 mins. 600W (*2½ mins. 700W; 3½ mins. 500W*); turn often. Serve hot.

 Preparation: 15 minutes

 Cooking time: 7 minutes

 Power setting: HIGH

◎ **Serves 4**

Illustrated below

From left to right: **Summer compote** (*see opposite*); **Apricot petit pots** (*see p. 131*); **Plum and banana crumble** (*see above*)

Summer compote

INGREDIENTS

½ lb black currants
½ lb red currants
2 teaspoons cornstarch
3 tablespoons honey

This refreshing fruit dessert is simple to make in the microwave.

1 Remove stems from currants, then purée or mash half of them. Dissolve cornstarch in 2 tablespoons honey and 2 tablespoons water. Add honey and stir into fruit purée.

2 Put in a medium bowl, cover and ⊠ HIGH for 4 mins. 600W (*3 mins. 700W; 5 mins. 500W*); stir once. Add other fruit and ⊠ HIGH for 1 min. 600W (*30 secs. 700W; 1 min. 500W*). Serve chilled.

Preparation:
15 minutes, plus chilling

Cooking time:
5 minutes

Power setting:
HIGH

Serves 4

Top with yogurt and red currants.

Illustrated below

Baked pears with mango sauce

INGREDIENTS

4 large pears
2½ cups orange juice
juice of ½ lemon
1-inch piece fresh ginger, cut into slivers
1 mango, peeled and diced
2 teaspoons cornstarch

A delicious, light dessert with an interesting combination of fruits. Use ripe Bartlett or Comice pears and choose a ripe mango by its distinctive scent.

1 Peel the pears, halve and core them. Arrange around the outside of a large round baking dish, cut side down, with the thicker ends pointing outward.

2 Pour over the orange and lemon juices and add the ginger. Cover and 🍲 HIGH for 5 mins. 600W (*4 mins. 700W; 6 mins. 500W*), giving the dish a quarter turn every 1½ mins.

3 Strain off the excess juice, then purée the mango in the fruit juices until smooth.

4 Dissolve the cornstarch in a little of the purée, then stir into the remainder.

5 Pour into a small bowl and 🍲 HIGH for 4 mins. 600W (*3 mins. 700W; 5 mins. 500W*), stirring once every minute until the sauce has boiled and thickened.

6 Pour the sauce over the pears and 🍲 HIGH for 1 min. to reheat if necessary.

  Preparation: 15 minutes

 Cooking time: 9 minutes

Power setting: HIGH

Serves 4

Cocoa sour cream pie

INGREDIENTS

⅓ cup butter or margarine	
1 tablespoon apple butter (optional)	
1¼ cup graham-cracker crumbs	
¼ cup quick-cooking oats, uncooked	
3 tablespoons brown sugar	

For the filling

1 cup, plus 2 tablespoons sugar
1½ tablespoons cornstarch
2 teaspoons cocoa
¼ teaspoon cinnamon
dash nutmeg (optional)
1½ cups sour cream
3 egg yolks
1 cup raisins

Decoration

shaved chocolate curls

This variation of the traditional sour cream and raisin pie is guaranteed to have chocolate and raisin lovers asking for seconds.

1 Place butter or margarine in 9-inch pie plate and ▨ HIGH 45 secs.-1½ mins. or until just melted. Stir in apple butter until well blended; add graham-cracker crumbs, oats and brown sugar, stir until well blended. Press mixture into bottom and up sides of dish. ▨ HIGH for 2½-3 mins. 600W *(2-2½ mins. 700W; 3-3½ mins. 500W)*. Cool.

2 Place sugar, cornstarch, cocoa powder and cinnamon in large bowl, stir until well blended.

3 In medium bowl, beat sour cream and eggs until well blended, stir into sugar mixture, until well blended. ▨ HIGH for 7-7½ mins. 600W *(6-6½ mins. 700W; 8-9 mins. 500W)* or until top surface appears to be boiling, stirring 2-3 times during cooking. Remove bowl from oven, whisking mixture until it appears smooth. Pour into prepared pie crust and chill until set. If you like decorate with shaved chocolate curls.

★ **Preparation:** 20 minutes, plus chilling time

〰 **Cooking time:** 10 minutes

⊘ **Power setting:** HIGH

◎ **Serves 8**

Illustrated on p. 136

Top left: **Cocoa sour cream pie** (*see p. 135*); Top right: **Low-calorie orange-ginger cheesecake** (*see opposite*);
Bottom: **Stuffed peaches in wine sauce** (*see p. 138*)

Low-calorie orange-ginger cheesecake

INGREDIENTS

5 tablespoons margarine
1⅓ cups graham-cracker crumbs
¼ cup quick-cooking oats, uncooked
3 tablespoons dark brown sugar
¼ teaspoon ground ginger
For the filling
1 15-ounce container ricotta cheese
½ cup skim milk
2 eggs
3 tablespoons honey
2 tablespoons orange juice
½ teaspoon vanilla extract
¼ cup unbleached all-purpose flour
1 teaspoon grated orange peel
Decoration
Orange slices and candied ginger pieces

The finished cheesecake is quite delicate, so handle it carefully. You may need to cook it a little longer than recommended here for a firmer texture but be careful not to dry out the mixture as it will continue setting as it cools.

1 Place margarine in 9-inch round baking dish and ▧ HIGH 45 secs.-1½ minutes until just melted. Stir in graham-cracker crumbs, oats, brown sugar and ground ginger until well blended. Press mixture into bottom and up sides of dish. ▧ HIGH 2-2½ mins. 600W *(1-1½ mins. 700W; 3-4 mins. 500W)* until heated through, rotating dish one half turn halfway through cooking time. Let stand on rack to cool.

2 In the meantime, combine ricotta cheese, skim milk, eggs, honey, juice and vanilla in 4-cup glass measure; beat until very smooth. Whisk in flour until well blended, then add orange peel. ▧ on HIGH 5½ mins. 600W *(4½ mins. 700W; 6½ mins. 500W)* or until mixture thickens, stirring 3 to 4 times during cooking.

3 Pour mixture into cooled crust. ▧ HIGH 3-3½ mins. 600W *(2-2½ mins. 700W; 4-5 mins. 500W)* or until edges are set (center will still be soft) rotating dish one-half turn halfway through cooking time. Let stand to cool; refrigerate at least 4 to 6 hours before serving. Garnish with orange slices and pieces of candied ginger.

 Preparation: 15 minutes plus 4 to 6 hours chilling

Cooking time: 10¾ mins.

Power setting: HIGH

Serves 8

 This makes a good low-calorie dessert.

Illustrated opposite

Stuffed peaches in wine sauce

INGREDIENTS

4 peaches
1¼ cups pitted cherries
2 tablespoons chopped nuts
1¼ cups rosé wine or apple juice
1 tablespoon cornstarch
½ teaspoon ground cinnamon

It's easy to heat fruit through without losing its color or texture, to make a distinctive and appetizing dish. Here, the peach halves are filled with cherries and nuts and topped with a light wine or fruit-based sauce.

1 Slice the peaches in half, remove pit and arrange skin-side down around the edge of a large round baking dish.

2 Chop the cherries very finely, mix with the chopped nuts and spoon this mixture on top of each peach.

3 Pour over the wine or apple juice, cover and ▩ HIGH for 4 mins. 600W (*3 mins. 700W; 5 mins. 500W*), rearranging halfway through the cooking time.

4 Strain off the juices into a small bowl. Mix the cornstarch with a little of this juice, then stir it back in to the remainder. Add the cinnamon and ▩ HIGH for 3 mins. 600W (*2½ mins. 700W; 3½ mins. 500W*), stirring once or twice.

5 Pour the sauce over the peaches and ▩ HIGH for 1 min. (*all powers*).

6 Serve hot or chilled, with cream or ice cream.

 Preparation: 10 minutes

 Cooking time: 8 minutes

Power setting: HIGH

Serves 4

 Other soft summer fruits such as raspberries, could be used in the filling instead of the cherries.

Illustrated on p. 136

Classic rice pudding

INGREDIENTS

1½ cups water
1 cup milk
1 cup long grain rice, uncooked
2 cups heavy cream
2 eggs, beaten
⅓ cup sugar
1 teaspoon vanilla
½ cup raisins (optional) cinnamon

Cooking rice in the microwave does not save time, however the results are always perfect and you do not need to worry about burned or scorched pans.

1 Stir water and milk in 2-quart bowl. Cover and ✷ HIGH for 6 mins. 600W (*5 mins. 700W; 8 mins. 500W*). Stir in rice. Cover and ✷ MEDIUM for 20 mins. 600W (*18 mins. 700W; ✷ HIGH 18 mins. 500W*), or until most of liquid is absorbed, stirring after 12 mins. Let stand, covered, for 5 mins.

2 Mix eggs, sugar, and vanilla in 4-cup glass measuring cup until well blended.

3 Place cream in 2-cup glass measuring cup and ✷ HIGH for 3 mins. 600W (*2½ mins. 700W; 3½ mins. 500W*). Whisking constantly to prevent eggs from cooking, gradually pour heated cream into egg mixture.

4 Stir cream mixture into rice; add raisins. If you like, transfer mixture into 2½-quart casserole; sprinkle with cinnamon. Cover and ✷ MEDIUM for 6-8 mins. 600W (*5-7 mins. 700W; ✷ MEDIUM-HIGH 10-12 mins. 500W*) or until just set. Serve warm or cool.

 Preparation:
15 minutes

 Cooking time:
35 minutes

 Power settings:
HIGH and MEDIUM

◎ **Serves 6**

★ For an eggnog-flavored pudding substitute rum extract for the vanilla and add a dash of nutmeg. To reduce calories, substitute 1 cup of milk for the cream.

Top: **Christmas plum pudding** (*see opposite*); Bottom: **Mixed fruit compote** (*see opposite*).

Christmas plum pudding

INGREDIENTS

heaping 1 cup flour
1 teaspoon apple pie spice mix
1 teaspoon ground cinnamon
½ teaspoon grated nutmeg
finely grated peel and juice of ½ lemon
2 oz cream of coconut.
1½ cups fresh bread crumbs
¼ cup dark brown sugar
1 cup grated carrots
1 dessert apple, grated
⅔ cup raisins
⅔ cup currants
⅔ cup golden raisins
scant ¼ cup chopped dried dates
2 tablespoons molasses
2 eggs
3 tablespoons brandy
1 tablespoon cocoa powder (optional)

Microwaving this type of pudding is a great time-saver. As the flavors have less time to develop during cooking, the raw mixture should be left to stand overnight.

1 Mix all the ingredients together in a large bowl, adding the cocoa powder if a darker color is preferred. The mixture should be moist enough to drop off the spoon – add more brandy or fruit juice if necessary.

2 Cover the bowl with plastic wrap and chill for several hours or overnight so the flavors combine well together.

3 Grease a 5-cup heat proof bowl. Spoon in the mixture, cover and HIGH for 5 mins. 600W (*4 mins. 700W; 6 mins. 500W*), then let it stand for 5 mins. Repeat this process 3 times to cook the pudding thoroughly.

4 If not serving immediately, store in a cool place wrapped in foil. Unwrap when required and cook, covered, in a bowl. Reheat for 5 mins. and stand for 5 mins. Serve with wine sauce if desired (see page 154).

 Preparation: 15 minutes, plus standing

 Cooking time: 20 minutes, plus standing

 Power setting: HIGH

Make in advance

Serves 8

If desired you can put a surprise inside of the pudding, as the English do, but remember not to use coins or metal objects.

Illustrated opposite

Mixed fruit compote

INGREDIENTS

¾ lb mixed dried fruit (prunes, peaches, apple rings, apricots, figs)
2 tablespoons raisins
1¼ cups red wine or grape juice
6 whole cardamoms
6 cloves
2-inch piece cinnamon stick
honey, to sweeten
Decoration
plain yogurt

Dried fruit are a good standby to have in the pantry, and with the microwave they come into their own for making emergency puddings or an instant breakfast.

1 Put all the ingredients, except the honey, in a large bowl, and add ⅔ cup warm water. Cover and HIGH for 10 mins. 600W (*8½ mins. 700W; 12½ mins, 500W*), stirring once or twice.

2 Leave to stand for 10-30 mins., then sweeten to taste with some honey. Discard the whole spices.

3 HIGH for 1 min. 600W (*30 secs. 700W; 1 min. 500W*) to reheat, then spoon into individual dishes.

4 Serve warm, topped with yogurt.

 Preparation: 15-35 minutes

 Cooking time: 11 minutes

 Power setting: HIGH

Make in advance

Serves 4

Try other spices, such as allspice or coriander, and different varieties of fruit juice.

Illustrated opposite

Steamed pudding

INGREDIENTS

½ cup margarine or butter
generous ½ cup dark brown sugar, packed
2 eggs
scant 1 cup flour
2 tablespoons cocoa or carob powder
2 teaspoons baking powder
1-2 tablespoons yogurt

This rich, dark pudding is quick to microwave and the end result is light with a crumbly, spongy texture. Serve the pudding with some yogurt and honey mixed together, a purée of dried or fresh fruit, or whipped cream. Carob is an alternative to chocolate for those concerned with their health or waistline.

1 Cream the margarine or butter and sugar together in a medium bowl until light and fluffy. ▨ HIGH for 5 secs.

2 Beat the eggs one at a time, blending well into the mixture, then fold in the flour, the cocoa or the carob and the baking powder.

3 Add enough yogurt to give the mixture a soft dropping consistency.

4 Line a 5-cup pudding bowl or heatproof bowl with waxed paper, then spoon in the pudding batter. Cover and ▨ HIGH for 5-6 mins. 600W (*4-5 mins. 700W; 6-7½ mins. 500W*), giving the dish a quarter turn every 1½ mins.

5 Leave to stand for 5 mins. before serving, while it is still hot, with the accompaniment you have chosen from those listed above.

★ **Preparation:** 10 minutes

≋ **Cooking time:** 5-6 minutes

⊘ **Power setting:** HIGH

◎ **Serves 4**

★ Once the mixture is made up it should be cooked right away to get the full benefit of the baking powder.

Bread and butter pudding

INGREDIENTS

6 large slices whole-wheat bread
¼ cup butter
grated peel of 1 orange
⅓ cup golden raisins
3 eggs, beaten
2 tablespoons light brown sugar
2 cups milk
few drops of vanilla extract
1 tablespoon light brown sugar

Traditionally, this pudding was made to use up stale bread. It microwaves extremely well; the bread layers, naturally sweetened by the golden raisins, soak up the orange-flavored custard, which sets softly to give a deliciously light pudding.

1 Cut the crusts from the bread, then spread the slices with butter and cut each into four triangles.

2 Layer the bread slices, butter-side up with the orange peel and golden raisins in a buttered 5-cup deep baking dish.

3 Beat together the eggs and sugar until light and fluffy. Put the milk in a bowl and ▧ HIGH for 2 mins. 600W (*1 ½-2 ½ mins. 700W; 2 ½-3 ½ mins. 500W*).

4 Beat the hot milk into the egg mixture, then stir in the vanilla extract. Pour over the bread, ▧ HIGH for 5 mins. 600W (*4 mins. 700W; 6 mins. 500W*), give the dish a half turn and ▧ MEDIUM for 15 mins. 600W (*12 ½ mins. 700W; 18 mins. 500W*) until just set, giving the dish a half turn twice.

5 Cover and leave to stand for 5 mins., then sprinkle with light brown sugar and serve the pudding at once.

 Preparation:
15 minutes

 Cooking time:
20 minutes

 Power settings:
HIGH and MEDIUM

 Serves 4

For a crispy top, brown the pudding under a conventional broiler.

Illustrated on p. 145

Tropical trifle

INGREDIENTS

1 3¼-ounce package vanilla pudding and pie filling
2 cups milk
2 tablespoons rum or 1 teaspoon rum extract (optional)
1 10¾-ounce ready-to-serve pound cake or 8 ounces ready-to-serve angel food cake
1 15½-20-ounce can pineapple chunks
1 11-ounce can mandarin orange segments, drained
2 medium bananas, peeled and sliced
1 cup heavy cream, whipped or 1 8-ounce container non-dairy whipped topping
2 tablespoons toasted coconut

Pudding is so easy to make in the microwave. Use it for this fruity dessert with a blend of tropical flavors that is special enough for a dinner party. Leave out the rum and it is ideal for children as well.

1 Mix contents of pudding package and milk in 4-cup glass measuring cup until smooth. HIGH for 7½-8 mins. 600W *(6½-7 mins. 700W; 8½-9 mins. 500W)* until mixture comes to a boil and thickens; stirring 3 to 4 times. Stir in rum or rum extract and allow to cool slightly.

2 Cut the cake into 1-inch cubes and arrange in 12 in × 8 in baking dish. Drain pineapple chunks reserving 6 tablespoons of the juice. Sprinkle juice over cake pieces.

3 Combine pineapple chunks, mandarin oranges, and bananas in medium bowl. (If you like set aside six pieces of each type of fruit to use as garnish. Banana slices used for garnish should be brushed with lemon juice to prevent browning.) Spoon fruit mixture over the cake in an even layer. Pour the pudding over fruit; chill for one hour or until set.

4 Spread and swirl the whipped cream or non-dairy topping over the pudding; garnish with reserved fruit and toasted coconut.

 Preparation: 25 minutes, plus chilling

 Cooking time: 8 minutes

Power setting: HIGH

Make in advance

Serves 8

Illustrated opposite

Top left: **Chocolate cheesecake** *(see p. 146)*; Center: **Tropical trifle** *(see opposite)*; Bottom: **Bread and butter pudding** *(see p. 143)*,

Chocolate cheesecake

INGREDIENTS

5 tablespoons butter

2½ cups chocolate-coated graham-crackers, crushed

For the filling

1½ cups cream cheese

1½ cups ricotta cheese

2 eggs plus 1 egg yolk, beaten

2 tablespoons cornstarch

11 squares semi-sweet chocolate

By using a mixture of cheeses this cheesecake has a wonderful soft texture. Cook it until it just begins to set, then chill thoroughly so it can set completely.

1 Put the butter in a medium bowl and ▨ HIGH for 1½ mins. 600W *(1 min. 700W; 1½-2 mins. 500W)* to melt. Stir in the cookie crumbs and mix well. Press into the bottom of a deep 9-inch pan.

2 To make the filling: Put the cheeses into a large bowl and ▨ MEDIUM for 2 mins. 600W *(1½ mins. 700W; 2½ mins. 500W)* to soften. Add the beaten egg and cornstarch and beat until smooth.

3 Put 9 squares of the chocolate into a small bowl and ▨ MEDIUM for 3½-4 mins. 600W *(3 mins. 700W 4½-5 mins. 500W)* to melt, stirring once. Stir into the cheese mixture, blending well.

4 Pour into the cake pan over the cracker base and smooth the surface. ▨ MEDIUM for 20-25 mins. 600W *(17-21 mins. 700W; 25-30 mins. 500W)* or until just set in the center.

5 Grate the remaining chocolate coarsely and sprinkle over the top. Leave the cheesecake to cool, then chill for at least 2 hours until firm.

★ **Preparation:**
20 minutes, plus chilling

▨ **Cooking time:**
28 minutes

⊘ **Power settings:**
HIGH and MEDIUM

▤ **Make in advance**

◎ **Serves 8-10**

Illustrated on p. 145

SAUCES
AND PRESERVES

Spiced tomato and coconut sauce

INGREDIENTS

1 tablespoon vegetable oil
1 medium onion, finely chopped
1 clove garlic, crushed
1 small chili, seeded and chopped finely
1 cup cream of coconut
1 ¼ cups boiling water
½ teaspoon ground cloves
½ teaspoon ground allspice
2 tablespoons tomato paste
⅔ cup tomato juice or equivalent in fresh tomatoes, puréed
salt

Cream of coconut makes a marvelous addition to sauces, adding a velvet texture and extra rich flavor. Serve this sauce with meatloaves, nut roasts or vegetables.

1 Put the oil in a medium bowl and ❀ HIGH for 1 min. 600W (*30 secs. 700W; 1 min. 500W*). Stir in the chopped onion, garlic and chili and ❀ HIGH for 2 mins. 600W (*1 ½ mins. 700W; 2 ½ mins. 500W*).

2 Add the coconut milk to the onion with the remaining ingredients, except the salt. Cover and ❀ HIGH for 7 mins. 600W (*6 mins. 700W; 8 ½ mins. 500W*), stirring once or twice.

3 Season to taste. Purée to make a smooth sauce.

★ **Preparation:**
10 minutes

❀ **Cooking time:**
10 minutes

⊘ **Power setting:**
HIGH

≋ **Good reheated**

❄ **Freezes well**

◎ **Makes about 2 ½ cups**

Illustrated on pp. 148-149

Sweet-and-sour sauce

INGREDIENTS

1 tablespoon margarine or butter
½ medium onion, finely chopped
1 clove garlic, crushed
½ cup water
½ cup pineapple juice
1 tablespoon cider vinegar
2 teaspoons honey
1 teaspoon soy sauce
½ teaspoon grated fresh ginger or ⅛ teaspoon dried ginger
⅔ cup plums, pitted and chopped
2 teaspoons cornstarch
salt and black pepper

Leaving the plums coarsely chopped gives this sauce a good texture. Take care not to over-thicken with cornstarch or the sauce will become gluey.

1 Put the margarine or butter in a bowl and 🔲 HIGH for 30 secs. (*all powers*). Stir in the onion and garlic and 🔲 HIGH for 2 mins. *600W (1 ½ mins. 700W; 2 ½ mins. 500W).*

2 Add the water, fruit juice, vinegar, honey, soy sauce, ginger and plums. Cover and 🔲 HIGH for 5 mins. *600W (4 mins. 700W; 6 mins. 500W),* stirring once.

3 Dissolve the cornstarch in a little water, then stir into the sauce and 🔲 HIGH for 2 mins. *600W (1 ½ mins. 700W; 2 ½ mins. 500W),* stirring once. Season to taste.

⭐ **Preparation:**
15 minutes

〰 **Cooking time:**
9½ minutes

⊘ **Power setting:**
HIGH

◎ **Makes about**
1¼ cups

Illustrated below

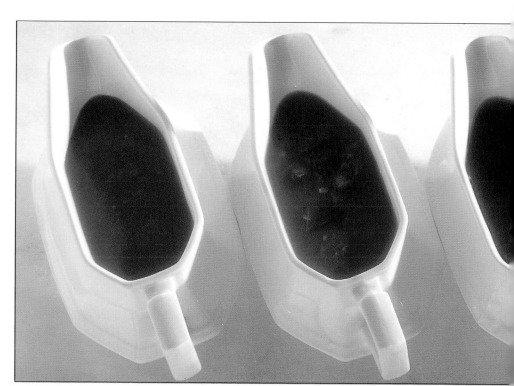

From left to right: **Spiced tomato and coconut sauce** (*see p. 147*); **Sweet-and-sour sauce** (*see above*); **Concentrated vegetable broth** (*see p. 151*); **White sauce** (*see p. 150*); **Savory brown sauce** (*see opposite*)

Brown sauce

INGREDIENTS

2 tablespoons margarine
½ teaspoon celery seeds
1 bay leaf
1 medium onion, finely chopped
1 clove garlic, crushed
2 tablespoons flour
1 teaspoon chopped fresh thyme or ½ teaspoon dried thyme
1 tablespoon soy sauce
1-2 teaspoons miso (optional) dissolved in a little broth or water (see p. 101)
2 cups broth or water
black pepper

This is an easy recipe for a rich gravy which is good served with any bowl bakes or roasts.

1 Put the margarine, celery seeds and bay leaf in a medium dish and ▓ HIGH for 1 min. 600W (*30 secs. 700W; 1 min. 500W*). Stir in the onion and garlic and ▓ HIGH for 2 mins. 600W (*1 ½ mins. 700W; 2 ½ mins. 500W*).

2 Stir in the flour and ▓ HIGH for 30 secs. Add the chopped thyme and soy sauce.

3 Dissolve the miso in a little of the broth or water and mix into the sauce, then add the rest of the broth.

4 Cover and ▓ HIGH for 5 mins. 600W (*4 mins. 700W; 6 mins. 500W*), stirring once or twice. Season with pepper.

Preparation: 10 minutes

Cooking time: 11 minutes

Power setting: HIGH

Freezes well

Makes about 2 cups

Soy sauce and miso are good combined, and can make a flavorsome sauce with water.

Illustrated below

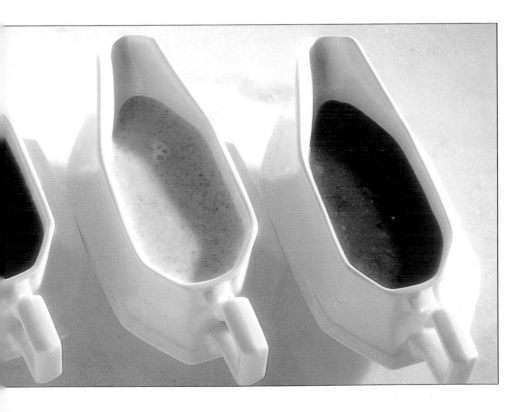

White sauce

INGREDIENTS

1¼ cups milk
½ medium onion
1 bay leaf
6 peppercorns
sprig of parsley or bouquet garni
2 tablespoons margarine
2 tablespoons flour
salt and black pepper

Milk-based sauces work particularly well in a microwave as there is little chance of scorching or sticking. Use a container large enough (4-cup minimum) to allow for the liquid's expansion as it heats up.

1 Put the milk, onion, bay leaf, peppercorns, and herbs in a bowl. ❊ HIGH for 2 mins. 600W (*1 ½ mins. 700W; 2 ½ mins. 500W*). Stand for 5 mins., then strain.

2 Put the margarine in a medium bowl and ❊ HIGH for 30 secs. Stir in the flour and ❊ HIGH for 30 secs.

3 Stir in the milk, blending very well. Season and ❊ HIGH for 2-3 mins. 600W (*1 ½-2 ½ mins. 700W; 2 ½-3 ½ mins. 500W*) until thickened, stirring 2-3 times.

★ **Preparation:** 10 minutes

≋ **Cooking time:** 5 minutes

∅ **Power setting:** HIGH

◎ **Makes about** 1¼ cups

★ For smooth results, stir milk-based sauce once a minute during cooking. You can even leave a wooden spoon in the mixture while it is in the oven.

Illustrated on pp. 148-149

VARIATIONS
Cheese sauce

INGREDIENTS

As for white sauce plus
½ cup grated cheese
pinch of mustard powder or cayenne pepper

Make a white sauce following the recipe above. Once cooked, add the cheese and spices. Stir well, then ❊ HIGH for 30 secs. (*all powers*) or until the cheese is just melted.

◎ **Makes about** 1¼ cups

Mushroom sauce

INGREDIENTS

As for white sauce plus
1½ cups thinly sliced button mushrooms
1 teaspoon paprika
pinch of cayenne pepper

1 Heat and flavor the milk as described in the basic recipe above, or simply use plain milk and start the sauce by heating the margarine.

2 Put the margarine in a medium bowl and ❊ HIGH for 30 secs. Stir in the mushrooms, spices and seasoning. Cover and ❊ HIGH for 4 mins. 600W (*3 mins. 700W; 5 mins. 500W*).

3 Stir in the flour and ❊ HIGH for 30 secs.

4 Pour in the milk, stir well, then re-cover ❊ HIGH for 3 mins. 600W (*2 ½ mins. 700W; 3 ½ mins. 500W*), stirring regularly.

◎ **Makes about** 1¼ cups

▤ If you don't want to use the sauce immediately, cover the surface with some waxed paper to prevent a tough skin forming.

Concentrated vegetable broth

INGREDIENTS

1 tablespoon vegetable oil
½ medium onion, with the skin left on
1 medium carrot. chopped in large chunks
⅔ cups chopped leeks
handful of celery leaves
¼ teaspoon celery seeds
sprig of parsley and thyme
salt and black pepper

Make a strongly flavored broth using less water – anything cooked with a high proportion of water doesn't save much time in the microwave. Dilute the broth to taste when using in soups and sauces.

1 Put the oil in a deep bowl and ⊠ HIGH for 1 min. 600W (*30 secs. 700W; 1 min. 500W*).

3 Stir in the vegetables and celery seeds and ⊠ HIGH for 3 mins. 600W (*2½ mins. 700W; 3½ mins. 500W*), stirring once or twice.

3 Add 2½ cups water and herbs. Cover and ⊠ HIGH for 12 mins. 600W (*10 mins. 700W; 15 mins. 500W*).

4 Strain, season and dilute as required.

★ **Preparation:** 10 minutes

⧈ **Cooking time:** 16 minutes

⊘ **Power setting:** HIGH

❋ **Freezes well**

◎ **Makes about 2½ cups**

★ To make a darker broth add soy sauce or tomato paste.

Illustrated on pp. 148-149

Concentrated meat stock

.INGREDIENTS

1 tablespoon vegetable oil
1 small onion, with skin left on, halved
1 carrot, chopped in large chunks
2 celery stalks, quartered
1 lb cooked meat bones or chicken carcasses, broken into small pieces
sprigs of parsley and thyme
1 bay leaf

This is a quick recipe for meat stock, using a mixture of any bones or meat scraps. This concentrated stock has the added advantage of taking up less room in the freezer than conventional stock.

1 Put the oil in a deep bowl and ⊠ HIGH for 1 min. 600W (*30 secs. 700W; 1 min. 500W*).

2 Stir in the vegetables and ⊠ HIGH for 3 mins. 600W (*2½ mins. 700W; 3½ mins. 500W*), stirring once.

3 Add the bones, 2½ cups water and herbs. Cover and ⊠ HIGH for 30 mins. 600W (*25 mins. 700W; 35 mins. 500W*), stirring two or three times.

4 Strain, season and dilute as required.

★ **Preparation:** 10 minutes

⧈ **Cooking time:** 30 minutes

⊘ **Power setting:** HIGH

❋ **Freezes well**

◎ **Makes about 2½ cups**

★ To make a darker stock, brown all the bones in a conventional oven before you start.

Fruit sauce

INGREDIENTS

⅓ cup raisins

⅔ cup orange juice

1 ripe banana

A refreshing, tangy sauce for serving with baked bananas, ice cream or other desserts.

1 Put the raisins and orange juice in a bowl, cover and ▦ HIGH for 2 mins. 600W (*1 ½ mins. 700W; 2 ½ mins. 500W*). Leave for 15-20 mins. until the raisins are plump. Drain, reserving the orange juice.

2 Purée the banana with the orange juice until smooth. Add the raisins and purée.

3 Return the sauce to the bowl and ▦ HIGH for 2 mins. 600W (*1 ½ mins. 700W; 2 ½ mins. 500W*) to reheat. Stir well, then leave to stand for 2-3 mins. before serving.

★ **Preparation:**
20 minutes

≋ **Cooking time:**
4 minutes

▨ **Power setting:**
HIGH

◎ **Makes about**
1 ¼ **cups**

Illustrated opposite

Barbecue sauce

INGREDIENTS

2 tablespoons butter

1 cup sliced mushrooms

⅔ cup tomato ketchup

¼ cup soft light brown sugar

2 teaspoons lemon juice

pinch of garlic salt

pinch of ground allspice

pinch of chili powder

This versatile sauce can either be served as an accompaniment to cooked meats and poultry, or used to baste them during microwaving.

1 Put the butter in a small bowl and ▦ HIGH for 1 min. 600W (*30 secs. 700W; 1 min. 500W*) to melt. Add the mushrooms and ▦ HIGH for 2 mins. 600W (*1 ½ mins. 700W; 2 ½ mins. 500W*), stirring once.

2 Stir in the ketchup, sugar, lemon juice, garlic salt and spices. ▦ HIGH for 3-5 mins. 600W (*2 ½-3 mins. 700W; 3 ½-5 mins. 500W*) until boiling, stirring two or three times. Serve hot.

★ **Preparation:**
5 minutes

≋ **Cooking time:**
6 minutes

▨ **Power setting:**
HIGH

≋ **Good reheated**

◎ **Serves 4**

Top: **Fruit sauce** (*see opposite*); Center. **Chocolate or carob sauce** (*see p. 154*); **Wine sauce** (*see p. 154*)

Chocolate or carob sauce

INGREDIENTS

2 tablespoons butter

2 squares baking chocolate or 2 oz sugar-free carob, broken into pieces

1 egg yolk, beaten

1 cup skim milk

This versatile and rich sauce can be used as a topping for desserts, served with poached fruit, fruit salads, bananas or ice cream.

1 Put the butter and chocolate or carob in a medium bowl and ▨ HIGH for 2 mins. 600W *(1 ½ mins. 700W; 2 ½ mins. 500W)* until melted. Stir well.

2 Beat in the egg yolk and milk and ▨ HIGH for 2½ mins. 600W *(2 mins. 700W; 3 mins. 500W)*, stirring 2-3 times. Leave to stand for 2-3 mins. Serve warm.

 Preparation: 5 minutes

 Cooking time: 4½ minutes

 Power setting: HIGH

Makes about 1¼ **cups**

Illustrated on p. 153

Wine sauce

INGREDIENTS

½ cup dry white wine or Champagne

2 egg yolks, plus 1 whole egg

6 tablespoons sugar

⅛ teaspoon grated lemon peel (optional)

Egg-based sauces and custards work well in the microwave as long as you are careful with the timing. Although this sauce needs to be stirred every 15 seconds it takes less than 5 minutes to cook. Served warm or cool, it adds an elegant touch to fresh or poached fruits or plain cakes.

1 Pour wine into 1-cup glass measuring cup. ▨ HIGH for 1-3 mins. *(all ovens)* to reduce the alcohol. Refrigerate until just cool.

2 Whisk the wine, eggs and sugar in 4-cup glass measuring cup until well blended. ▨ HIGH for 1¾-2 mins. 600W *(1 ¼-1 ½ mins. 700W; 3 ½-3 ¾ mins. 500W)*, whisking every 15 secs., until thickened. Do not allow to boil.

Preparation: 5 minutes, plus time to cool wine

Cooking time: 1¾ minutes

Power setting: HIGH

Makes about 1½ **cups**

If you choose to serve the sauce cool, cover the surface with plastic wrap to prevent skin from forming.

Illustrated on p. 153

Blackberry and apple purée

INGREDIENTS

3 heaping cups blackberries
½ lb eating apples
2 tablespoons honey
1 tablespoon lemon juice
2 teaspoons cornstarch (optional)

This thick fruit purée can easily be used as a jam, thinly spread on toast or crispbreads, or as a sauce topping. The purée will keep in the refrigerator for about two weeks.

1 Wash all the fruit carefully. Core and chop the apples. Place all the ingredients in a large bowl and HIGH for 8 mins. 600W (*6 ½ mins. 700W; 10 mins. 500W*), stirring twice.

2 If you want a thicker consistency, add the cornstarch. Dissolve it in the fruit, then HIGH for 2-3 mins. 600W (*1 ½-2 ½ mins. 700W; 2 ½-3 ½ mins. 500W*).

3 Leave to cool, then purée and sieve to remove the pits. Store in sterilized jars.

 Preparation:
10 minutes

Cooking time:
8 minutes

Power setting:
HIGH

Freezes well

Makes about 2 cups

Illustrated on p. 157

Tomato relish

INGREDIENTS

⅔ cup slivered large dried apricots
¼ cup cider vinegar
8-ounce can crushed tomatoes
1 medium onion, diced
1 small green pepper, seeded and chopped
¼ teaspoon salt
1 dried chili, finely chopped
½ teaspoon cumin seeds
½ teaspoon mustard seeds
2 bay leaves
8 peppercorns

A colorful, spicy relish that complements all savory dishes perfectly.

1 Put the apricots and vinegar in a medium bowl and HIGH for 2 mins. 600W (*1 ½ mins. 700W; 2 ½ mins. 500W*). Leave to stand for 30 mins.

2 Mix the remaining ingredients with the apricots. Cover and HIGH for 14 mins. 600W (*11 mins. 700W; 17 mins. 500W*), stirring several times.

3 Leave to cool, then pour into sterilized jars. Store for up to two months.

 Preparation:
15 minutes

Cooking time:
16 minutes

Power setting:
HIGH

 Makes about 1 ¼ lb

 Sterilize the jars before you fill them with relish.

Illustrated on p. 157

Plum and pear jam

INGREDIENTS

1 lb plums
1 pear, peeled, cored and chopped
¼ cup honey
1 tablespoon orange juice
½ cup brown sugar (optional)

This recipe can be used to make a conventional jam or a sugar-free fruit paste, to spread on toast or use as a filling for cakes. Store in the refrigerator for one week, or freeze in small portions.

1 Chop the flesh of the plums coarsely. Mix with the pear and honey and orange juice in a large bowl.

2 Crack the plum pits using a rolling pin, and add to the fruit. Count how many are added so that they can all be taken out afterward.

3 ▣ HIGH for 8 mins. 600W (*6 ½ mins. 700W; 10 mins. 500W*), stirring once or twice.

4 Leave to cool, remove the pits, then purée the jam. Stir in sugar, if using, and ▣ HIGH for 12 mins. 600W (*10 mins. 700W; 15 mins. 500W*), stirring every 3 mins. Leave to cool, then bottle.

★ **Preparation:** 25 minutes

≋ **Cooking time:** 20 minutes

⊘ **Power setting:** HIGH

◎ **Makes about** 1 ¼ lb

★ For a sugar-free purée, omit the sugar and refrigerate after puréeing. The purée will thicken in the refrigerator.

Illustrated opposite

Apple and date chutney

INGREDIENTS

2 cups pared, cored, and chopped eating apples
⅔ cup chopped onions
1 clove garlic, crushed
heaped ⅔ cup dates
6 tablespoons cider vinegar
⅔ cup raisins
½-inch piece fresh ginger, grated
½ teaspoon apple pie spice mix
1 teaspoon mustard seeds
pinch of salt
pinch of cayenne pepper

The smell of vinegar and spices doesn't dominate the kitchen when making chutneys and relishes in the microwave, and you can make them in small quantities.

1 Put the apples, onions, garlic, dates and vinegar in a large bowl. Cover and ▣ HIGH for 5 mins. 600W (*4 mins. 700W; 6 mins. 500W*), stirring once.

2 Add the remaining ingredients and ▣ HIGH for 12 mins. 600W (*10 mins. 700W; 15 mins. 500W*), stirring once or twice.

3 Leave to stand overnight, then pour into sterilized jars and store in the refrigerator.

★ **Preparation:** 20 minutes

≋ **Cooking time:** 17 minutes

⊘ **Power setting:** HIGH

◎ **Makes about** 1 ¼ lb

Illustrated opposite

From top to bottom: **Blackberry and apple purée** (*see p. 155*); **Plum and pear jam** (*see opposite*); **Apple and date chutney** (*see opposite*); **Tomato relish** (*see p. 155*)

Red cherry jam

INGREDIENTS

4 cups pitted red cherries, pits reserved

2 tablespoons lemon juice

2¼ cups granulated sugar

Small quantities of jam microwave very quickly. Make sure the bowl is heatproof and always use pot holders as the bowl can get very hot. Sterilize jars conventionally for jams.

1 Put the cherries in a deep, heatproof bowl with the lemon juice. Tie the cherry pits in a cheesecloth bag and tuck under the cherries.

2 Cover and ▓ HIGH for 10-12 mins. 600W *(8½-10 mins. 700W; 12½-15 mins. 500W)* until soft, stirring two or three times.

3 Stir the sugar into the cherries and ▓ HIGH for 2-3 mins. 600W *(1½-2½ mins. 700W; 2½-3½ mins. 500W)*, then stir to dissolve the sugar.

4 Half-cover the bowl and ▓ HIGH for 13-15 mins. 600W *(10½-12½ mins. 700W; 16-18 mins. 500W)*, until setting point is reached.

5 Leave to settle for 10 mins., then remove the pits and ladle the jam into clean jam jars and seal.

Preparation: 15 minutes, plus cooling

Cooking time: 25 minutes

Power setting: HIGH

Make in advance

Makes about 1¾ lb

To help the sugar dissolve, warm it in a conventional oven at 300°F for 10 minutes.

BREADS, CAKES AND COOKIES

Remember never to put the dough into traditional metal loafpans, use bakeware especially designed for use in microwave ovens.

Whole-wheat bread

INGREDIENTS

2 cups whole-wheat flour
1 package active dry yeast
1 teaspoon salt
2 tablespoons margarine
¾ cup milk
¼ cup water
3 tablespoons molasses
1 egg, slightly beaten
1¼-1½ cups unbleached all-purpose flour
2 teaspoons milk
2 teaspoons quick-cooking oats, uncooked

A microwave oven makes the actual baking of bread a very speedy process. You can also raise the dough on Low for 15 to 20 minutes but the flavor of the results are not as good.

1 Stir whole-wheat flour, yeast and salt in a large bowl.

2 Place margarine in 2-cup glass measuring cup and ▨ HIGH 30 secs.-1 min. until melted. Stir in milk, water, and molasses. ▨ HIGH about 30 secs.-45 secs. until mixture reaches 120°F-125°F.

3 Pour liquid mixture into whole-wheat mixture; beat until smooth. Stir in egg until well blended. Stir in all-purpose flour.

4 Turn dough onto lightly floured surface; knead until smooth and elastic. Shape dough into ball; place in large greased bowl, turning dough to grease top. Cover tightly with plastic wrap; let rise in warm, draft-free place until doubled, about 1 hour.

5 Punch down dough. Turn onto lightly floured surface; cover with bowl; let dough rest for 15 minutes. Lightly grease 8½ × 4½ in loaf dish.

6 Shape into loaf; place seam side down in loaf pan. Brush top with milk; sprinkle with oats. Cover with plastic wrap; let rise in warm place until doubled, about 45 mins.-1 hour.

7 Remove plastic wrap; ▨ MEDIUM for 6 mins. 600W (*5 mins. 700W; 8 mins. 500W*) rotating dish one-half turn halfway through cooking time. ▨ HIGH for 5-5½ mins. 600W (*4-4½ mins. 700W; 6-7 mins. 500W*) or until top springs back when touched lightly. Stand in dish 10 mins., transfer to rack and cool.

★ Preparation:
25 minutes, plus 1¾ hours-2¼ hours rising time.

〰 Cooking time:
12 minutes

⊘ Power settings:
MEDIUM and HIGH

〰 Good toasted

◎ Makes 1 large loaf

〰 Use microwave thermometer or temperature probe to determine temperature while cooking. When bread is removed from pan the sides may appear to be moist. Bread will dry as it cools.

Soda bread

INGREDIENTS

3¾ cups flour
½ teaspoon salt
1 teaspoon baking soda
¼ cup butter
1 cup buttermilk

Bake the mixture right away, so as not to lose the full effect of the baking soda.

1 Mix the flour, salt and baking soda together, then cut in the butter. Add the buttermilk and mix to a stiff dough.

2 Knead the dough into a slight mound. Place on a small plate or flat dish and make a deep cross on the top.

3 ▨ HIGH for 7 mins. 600W (*6 mins. 700W; 8½ mins. 500W*), giving the plate or dish a half turn every 2 or 3 mins. Leave to stand and cool on a wire rack.

 Preparation: 15 minutes, plus cooling

 Cooking time: 7 minutes

 Power setting: HIGH

 Makes an 1½-lb loaf

 Remember never to put the dough into traditional metal loaf pans; use bakeware especially designed for use in microwave ovens.

Cheese and oat loaves

INGREDIENTS

3¾ cups flour
2⅓ cups quick-cooking oats, uncooked
1 package active dry yeast
1 teaspoon caraway seeds
1 teaspoon paprika
1 teaspoon salt
½ cup grated cheddar cheese
2 cups water
1 tablespoon molasses

This makes a tasty, pleasantly chewy, cheesey bread which is delicious served with soups.

1 Stir ingredients except water and molasses in large bowl.

2 Measure water and molasses in 2-cup glass measuring cup. ▨ HIGH 30-45 secs. until mixture reaches 120°F-125°F.

3 Pour warm liquid into flour mixture and stir until dough is formed. Turn dough onto lightly floured surface and knead until smooth and elastic. Shape into ball; place in large greased bowl, turning dough to grease top. Cover tightly with plastic wrap; let rise in warm, draft free place until doubled, about 30 mins. Meanwhile lightly grease two 8½ × 4½-in loaf pans.

4 Punch down dough. Turn onto lightly floured surface. Knead for 2-3 mins., divide dough into half. Shape each half into loaf; place seam side down into loaf pan. Cover with plastic wrap; let rise in warm place until doubled, about 1 hour.

5 Remove plastic wrap; ▨ HIGH for 7 mins. 600W (*6 mins. 700W; 8½ mins. 500W*), or until top springs back when lightly touched, rotating pan one-half turn halfway through cooking time. Transfer to rack and cool.

 Preparation: 25 minutes, plus 1½ hours rising time.

Cooking time: 14½ minutes

Power setting: HIGH

Makes 2 loaves

 When bread is removed from pan the sides may appear to be moist. Bread will dry as it cools.

Top: **Savory swirl loaf** (*see p. 163*); Bottom right: **Honey and sesame scones** (*see p. 162*); Left: **Orange cake** (*see p. 162*)

Honey and sesame scones

INGREDIENTS

1¾ cups self-rising flour
pinch of salt
1 teaspoon baking powder
1 teaspoon apple pie spice mix
¼ cup vegetable margarine
2 tablespoons sesame seeds
2 tablespoons honey
1 egg, beaten
2-3 tablespoons milk

Scone dough microwaves well and the apple pie spice mix gives the scone a good color. The sesame seeds provide a delicious crunchy quality and the honey adds just enough sweetness.

1 Mix the flour, salt, baking powder and spice mix together. Cut in the fat, then mix in the sesame seeds.

2 Add the honey, beaten egg and enough milk to make a soft, pliable dough.

3 Quickly pat out the dough to a large round and mark into eight sections. Place on a dish lined with waxed paper and ▒ HIGH for 4 mins. 600W (*3 mins. 700W; 5 mins. 500W*), giving the dish a half turn every 2 mins. Leave to stand for 4 mins. Serve while scones are still warm.

Preparation: 15 minutes

Cooking time: 4 minutes

Power setting: HIGH

Freezes well

Serves 8

Illustrated on p. 161

Orange cake

INGREDIENTS

1 orange
1 tablespoon honey
½ cup sugar
½ cup vegetable oil
heaped 1¾ cups flour
1 teaspoon apple pie spice mix
pinch of salt
1 teaspoon baking powder
Decoration
fresh orange slices
desiccated coconut

This simple cake has a good texture and delicious flavor. The cake can be made with lemon, if preferred.

1 Scrub the orange well, and chop into small pieces. Purée with 7 fl oz water and the honey until fairly smooth. Add the sugar and oil and purée again.

2 Mix the flour with the spice, salt and baking powder. Stir in the orange mixture and mix until smooth.

3 Line a 5-cup tube pan or savarin mold with waxed paper. Spoon in the cake batter and ▒ HIGH for 8 mins. 600W (*6½ mins. 700W; 10 mins. 500W*), giving the dish a quarter turn every 2 mins.

4 Leave to stand for 5-10 mins. before turning out on a wire rack to cool. Remove the paper at the end of the standing time to prevent it sticking to the cake.

5 Decorate with orange slices and coconut.

Preparation: 10 minutes

Cooking time: 8 minutes

Power setting: HIGH

Freezes well

Serves 8

★ At the end of the cooking time most cakes still look damp on top. Leave to stand for the time specified, then insert a skewer into the center. If the skewer comes out clean the cake is cooked; if not, cook the cake for a further 1-2 mins., then leave to stand again.

Illustrated on p. 161

Savory swirl loaf

INGREDIENTS

For the filling-makes about 1 cup

1 tablespoon olive or salad oil
1 medium onion, finely chopped (about ¾ cup)
1 garlic clove, minced
1 tablespoon prepared chutney
1 tablespoon tomato paste
⅔ cup walnuts, chopped
salt and black pepper

For the dough

1 cup self-rising flour
¾ cup flour
2 teaspoons baking powder
dash cayenne pepper
dash salt
¼ cup butter or margarine
1 egg, beaten
5-6 tablespoons milk

This is a useful recipe for a quick snack at home, or for picnics and packed lunches. The filling can be varied by using different nuts and adding extra herbs and vegetables, but be sure that they are all finely chopped.

1 For the filling; put the oil, onion, and garlic in a 1-quart casserole. Cover and ☷ HIGH for 2½ mins. 600W (*2 mins. 700W; 3 mins. 500W*).

2 Stir in the remaining ingredients; season with salt and pepper according to taste.

3 For the dough; mix the flours, baking powder, cayenne pepper, and salt in a large bowl. Cut in margarine until mixture resembles coarse crumbs; add the egg and enough milk to make a soft dough. On lightly floured waxed paper, with lightly floured rolling pin, roll dough into a 9 × 6-in rectangle. Spread filling within ½-in of edges. Starting at 9-inch end, carefully roll dough jelly roll fashion; pinch seam and tuck ends under.

5 Wrap loosely in waxed paper, seam down, and place in a 12 × 8-in dish. ☷ HIGH for 4½ mins. 600W (*3½-4 mins. 700W; 5½-6 mins. 500W*), giving a half turn every 2 mins. Allow to cool uncovered, on a rack, at least 30 mins. before slicing. Serve warm or cold.

⭐ **Preparation:** 20 minutes

〰 **Cooking time:** 8½ minutes

▱ **Power setting:** HIGH

❄ **Freezes well**

◎ **Serves 4**

⭐ Wrapping the roll in waxed paper helps retain the moisture and keep the dough soft.

Illustrated on p. 161

Spice and currant cookies

INGREDIENTS

2 cups unbleached all-purpose flour
1 cup whole-wheat flour
1 teaspoon cinnamon
1 teaspoon ginger
1 teaspoon baking soda
½ teaspoon salt
¼ teaspoon ground cloves
¼ teaspoon nutmeg
⅓ cup currants
½ cup margarine or vegetable shortening
⅓ cup packed brown sugar
½ cup molasses
¼-⅓ cup milk

Soft cookie doughs work well in the microwave, specially if they are a dark color to begin with.

1 Stir flour, cinnamon, ginger, baking soda, salt, cloves, nutmeg, and currants in a medium bowl. Set aside.

2 Cream margarine or shortening and sugar in a large bowl. Stir in molasses and milk. Gradually add flour mixture, stir until well mixed. Wrap dough in plastic wrap and refrigerate for at least 3 hours.

3 Using lightly floured rolling pin, roll dough ¼-inch thick on lightly floured surface. Cut out cookies with 2½-3-inch round cookie cutter.

4 Transfer cookies to baking dish. For 600W and 700W ovens arrange 6 cookies around outer edge of 12-inch dish. ▧ HIGH for 3-3½ mins. 600W (*2-2½ mins. 700W*), rotating dish one-half turn halfway through cooking; for 500W ovens arrange 4 cookies around outer edge of 10-inch dish. ▧ HIGH for 3½-3¾ mins. Stand for 1 minute. Sprinkle with sugar and cool on a wire rack.

 Preparation: 15 minutes, plus 3 hour chilling time

 Cooking time: 3-3½ minutes per 6 cookies

 Power setting: HIGH

Makes about 2 dozen

Take care not to overcook. The cookies should be soft at the end of the cooking time. They will harden as they cool.

Illustrated opposite

Light yellow cake

INGREDIENTS

¾ heaping cup self-rising flour
½ teaspoon baking powder
½ cup superfine sugar
½ cup butter softened
2 eggs, beaten
¼ cup milk
½ teaspoon vanilla extract
For the filling
⅔ cup heavy cream, whipped
confectioners' sugar, to dust

A microwaved cake is very light and moist, but remember it cooks while standing.

1 Sift the flour and baking powder into a mixing bowl and add the sugar, butter, eggs, milk and vanilla. Beat until well blended.

2 Grease and line two 8-inch cake pans with waxed paper. Divide the batter between the pans and smooth.

3 Cook one layer at a time, ▧ HIGH for 3-4 mins. 600W (*2½-3 mins. 700W; 3½-5 mins. 500W*) until just shrinking from the sides, giving the dish a quarter turn 2-3 times.

4 Leave to stand for 5 mins., then turn out on to a wire rack to cool. Sandwich with the cream and dust with confectioners' sugar.

 Preparation: 15 minutes

 Cooking time: 6 minutes

 Power setting: HIGH

 Freezes well

 Serves 6

Clockwise from the top: **Date and chocolate or carob slice** (*see p. 166*); **Crunch bars** (*see p. 166*); **Spice and currant cookies** (*see opposite*).

Crunch bars

INGREDIENTS

6 tablespoons margarine
2 ½ tablespoons brown sugar
2 cups quick-cooking oats, uncooked
1 tablespoon honey

Crunch bars cook successfully in the microwave. They do tend to soften and become more crumbly during storage so don't leave too long before eating them.

1 Put the margarine in a medium bowl and ▓ HIGH for 1 min. 600W *(30 secs. 700W; 1 min. 500W)*. Mix in all the remaining ingredients, stirring thoroughly.

2 Press the mixture into an 8-inch square dish and level out the surface. ▓ HIGH for 3 mins. 600W *(2 ½ mins. 700W; 3 ½ mins. 500W)*.

3 Press down the top with a fork and leave to cool in dish. While still slightly warm, cut into nine squares.

★ **Preparation:**
5 minutes

≈ **Cooking time:**
4 minutes

⊘ **Power setting:**
HIGH

◎ **Makes 9**

★ Substitute molasses for the honey to darken the color of the crunch bars.

Illustrated on p. 165

Date and chocolate or carob slice

INGREDIENTS

4 oz of pitted dates (about ½ cup, packed)
⅔ cup boiling water
½ cup margarine
1 medium banana, mashed (about 1 cup)
⅔ cup all-purpose flour
⅔ cup cocoa or carob powder
1 teaspoon baking powder
pinch of salt
⅓ cup orange juice
⅓ cup whole blanched almonds or walnuts, chopped

Chocolate or carob mixtures work well in a microwave. This slice is best when left to cool completely.

1 Put the dates in a small bowl and pour over the boiling water. Cover and ▓ HIGH for 3 mins. 600W *(2 ½ mins. 700W; 3 ½ mins. 500W)*. Cool thoroughly, then beat to a smooth purée by hand or in a food processor.

2 Cream the purée with the margarine until fluffy, then add the banana. Stir in the flour, soybean flour, cocoa or carob, baking powder and salt. Add the fruit juice to make a soft mixture. Mix in the chopped nuts.

3 Line the bottom of an 8-inch baking dish with waxed paper. Using a spatula spread batter evenly into baking dish. Cover with waxed paper and then ▓ HIGH for 7 mins. 600W *(6 mins. 700W; 8 ½ mins. 500W)*, giving the dish a quarter turn once every 2 mins.

4 Cool in dish, uncovered, on wire rack for 5 to 10 minutes. Turn out onto a wire rack, carefully peel off waxed paper and allow to cool completely. Transfer back to baking dish or serving dish and cut into 2-inch squares.

★ **Preparation:**
15 minutes, plus cooling

≈ **Cooking time:**
10 minutes

⊘ **Power setting:**
HIGH

◎ **Makes 16**

★ Drain the cooked dates if necessary, as the purée should be thick and not runny like a sauce.

GETTING TO KNOW YOUR MICROWAVE

Buying a microwave might seem a good idea, but with so many different models on the market where do you start? This section tells you what types of microwaves are available and describes in non-technical detail how they work, how to clean and maintain them, and what is best to cook in them.

You needn't throw away all your conventional cook books; just follow the details given on how to convert recipes to the microwave style of cooking. A great deal of normal cookware can be used in the microwave, but study the information given on special cookware and materials that work particularly well in the microwave. To make sure all your microwave dishes cook evenly, learn the art of rearranging, turning and stirring food from the different cooking techniques described.

One of the joys of having a microwave is that it can so often save you time, especially with tasks like defrosting food. A comprehensive defrosting and reheating chart is included so that you can see the timings for all types of food at a glance. Helpful hints and tips are also included on other ways the microwave can become an indispensable cooking aid – you will be surprised at just how easy it is to heat up bread, to dry fresh herbs or to toast nuts.

Converting recipes for the microwave

There is no need to abandon all your favorite conventional recipes when you start to use a microwave oven. Recipes for foods that are naturally moist or cooked by boiling, steaming or poaching can all be adapted quite easily and very successfully for the microwave, usually just by reducing the cooking time and the liquid content. However, it's best not to attempt to adapt recipes until you feel fully familiar with your microwave and understand the different microwave techniques, knowing just when and why they should be employed. The only way to do this is to learn by practice and experimentation.

For the best results when converting a conventional recipe, use an existing microwave recipe with similar ingredients and quantities as a model, refer to pages 8-48 for ingredients' cooking times and techniques, and then just keep to the following guidelines.

■ Preparation is usually the same for microwaved food as for conventionally-cooked food, only it is always far more important that ingredients such as vegetables are cut to a small and uniform size for even cooking in the microwave.

■ Foods that are normally cooked covered should also be covered in the microwave.

■ When cooking a variety of ingredients in a dish, remember to stir thoroughly every few minutes in the microwave.

■ Dishes that cannot be stirred, such as quiches, roasts or meatloaves, should be turned every few minutes for even cooking.

■ When cooking separate food items, remember to follow the rules for arrangement (see pp. 198-9) and to rearrange them during the cooking time.

■ As a general guide, reduce the amount of liquid required in a conventional recipe by a quarter or a third. More liquid can always be added during the cooking period if needed.

■ For steamed vegetables, put them in a bowl with 2-3 tablespoons water and they will steam themselves.

■ Cut the cooking time by at least a half, although there is no standard rule on this. Follow the timing used in a similar existing microwave recipe rather than guessing.

■ Always underestimate the cooking time and test frequently for doneness. Take particular care when cooking foods like eggs, milk and custards, and foods with high fat or sugar contents, as they cook quickly.

■ Remember that foods will continue to cook after being removed from the microwave, so take this into account. The denser the food, the longer the standing time required.

■ Casseroles cook very quickly in the microwave but often improve in flavor by being cooked in advance and then being reheated so that the flavors really have time to develop and blend together.

■ You may prefer to add more herbs and spices to some dishes than you would when cooking them conventionally as the quick cooking times do not allow their flavors to permeate through a dish in the same way. Test for taste and adjust seasonings to suit your palate.

■ Do not add salt at the beginning of the cooking time as it has a dehydrating effect. Add to taste before serving.

■ Cake and pudding mixtures should be slightly wetter than in conventional recipes. Because they rise so much in the microwave, only half fill containers with the batter. Allow them to finish cooking through by standing for 5 to 10 minutes.

■ Pastry shells must be baked empty before being filled. Cover with paper towels and a plate to keep fairly crisp. Allow for shrinkage.

■ Dried beans should be pre-soaked in the normal way.

■ Cook dried beans, grains and pasta in the microwave in the usual amount of boiling water. Use slightly larger containers than usual to allow for swelling and prevent the water from boiling over.

■ Red kidney beans should be boiled rapidly for the first 10 minutes. Do this conventionally.

WHICH FOODS WILL WORK IN THE MICROWAVE

A wide range of foods cook extremely well in the microwave, but you must accept that this is a different method of cooking requiring a new approach and yielding cooked foods that may look and taste slightly different to those you are used to.

■ Whole fruits and vegetables cook very successfully in the microwave. The flavors tend to be fresher and the texture slightly different; for example, baked potatoes do not become crisp. Remember when baking whole fruit and vegetables that the skin must be pierced beforehand or steam will build up and cause them to burst during cooking.

■ Ready-prepared dishes cook well by microwave energy, but the result may seem pale. These can often be browned under a conventional broiler if you prefer a golden look.

■ Pasta and grain dishes cook well, provided the raw mixture is well flavored and quite moist.

■ Casseroles and dried-bean dishes benefit from being made in advance and then reheated so their flavors have time to develop.

■ Most cake and bread mixtures bake successfully by microwave, although the batter or dough should be slightly wetter than in conventional recipes. Allow for considerable rising, and see p. 201 for tips on improving their appearance.

■ Fish cooks extremely well and the flesh becomes beautifully moist and flaky. Poached and steamed fish work best, and recipes where the fish is traditionally baked or broiled are also good – the skin of whole fish can be quickly crisped and browned under a hot, conventional broiler or browning element, after, if you wish.

■ Small shellfish such as mussels and clams are very tasty cooked in the microwave, although care must be taken not to overcook them as they have a very short cooking time and can quickly become tough and rubbery in texture.

■ All types of poultry will microwave very successfully. However, the short cooking times mean that the skin doesn't have time to brown. You can get around this by cooking them in a roasting bag, which helps to promote browning, or you can brush the skin with a browning agent before cooking.

■ Small meaty foods that are usually broiled or fried such as sausages, bacon and chops cook very well in the microwave. They can be done either on a microwave roasting rack, or in a browning dish which helps to brown and seal the food.

■ Meatballs and hamburgers cook very evenly, and the small portions can be put in the microwave straight from the freezer, if necessary.

■ Good cuts of meat microwave very well, especially meats with evenly marbled fat. However, large areas of fat attract more microwave energy and as a result the meat cooks unevenly. For this reason, it's best to trim off excess fat from around chops or roasts first. Tougher cuts of meat can be cooked in the microwave too, although they need to spend almost as long as in a conventional oven to make them really tender and appetizing.

■ Sauces and puddings are cooked in the microwave with amazing ease – there's no direct bottom heat to make them scorch or stick so there's no need for continuous stirring. As long as the sauce or custard pudding is stirred two or three times during cooking it will always be smooth and lump-free.

■ Pastry shells work well when cooked empty and covered with paper towels and a plate. Do not make their fillings too moist, and never fill an unbaked crust or the pastry will become soggy and unappetizing.

■ Steamed puddings cook very quickly in the microwave and have a good texture.

■ Pasta, grains and dried beans will cook in the microwave, but be sure to cook them in already boiling water, and do not attempt to do too much at one time. If you want to cook more than ½ lb, it's better to boil conventionally.

■ Cornstarch, gelatin and bouillon cubes can all be dissolved in minutes.

■ Milk can be heated in minutes.

FOODS THAT CANNOT BE COOKED IN THE MICROWAVE OVEN

Some recipes and cooking techniques will not work in a microwave oven and should not be attempted.

● Eggs cannot be hard-boiled. The pressure of steam inside the egg shell causes them to explode.

● Crepes and pancakes cannot be microwaved successfully as they will not become crisp and dry.

● Deep frying should not be attempted because it is virtually impossible to control the temperature of the oil.

● Double-crust pies rarely work successfully as the fillings tend to cook much faster than the pastry.

● Large turkeys cook very unevenly so are best cooked conventionally.

● Large shellfish with hard shells like crab and lobster should not be microwaved as they explode when steam builds up inside.

● Smoked ham becomes very dry because of its high salt content and should not be cooked in the microwave.

Cooking for one

Microwave cooking is a marvelous way to cook for one. It makes it easy to prepare quick, healthy snacks and meals so you can avoid resorting to convenience foods, cookies and cakes when you want to eat in a hurry. Vegetable dishes can be made in minutes from whatever ingredients you have on hand. Cook them in a little broth or sauce to make a simple casserole, or steam them and enjoy their full, fresh flavors. Garnish the dish by adding a few chopped fresh herbs, toasted nuts or grated cheese for extra nourishment and flavor.

Fish and shellfish are ideal for single portions, especially as they cook so quickly. Chops, steaks and poultry portions are all microwaved very fast. After taking them out, cover them with foil and leave to stand for a few minutes while you cook a few fresh or frozen vegetables. Or to make a more substantial meal, bake a potato while you are preparing the meat or fish, or if you have any leftover cooked grains, pasta or dried beans in the refrigerator, they can be reheated in minutes and will taste as if freshly cooked.

Most dishes can be cooked in the dish or container you want to serve them in, which means that you save on messy dishwashing. The microwave also allows you to cook small portions without any worry of them burning as they often do on the stove. Nor do you have the cost of heating up a conventional oven just to cook one portion of food. You can cook small quantities of any of the recipes in this book. Remember to reduce the cooking time accordingly: For half the quantity, cook for approximately two-thirds of the original time; for a quarter of the quantity, cook for aproximately one-third of the original time.

If you have a freezer too, cooking for one with a microwave becomes even more economical. You can take advantage of seasonal gluts and bargains, and blanch vegetables in the microwave (see pp. 210-11). They can then be stored in the freezer until you are ready to use them. You can cook extra portions or even several dishes at a time when you are in a cooking mood, and then freeze them for future use. Read in particular the notes on blanching, freezing and defrosting on pp. 204-11.

Menu planning

When you want to combine several dishes into a meal, you'll need to plan the order in which you cook them because the timing factor is so important and varies from food to food. Take your time at the planning stage and read through the recipes carefully, taking note if some dishes are marked as being better cooked in advance and served after being reheated.

Many food items can be reheated as required. One of the major benefits of the microwave is that most dishes that are reheated remain moist and taste freshly cooked. However, vegetables are less flexible because they cook so quickly and although reheating is possible, they can easily become overcooked.

The fact that denser foods require standing times means that you can microwave any accompanying vegetables after the main dish has been removed from the oven. On the other hand, vegetables like baked potatoes, corn-on-the-cob and stuffed vegetables will retain their heat for about 20 minutes once cooked if you wrap them in some foil immediately after removing them from the microwave.

Recipes containing egg or cheese do not usually reheat well; they cook so quickly it is very easy to overcook them, so dishes that include these as ingredients are usually better cooked just before serving. Dishes that have cheese as a garnish can always be cooked in advance without the cheese, and then the cheese can be added for reheating.

Grains, dried beans and pasta all reheat well by microwave. You may even prefer to cook them conventionally and just use the microwave to reheat them before serving.

Cook foods in the dishes you plan to serve them in whenever possible as this helps to retain their heat. Single portions can be reserved on a plate for any latecomers and then simply covered and reheated in the microwave when required.

Microwave trouble-shooting guide

Some common questions and problems answered and explained

Q I notice that dish size is always specified in microwave recipes. Is the size more important than in conventional recipes?

A Dish size can make all the difference to a microwave recipe. If the dish is too large the food will spread out and may overcook at the edges before the center is done. On the other hand, if it is too small or narrow, the food may bubble over the top or be squeezed into a dense mass that may not cook through to the center. Always use the dish size recommended.

Q I thought that dishes stayed cool in the microwave, yet I find that I frequently need to use pot holders when taking cooked items out of the oven. Does this mean that I am using the wrong kind of dishes?

A Dishes frequently do become hot from the food conducting heat to them. As long as the food in the dishes is cooking in the time specified in the recipes, it simply means that the hot food is heating the dish. If food is taking much longer than the recipes state, then test the dish to make sure it is suitable, following the instructions on p. 191.

Q I have heard that it is a good idea to keep a cup of water in the microwave oven when it is not in use. Why is this?

A This is a good safety precaution in case the oven is accidentally switched on, and it is a particularly good idea when there are children in the house. If the oven is switched on and there is nothing to absorb the microwaves, the waves will bounce off the walls and floor and may damage the oven. A cup of water will absorb the microwaves, preventing them from causing any damage.

Q Is cooking in the microwave a cheaper method than using a conventional oven?

A Microwave ovens are much more economical than conventional ones. They cook very quickly, there is no need for preheating and part of the cooking process takes place after microwaving during standing time – using no power at all!

Q How do you convert the cooking times in recipes that do not give alternative timing for machines with other wattages?

A As a general guide, if recipes have been tested on a 600 watt machine on High power, then reduce the cooking time by 10 seconds per minute if you have a 700 watt machine. If you have a 500 watt machine, increase the time by 15 seconds per minute, checking frequently to make sure the food does not overcook.

Q If you can sear and brown foods in a special browning dish, why can't you fry foods in them?

A It is impossible to control the temperature of oil in a microwave and this could be dangerous, particularly if deep-frying when a large quantity of oil is used. The only frying that should be done in the microwave is "stir-fry style," using a very small amount of oil. This method produces beautifully crunchy, tender vegetables.

Q Is microwaving a healthier way of cooking vegetables?

A It is the perfect way to cook vegetables as it keeps vitamin loss to a minimum. Water-soluble vitamins, such as vitamin C, are easily lost in cooking water, but because so little water is needed for microwave cooking this loss is kept to a minimum. It can be reduced still further by using the cooking water for broth or soup.

The very fast cooking times also mean that vegetables keep their bright colors and natural crunchy textures. Try to prepare vegetables just before you want to cook them, and serve them as soon as possible after cooking; if they are kept warm for a long time more vitamins will be lost.

Foods can also be cooked with less fat and, because vegetables retain more flavor, very little salt is needed – and fats and salt are two of the things that nutritionists are urging us to cut down on for good health.

Q If the microwaves can pass straight through glass, what stops them coming through the glass door of the oven?

A The glass panel on a microwave door is covered with a very fine metal mesh screen that is especially designed to prevent the microwaves passing through it, but still allows you to see into the oven during the cooking process.

Q How safe are microwave ovens?

A All microwave ovens are designed with a safety mechanism that ensures the oven cannot operate unless the door is shut and the Start button has been operated. Opening the oven door immediately stops the generation of microwaves which cannot re-start until the door is shut and the Start control operated again.

When buying a microwave oven, check that the model you wish to purchase is approved by a national electrical safety agency. This means that it has been subjected to stringent tests for safety and microwave leakage, including opening and closing the door 100,000 times – which represents many years of normal wear.

Microwave cooking is also safer as the sides of the oven do not become hot like a conventional oven, although the bottom of the cooker may become warm by conduction.

Q If my microwave has a Defrost button, do I still need to leave foods to stand during defrosting?

A It depends on the food. For many items the Defrost power level is low enough to ensure gentle defrosting without switching off the machine during the defrosting time, but with a dense quantity of food, such as a cooked moussaka or lasagne, it is better to allow some standing time during defrosting. This enables the center to defrost without the edges overheating.

Q Why is salt added before cooking in some recipes, while others recommend adding it afterward?

A Vegetables are usually cooked in very tiny amounts of water, and if salt is sprinkled on the vegetables it will cause dehydration of the surface of the food. If food is cooked in a larger quantity of water and the salt can be completely dissolved, then it can be added before cooking in the microwave. The texture of pork rind, for example, is improved if it is rubbed with salt before cooking, but you should avoid salting the surface of other meats or fish. You can, however, season inside meat or fish before cooking if you like.

Q Why is it possible to use aluminum foil to shield food inside the oven when you cannot use metal dishes for cooking?

A Foil is used in very small quantities for shielding. The amount of food unshielded must be greater than the amount covered with foil, so that there is plenty of food to absorb all the microwave energy. This is not the case when metal dishes are used as the microwave energy does not even reach the food.

Q What should you do if you suddenly realize you've put a metal trimmed dish in the microwave and it starts sparking?

A Switch off the microwave immediately and the sparking will stop. As long as you turn off immediately, you are unlikely to do any harm to the oven, but if sparking is allowed to continue the walls of the cooker may become pitted, and this will distort the microwave pattern. In extreme cases, sparking may even damage the magnetron. If in doubt, have your microwave checked by a qualified engineer – never try and repair or dismantle your microwave yourself.

Q Why do some sauces and hot drinks bubble over the rim of the container once they have been stirred?

A When you microwave liquids in a confined space, particularly those with a high milk content, the temperature gets much higher below the surface than on the surface. When you stir it, the gases produced by the heating process escape and spill over the edge. To overcome this problem, never allow liquid to fill a container more than three-quarters and stir at least halfway through the cooking time.

Q Why was my cake hard and dry by the time it had cooled?

A This is the result of overcooking. The cake should still look moist when removed from the microwave as it will cook through during the standing time. Always aim to undercook rather than overcook in the microwave, and remember not to expect items to look cooked until after their standing times. A cake is ready to come out of the oven when the sides come away from the edge and a wooden tooth pick inserted in the center comes out clean.

Q What does it mean when recipes talk about heat equalizing?

A Microwaves only penetrate food to a depth of about 2 inches, and this area becomes very hot while the center of the food is still quite cool. During standing time, heat is conducted through to the center of the food and the two areas become equally hot.

Q Why do some cakes rise well in the microwave and then sink after being removed?

A This is due to overbeating when mixing the cake. Too much air is trapped in the mixture causing it to rise well in the oven, but then the cake sinks as air is released during cooling.

Q Why do I have to extend the cooking time when I am cooking a larger quantity of food than that specified in a recipe?

A When microwaves enter the food they have to spread themselves through the total quantity for the food to cook. On the whole, microwave ovens should only be used to cook moderate quantities – up to four to six portions at a time.

Q Is there any way of rescuing overcooked foods?

A Because food cooks so quickly in the microwave, it's always better to undercook and then return food to the oven for another minute or so if necessary. Once overcooked, there is no way of restoring texture and flavor to vegetables. They can, however, be puréed to make soups or sauces. Overcooked fruits can also be puréed, then sieved if necessary, to make pastes or sauces. Overcooked cakes can be used for trifles, and plain cookies for making cookie-crumb bases for sweet tarts and cheesecakes.

Overcooked fish dries out, but can be rescued by flaking it into a flavorsome sauce. Overcooked shellfish are more of a problem because they become tough and inedible. However, if you catch them quickly enough – before they are too overdone – stop them cooking immediately by plunging them into cold water.

Q Can I heat up plates in the microwave?

A Yes, so long as they are microwave-safe and don't contain any metal. Stack up to six plates, putting a little water between each one and sprinkling some water on the top one. ▨ HIGH for up to 1 minute. Remember to use a pot holder when removing them and dry off any excess water before serving the food.

Q If chicken and meats don't brown, how can I tell that they are ready?

A If you insert a knife into the thickest, fleshiest part of poultry, pork or another well-done meat the juices should run clear. They should still be slightly pink for rare and medium lamb and beef.

Q Duck always seems to take much longer to cook than the recommended time; what could I be doing wrong?

A During the cooking process duck releases a great deal of fat and juice, which collects in the roasting dish. This liquid absorbs some of the microwave energy, leaving less for the duck – so it cooks more slowly. You should always remember to pour off the juices several times during cooking.

Q Why is it necessary for roasts to stand for such a long time – surely the meat will be cold when it is carved?

A Because meat and poultry are so dense, they benefit from a long standing time. After microwaving, as long as the meat is wrapped in foil, the internal temperature actually continues to rise for about an hour. Initially the outside is much more cooked than the center, but on standing the heat travels to the center, cooking that too. At the same time, the juices are re-absorbed by the meat and the fibers "settle" so the meat carves more easily and stays very moist.

Q My meat thermometer seems to be very inaccurate – the temperature sometimes goes down rather than up after more cooking. Why is this?

A The thermometer is probably working very well. It must be pushed into the fleshiest and thickest part of the roast each time you check or you will always get different readings. The thickest part is likely to be last to cook so it gives the lowest reading. If the thermometer tip presses against bone instead of flesh or if it is pushed in too far (or not far enough) the reading will be much higher.

Choosing a microwave oven

When it comes to buying a microwave oven, there appears to be a bewildering range to choose from. They can be portable or built-in; they have different capacities, wattages and systems of power control; they may offer a choice of additional features as shown on page 178; or even combine microwave power with conventional cooking facilities. Your choice will depend upon such factors as size, price, availability and how you plan to use the microwave power. Consider your present and your future needs: How many people will be using the oven; what other cooking facilities you have, etc. After examining different models for their facilities, check that your final choice complies with national safety standards and that it also has good servicing arrangements.

TYPES OF MICROWAVE OVEN

There are three basic categories of microwave oven, which are described and illustrated below.

Countertop ovens

These come in various sizes and wattages. The larger the oven, the higher the output has to be. Installation is straightforward. They simply require a firm work surface, table or cart to stand on and a nearby electrical socket. Some models can be built into your kitchen units so long as you ensure that there is sufficient space between the machine's air vent and any neighboring surfaces so that air can circulate freely and steam can escape. If the vents are at the back of the machine, don't push or fit it

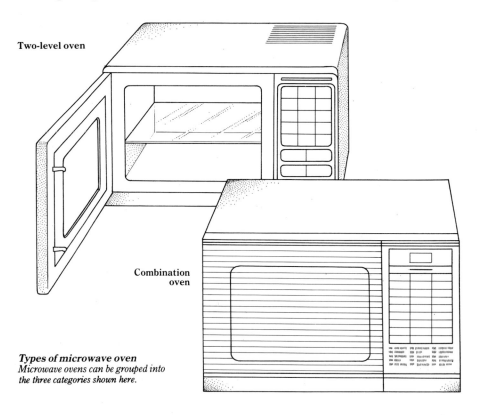

Two-level oven

Combination oven

Types of microwave oven
Microwave ovens can be grouped into the three categories shown here.

against a wall; if they're on top, don't put the machine directly under a shelf or cupboard.

Two-level microwave ovens

Some microwave ovens are fitted with a shelf which allows cooking on two levels. In this type of oven, the microwave energy usually enters the oven cavity through the sides rather than the top. About 60 percent of the energy is fed to the upper section of the oven and 40 percent to the bottom part. Foods which require more microwave energy for thorough cooking can be placed on the shelf, while those needing slower, gentler cooking can be put on the floor of the oven. This type of microwave gives greater flexibility, especially if you want to cook a whole meal at one time or if you regularly cook for a number of people, but it does need a certain amount of planning and calculation. Also, with more food in the oven, cooking times will be longer than in other types of microwave oven. Shelves

cannot be added to other models, they can only be used in microwave ovens that have been designed to take them.

Hi-low ovens

This all-in-one unit combines a conventional oven and a microwave oven. The cooking operations are quite separate, but the two are situated conveniently close together. Food can be microwaved for speed, then browned in the conventional oven or under the broiler. You can, however, use a countertop model with an existing conventional oven in much the same way.

Combination ovens

Combination ovens provide microwave and convection cooking facilities in the same oven cavity. They are particularly good for roasting and baking, as you can combine fast cooking in the microwave with conventional browning. A whole meal can be produced in a very short time, but with all the look of traditionally cooked food. The microwave and conventional cooking facilities may be used simultaneously or in sequence, depending upon the model. You can also use them separately. The microwave oven's maximum output, however, is usually lower than in countertop or double-oven models.

ADDITIONAL FEATURES

Most microwave ovens, whatever category they come under, also incorporate some or all of the following features. Consider these carefully when making your choice and select those that will suit your needs: for example, if you frequently use frozen foods, a separate Defrost button is an advantage. You should also consider the design of the controls and make sure you understand how to operate them. Some of the more technologically advanced systems may seem rather daunting.

Timing control

In microwave cookery, control is by time rather than by temperature and most microwave ovens incorporate some means of time control. This may be set by a touch pad, push buttons or a dial. Some controls

Hi-low oven

Microwave oven

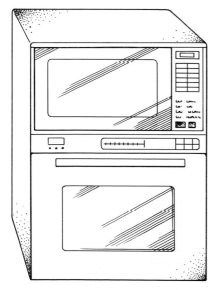

Conventional oven

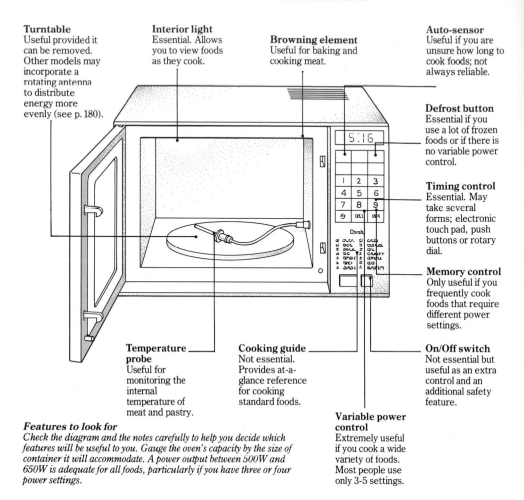

Turntable
Useful provided it
can be removed.
Other models may
incorporate a
rotating antenna
to distribute
energy more
evenly (see p. 180).

Interior light
Essential. Allows
you to view foods
as they cook.

Browning element
Useful for baking and
cooking meat.

Auto-sensor
Useful if you are
unsure how long to
cook foods; not
always reliable.

Defrost button
Essential if you
use a lot of frozen
foods or if there is
no variable power
control.

Timing control
Essential. May
take several
forms; electronic
touch pad, push
buttons or rotary
dial.

Memory control
Only useful if you
frequently cook
foods that require
different power
settings.

**Temperature
probe**
Useful for
monitoring the
internal
temperature of
meat and pastry.

Cooking guide
Not essential.
Provides at-a-
glance reference
for cooking
standard foods.

On/Off switch
Not essential but
useful as an extra
control and an
additional safety
feature.

**Variable power
control**
Extremely useful
if you cook a wide
variety of foods.
Most people use
only 3-5 settings.

Features to look for
Check the diagram and the notes carefully to help you decide which
features will be useful to you. Gauge the oven's capacity by the size of
container it will accommodate. A power output between 500W and
650W is adequate for all foods, particularly if you have three or four
power settings.

can be set very accurately to as little as one
second, others are programmed in minutes.
Once the cooking time is set, the timer
works back to 0 and a bell or buzzer
will alert you when the cooking time is
completed. The timer will also turn off the
microwave energy automatically at the end
of the cooking period. If you find you
frequently require cooking timings in
seconds and your oven cannot set them,
invest in a mechanical cooking timer that
registers seconds.

Interior light
This lights up the cooking chamber once
the machine is turned on and enables you

to keep an eye on foods as they cook. It
normally goes off automatically when the
cooking time is completed and the oven has
turned itself off.

Defrost button
Most microwave ovens have a separate
Defrost facility. This lowers the microwave
energy emitted either by pulsing it on and off
in a regular pattern, or by reducing the
overall wattage. Less energy is necessary to
ensure that frozen foods are completely
thawed rather than just thawed on the
surface, and to prevent them from starting
to cook at the edges before the center has
thawed. On models that do not offer variable

power control, the Defrost setting can also be used to cook and reheat foods at a more gentle speed.

On/Off switch

Some models require a power On button to be operated separately once the cooking and timing controls have been selected, the food placed in the cavity and the oven door closed. This often turns on the interior light and a cooling fan, which prevents the electrical components becoming overheated and helps to disperse steam. The Off switch turns the power off during cooking if desired. It is really supplementary to the Door Release button, which cuts off all circuits before the door can be opened, but it acts as an additional safety control.

Memory control

A few models have a memory control panel which can store instructions for cooking at a particular power setting for a specified amount of time. Other models incorporate memory

VARIABLE POWER CONTROL

Many microwave ovens offer a choice of anything up to ten different power settings. These provide you with far greater control of cooking and allow you to cook foods at a slower rate when this is necessary. However, power settings in different models have not been standardized and settings may be indicated in numerals, percentages, wattages or by various cooking descriptions. On most models, you can reduce or increase the cooking power by adjusting the control at any time during the cooking program.

COMPARATIVE POWER SETTINGS

This chart shows the different systems commonly used by manufacturers. The most accurate guide is by wattage.

Numerical setting	Percentage setting	Descriptive setting	Wattage setting
1	10%	Low	60W
2	20%	Warm	120W
3	30-35%	Defrost	200W
4	40%	Braise	250W
5	50-55%	Simmer	300W
6	60%	Bake	400W
7	70%	Roast	450W
8	80-85%	Reheat	500W
9	90%	Sauté	550W
10	100%	High	600W

controls that allow you to select a series of cooking times at different power settings; the oven will start with one then move onto the next. These models also offer a delayed start so that you can leave foods to cook while you are doing other things. Check that such controls are not too complicated.

Auto-sensor

On auto-sensor, the microwave is controlled in a slightly different way from other microwave functions. You indicate on the control panel the type of food that is going to be cooked. The machine calculates the required cooking time by measuring air temperature and the amount of steam released during cooking, and switches itself off automatically when the food is done.

Cooking guide

The oven front may have a display guide showing the different power settings available and the types of cooking they are most often used for.

Temperature probe

Some ovens incorporate a temperature probe which has a flexible connection to a socket inside the cooking cavity. The probe is usually used for cooking meat, but can be used with other foods. The point of the probe is inserted into the food and is left in position throughout the cooking process. The degree of cooking is selected and when the required temperature is reached, the microwave either turns off automatically or reduces the power setting to the right level to keep the food warm.

Browning element

Some models have a browning element fitted into the roof of the oven cavity. Although this is less powerful than a conventional broiler, it can be used for browning foods before or after cooking. When using this facility, however, you should take care to use suitable cookware.

Turntable

Many ovens incorporate a revolving turntable on the floor of the oven. This may be instead of or as well as a stirrer fan to aid the even distribution of microwaves through the cooking cavity. Turntables are usually made of toughened ceramic glass, some can be removed for cleaning, or if you want to use large or awkwardly-shaped cookware. You should never put a dish on the turntable if it is going to knock against the oven's walls as it rotates during cooking.

Rotating fan

This is a slatted metal disc which may be concealed below the oven floor or above the ceiling. It rotates, driven by air from the cooling system, and helps to distribute the microwaves more evenly around the complete cooking cavity.

Removable floor

Some microwave ovens without a turntable have a ceramic glass tray on the floor of the oven. Usually this is sited just above the oven's base to allow microwaves to be reflected. This also acts as a spillage tray and can be removed and thoroughly washed when necessary.

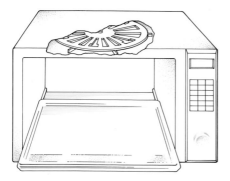

Rotating fan and removable tray
Microwave ovens that don't have a turntable may incorporate a stirrer fan and a removable tray instead, both to aid the distribution of microwaves.

Understanding microwave ovens

The microwave oven is a revolutionary electrical appliance that can cook, defrost and reheat foods with incredible speed and efficiency. But despite its increased popularity, it is probably the least understood of all kitchen appliances. Its mechanics and facilities are explained in more detail on the following pages but, basically, instead of generating heat like a conventional oven, it generates microwaves. These agitate the molecules in foods at such an incredibly high speed that they create instantaneous heat and start the cooking process, as shown on page 182.

Microwaves themselves are high-frequency electromagnetic waves of energy present in the atmosphere, similar to those that convey radio, television and radar signals. They are invisible and non-accumulative, unlike X-rays, gamma rays and ultra-violet rays, which can build up and cause irreversible damage to cellular and chemical structures in our bodies. But because microwave ovens are so different from conventional ovens, they are often regarded with unnecessary wariness. In fact, cooking by microwave is far safer than traditional methods that involve direct heat.

The basic microwave oven
All microwave ovens consist of the same basic unit. This may incorporate some of the additional facilities described on page 178. When the machine is turned on, the microwaves are produced by the magnetron. They travel along the wave guide and enter the oven, as shown here. The stirrer fan distributes them evenly throughout the metal cooking cavity. The especially designed safety door prevents any microwave leakage while the oven is in operation. The air vent allows any steam to escape during cooking.

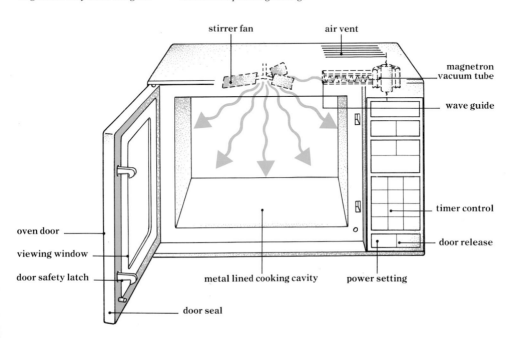

stirrer fan

air vent

magnetron vacuum tube

wave guide

timer control

door release

oven door

viewing window

door safety latch

metal lined cooking cavity

power setting

door seal

HOW MICROWAVE OVENS WORK

The mechanics of a microwave oven are really very simple. The machine is plugged into the regular electricity supply but converts the electrical energy emitted to electromagnetic waves by passing it through a magnetron vacuum tube. The high-frequency microwaves produced are directed into the oven cavity by a wave guide. The oven cavity is made of metal, a material which reflects microwaves without absorbing them. So once the door is closed and the machine is turned on, all the microwave energy produced is safely contained within the oven. The microwaves bounce off and across the oven's metal walls in a regular pattern and are distributed evenly throughout the cavity by a stirrer fan.

The three diagrams below show how microwaves react to different materials in the cooking cavity. They can be reflected, transmitted or absorbed according to the composition of the items they come into contact with. Microwave cooking exploits these properties in order to cook food safely and efficiently, as explained opposite.

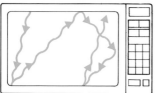

Reflection
Microwaves are reflected by metal; they cannot pass through it. Microwaves bounce off the metal surfaces (walls, ceiling and floor) of the oven cavity in a regular pattern.

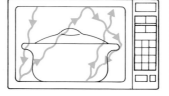

Transmission
Microwaves are transmitted by other materials, such as glass, ceramics, paper and some plastics. Microwaves can pass through these substances without heating them up.

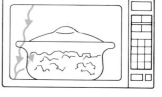

Absorption
Microwaves are absorbed by the moisture molecules in foods. The microwaves can only penetrate to about 2 inches but the food then heats through by conduction.

HOW MICROWAVES COOK FOOD

The unique properties of microwaves allow them to cook foods directly without heating up the cooking cavity. Microwaves are absorbed by the moisture molecules – water, fat and sugar – contained in foods. They make the molecules vibrate at an intense rate, millions of times per second, which causes friction and generates heat as shown below. The heat spreads rapidly through the food from the microwaves' initial point of penetration, which is all over the surface to a depth of about 2 inches, with one layer heating up the next by conduction. Those microwaves that do not hit the food

How microwaves affect food molecules

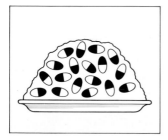

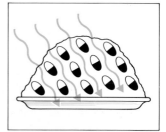

1 *All foods are composed of thousands of molecules; in particular, water, fat and sugar molecules which all attract microwave energy.*

2 *A pulse of microwave energy is absorbed by a piece of food and has the effect of aligning all the molecules in one direction.*

3 *The next pulse of microwave energy reverses their direction. This happens millions of times per second, producing instant frictional heat.*

initially continue being reflected to and from the oven's metal walls until they do penetrate the food.

Microwave energy is absorbed at different rates depending upon a food's density and composition. Foods which contain a lot of air, moisture, sugar or fat cook faster by microwave energy than foods that have a dense molecular structure, which takes longer to penetrate and heat through (see p. 194).

Microwaves pass through certain materials, such as glass, china, paper, and some plastics, without being reflected or absorbed by them. Items made from these materials make suitable utensils for microwave cooking as they do not use up any of the microwave energy produced, allowing it all to pass through to the food. Consequently, containers made from these materials remain comparatively cool, although they may heat up through conduction by being in contact with hot food.

Items made from or containing metals should never be used in microwave ovens. The fact that metals reflect microwaves means that they do not allow the energy to reach food but reflect it away. This can cause sparking in the oven cavity, disturb the carefully balanced electromagnetic field and the magnetron, and thus seriously damage the oven.

ARE MICROWAVE OVENS SAFE?

A microwave oven is one of the safest kitchen appliances you can have. Unlike a conventional cooker, it doesn't have any hot surfaces either inside or outside the machine; there aren't any flames and items are safely contained within the cooking cavity. The microwave oven's exterior casing is designed to be sturdy and stable so you cannot accidentally tip the oven over.

Tests, standards and maintenance

All microwave ovens undergo stringent tests at the manufacturers for both electrical safety and microwave leakage (the most common anxiety). These include opening and closing the door to simulate many years of usage. Tests are carried out after such operations to check that there is no deterioration in the machine's safety level.

Those models designed for domestic use that comply with national electrical safety standards will also have been independently tested and approved by the relevant government agency. All such microwave ovens have many special safety features. They have a series of door locks and switches that make it impossible to operate the oven unless the door is properly shut. Special tests are carried out on each of these locking devices. In particular, to check that if one interlock fails, the magnetron will immediately stop producing microwaves. Microwave oven doors are constructed to precise specifications to ensure that once they are shut, the cooking cavity is completely sealed against energy leakage, and when opened, the machine's generation of microwaves immediately ceases.

Provided you comply with the manufacturer's recommendations for installation, usage and maintenance (see pp. 184-5), your microwave should remain safe to use for many years. If your microwave oven becomes damaged in any way, do not use it until it has been repaired and checked by one of the manufacturer's qualified service technicians. Never attempt to repair it yourself.

Cleaning and maintaining your microwave oven

When you first buy a new microwave oven, inspect it for damage and check that all the components you expect are there. Pay particular attention to the oven door, seal and hinges, and to the oven interior, which should not be dented or scratched in any way. Do not attempt to repair any damage yourself. Always contact the manufacturer or dealer if you have any worries or problems. Follow the manufacturer's recommendations for installation, always read the instructions.

Cleaning a microwave oven

Clean the exterior occasionally by wiping with a damp cloth. Take care not to splash water onto or into the vents. The interior walls do not heat up so any splashing or spilling of foods that occurs during cooking does not get baked onto the surface and can be quickly wiped off. It is important to keep the oven cavity clean because any foods that do get spilled inside will absorb microwave energy and start to slow down the normal cooking process.

How to clean your microwave

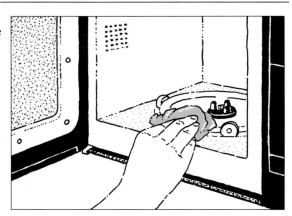

The cooking cavity
Clean the cooking cavity frequently with a cloth soaked in warm, soapy water. Take out and clean any removable parts.

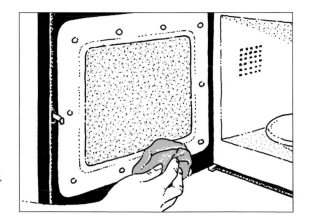

The door seals
Keep the door seals spotlessly clean. Use a mild detergent, rinse and wipe dry. Never use abrasive materials.

How to clean your microwave

Removing stains
Stubborn stains should be loosened by bringing a bowl of water to the boil in the oven. Then clean in the normal way.

Follow these cleaning guidelines:

Use a gentle dishwashing liquid to clean microwave ovens. Use a damp cloth to wipe over all the interior surfaces and the door after each use. Do not use any abrasive cleansing agents unless the manufacturer recommends it.

Take out and clean any removable parts such as turntable, ceramic tray, shelves, at regular intervals.

If a stain proves difficult to remove, heat a bowl of water in the oven to boiling point. The steam produced should loosen the food particles. Wipe off with a damp cloth. Use a cloth soaked in warm, soapy water to wipe off greasy stains. Then wipe the area with a clean cloth.

Pay particular attention to the oven door seal area. This should be kept spotlessly clean by wiping with a cloth soaked in warm, soapy water, then with a clean cloth and finally with a dry cloth.

To remove lingering smells from the oven, place a bowl containing three parts water to one part lemon juice in the oven cavity and heat on ▨ HIGH for about 5 minutes. Wipe thoroughly and dry the oven surfaces afterward.

Never use a knife, scouring pad or any type of abrasive cleaner in the microwave as these will scratch the surfaces and thus damage the oven by distorting the set wave patterns of the microwaves.

IMPORTANT POINTS TO REMEMBER

● Never turn the oven on when it is empty. Always put a mug of water in the oven cavity when it is empty if there is any chance that the oven may be switched on inadvertently.

● Never use the oven cavity as a storage cupboard.

● Never use a microwave oven to dry or heat clothes, papers or any items other than food.

● Never put any undue strain upon the door; for example, by hanging towels from it.

● Never attempt to close the oven door when there is an object between it and the oven or the door seal may become damaged.

● If the door seals or latches look damaged, do not use the oven until a service engineer has checked and replaced them.

● Do not tamper with the machine in any way, either with its casing or with the controls.

● Only use qualified microwave technicians when the machine is in need of repair or servicing.

Microwave cookware and equipment

One of the great advantages of a microwave oven is the wide range of utensils and containers you can use in it. In many cases, foods can even be cooked in the same dishes you wish to serve them in. Although a growing range of specialist microwave cookware is available in the stores, on most occasions you should be able to manage with cookware you already have in your kitchen cupboards.

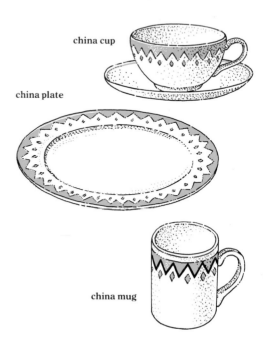

china cup

china plate

china mug

CHOOSING COOKWARE FOR THE MICROWAVE

When deciding which container to use, your first consideration should always be whether it will allow the microwaves to pass through it onto the food. Suitable cookware is made from glass and ceramic, natural substances such as paper, straw and cotton, and certain plastics. It should not contain any materials that will reflect or absorb microwaves. Metal dishes should never be used because metal reflects microwaves and prevents the food from heating up. More importantly, the introduction of metal into a microwave oven will cause sparking arcing which can damage the oven walls and cause pitting. Pitting will alter the pattern of the microwaves and so affect the oven's performance. In some cases, severe sparking may even damage the magnetron. Select items from those shown here and on the following pages.

Pottery and china
Containers made of sturdy china or pottery are suitable for microwave cooking. Ordinary china cups and plates can be used as long as they do not have any metal trimmings, such as a gold or silver pattern. When using china dishes, check that there isn't any gold lettering on the underside or metal screws in the handles. Do not use fine porcelain because it could be damaged in the microwave. Fully glazed earthenware and stoneware can be used, but food in these

dishes may take slightly longer to cook as these materials are often slightly absorbent. Avoid using unglazed earthenware as this is porous and will absorb microwaves, becoming extremely hot and slowing up the cooking process.

Ceramic baking beans
These gray beans look like small opaque marbles and can be used in place of traditional baking beans – which can't be used because they absorb microwave energy. Ceramic beans are excellent for keeping pie shells crisp and flat. Just spread a layer on top of a sheet of paper towels inside the uncooked dough shell and leave them there for two-thirds of the cooking time, then remove the beans and paper and cook without them for the last third.

Glassware
Glass dishes are ideal for microwave cooking. They transmit microwaves and

heatproof glass
measuring cup

glass quiche dish

glass
soufflé
dish

allow you to keep an eye on foods as they cook. When cooking foods with a high fat or sugar content, use heatproof glass as these foods can reach such high temperatures in the microwave oven. Heatproof glass measuring cups, soufflé dishes, bowls and quiche dishes are all particularly suitable. Never put delicate lead crystal in the microwave because it could be damaged.

Paper and cardboard
Paper towels and plain white paper napkins are very useful for soaking up excess moisture while microwaving foods,

particularly when defrosting breads and cakes, or baking potatoes. They can also be used to prevent foods like pastry shells drying out too much during cooking. Don't use patterned or colored paper towels because the dyes can transfer to foods or the oven bottom during the heating process. Waxed paper is good for lining loaf and cake pans,

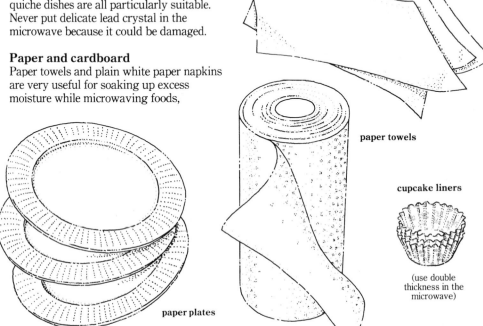

wax paper

paper towels

cupcake liners

(use double
thickness in the
microwave)

paper plates

and also for covering foods. Cardboard containers can be used in the microwave, although those with waxed linings should only be used for defrosting as the heat emitted by foods may melt the wax.

Wood, straw and linen

Equipment made from wood or straw can be used in the microwave oven for reheating foods such as bread rolls, but should not be used for long periods of cooking or they will dry out and eventually split. Wooden spoons may be left in the microwave for short periods of time when making sauces, although the handles start to get hot after about 2 minutes. Pure linen cloths and napkins may be used to line bread baskets or to wrap foods for short periods. Check that they do not contain synthetic fibers.

Plastics

Rigid plastic containers and utensils that are labeled dishwasher-safe are usually designed to withstand high temperatures and can be used in the microwave, too. Articles made from polypropylene and polysulfone are made in a range of shapes and sizes and these are suitable for freezer-to-microwave cooking. There is also a wide choice of specialized microwave cookware made from plastic, as shown overleaf. Lightweight plastic containers, such as yogurt or margarine tubs, can be used for defrosting but are unsuitable for cooking foods as they are likely to distort and may melt when the food becomes hot. Plastic microwave boiling bags and roasting bags make good containers, although they should always be pierced or fastened loosely so steam can escape during cooking. Be sure to secure the bags with plastic ties *not* metal ones, or use rubber bands. Ordinary plastic bags are not suitable for cooking.

Roasting bags are especially good for cooking meat and poultry because they also help to promote browning. You will still need to raise the roast or bird out of the cooking juices, so make sure you place the microwave rack inside the bag and not underneath it. If the bag is too small, slash it along one side and make a tent over the top. Tuck the ends underneath.

wooden skewers

wooden cocktail sticks

wooden spatula

wooden spoon

straw bread basket

cotton napkin
(ensure cloth napkins do not contain man-made fibers)

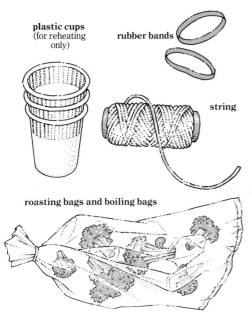

plastic cups
(for reheating only)

rubber bands

string

roasting bags and boiling bags

The use of **plastic wrap** in the microwave is a contentious subject at the moment. There has been increasing concern about this product and it is currently undergoing stringent tests and investigation. It has been noted that some of the plasticizer di-2-ethyhexyladipate (DEHA) used to soften plasticized polyvinyl chloride film (commonly known as plastic wrap) can migrate into closely wrapped foods, and the level of migration is markedly higher as foods increase in temperature. As a result of these findings, many authorities now recommend that ordinary plastic wrap should not be used in the microwave oven. Manufacturers are now producing a microwave-safe polythene film which does not contain these additives. Look for the label saying: "suitable for the microwave" when buying plastic wrap.

Alternatively, another option is to make

plastic wrap

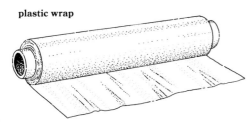

use of boiling bags, paper, casserole lids and plates when you want to cover foods.

Microwave thermometers

These especially designed plastic thermometers are used to determine the internal temperature of meats so you can tell more accurately how the meat is cooking. They can be inserted into the meat about halfway through the cooking time. As the meat cooks, you can check the temperature from time to time, through the glass door. Conventional meat thermometers must not be left in the meat during microwaving, but can be used to check the temperature after the roast or bird is removed from the oven.

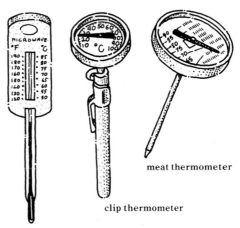

meat thermometer

clip thermometer

mercury thermometer

Especially designed microwave cookware

A large and varied range of microwave cookware made from glass, ceramic or thermoplastic materials is now available. It includes a wide selection of containers, such as round and loaf pans, ramekin dishes, baking molds, bowls, and stacking rings for reheating foods. Many of these cookware items are microwave and freezer safe, so foods can be cooked in the microwave, frozen, then defrosted and reheated all in the same dish.

The microwave cookware includes special browning dishes. These are the only dishes that can be put into the microwave when empty. They have a special coating on the base which absorbs microwave energy and

Special microwave cooking equipment

A wide range of containers made from thermoplastics and glass-ceramics have been designed specifically for microwave cooking

plastic ramekins

ceramic browning dish

plastic loaf pan

plastic cake pan

plastic stacking rings

plastic bowl

plastic roasting rack

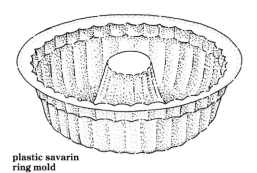

plastic savarin ring mold

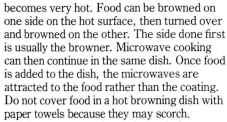

plastic measuring cup

becomes very hot. Food can be browned on one side on the hot surface, then turned over and browned on the other. The side done first is usually the browner. Microwave cooking can then continue in the same dish. Once food is added to the dish, the microwaves are attracted to the food rather than the coating. Do not cover food in a hot browning dish with paper towels because they may scorch.

Microwave roasting racks made from a ceramic or rigid plastic material are also available. They are especially designed for cooking meats and poultry as they raise them out of their cooking juices. Some racks come with a roasting dish underneath, otherwise put a shallow dish under the rack to catch the cooking juices. Racks are also effective for baking cakes, breads, and meat- and vegetable loaves, in fact anything that benefits from all-around microwave energy.

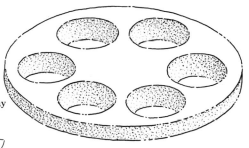

plastic muffin tray

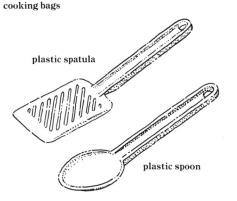

microwave cooking bags

plastic spatula

plastic spoon

HOW TO TEST WHETHER A CONTAINER SHOULD BE USED IN THE MICROWAVE

If you are not sure about using a dish in the microwave oven, you can carry out a simple test to check its suitability and efficiency. Place the dish in the microwave, then put a glass cup containing about 1¼ cups water in the dish and ⊠ HIGH for 1-2 minutes. At the end of the cooking time, if the dish is cool and the water in the jug is hot, the dish is suitable. If the dish is hot and the water is still cool, the dish should not be used as it contains moisture which is attracting some of the microwave energy and preventing it reaching the food.

CONTAINER SHAPES

The speed that foods cook at will be affected by the type of container and its shape. China and pottery, for instance, are slower cookers than special microwave plastic dishes. Round dishes give better results than rectangular ones, in which food tends to overcook in the corners, where it receives more microwave energy. Ring molds are extremely effective in microwave cooking as they provide even heat distribution and allow microwave energy to reach foods on all sides and in the center. You can easily improvise this shape by standing a plain glass tumbler in the center of a round dish. Hold the glass in position while you surround it with food.

Choose deep bowls or dishes when cooking foods that require a large quantity of fast boiling water, for example, pasta, dried beans or rice, otherwise the water may boil over. Allow space for foods to swell or rise during cooking. Pasta, dried beans and grains all expand as they cook, and milk-based sauces swell as they heat up. When cooking these items, they should only take up half to two-thirds the volume of a container. For other foods, make sure that the dish is not too large or the food will spread out thinly and overcook at the edges before the center has been cooked. A medium-sized shallow baking dish is suitable for many of the recipes in this book. Avoid using narrow-necked containers when heating liquids as the steam produced may not be able to escape fast enough and the container may explode due to the build-up of pressure. Do not use tall, narrow dishes for heating food either as it will be packed into too dense a mass to cook evenly.

WHAT NOT TO USE IN THE MICROWAVE

Never use the following cookware in a microwave oven:

● Metal dishes, such as baking trays, bread pans and foil trays, or dishes with metal trims. Anything metal will reflect the microwaves and cause harmful sparking. Use only special microwave-safe bakeware instead.

● Unglazed pottery and earthenware. These attract the microwave energy, becoming very hot, and will slow down the cooking of food.

● Dishes that have been repaired with glue or that have glued handles as the glue may absorb microwave energy and begin to melt.

● Tall, narrow-necked containers which may trap steam and cause it to build up dangerously.

● Wire fasteners on paper or plastic bags. The metal in the fastener becomes hot and could spark off a fire.

narrow-necked bottles

cracked and glued dish

foil tray

metal baking pan

metal trimmed china

wire fasteners

Factors that affect microwave cooking

Many factors affect the length of cooking time required by different foods in the microwave oven: The machine itself; the nature of the food and the quantity; the container used, and the recipe method. All these factors have to be taken into consideration for a recipe to work successfully in your microwave oven.

The microwave oven itself

Microwave ovens have yet to have their power levels standardized, so one machine can vary from another in power output, even if both have the same wattage and are made by the same manufacturer. Machines offering variable power control also use different systems to describe their various power levels (see p. 179). Whenever you consult microwave recipes, check how the power levels recommended in them compare with those of your own oven and make necessary adjustments. The recipes in this book use three different power levels as shown on the chart on p. 50. Compare these levels to the wattages offered on your microwave oven and select the nearest appropriate setting. In the recipes and cooking instructions provided, the alternative times given in brackets for 700W and 500W machines are the lowest times recommended to avoid any possibility of overcooking. You can always extend the cooking time but you can't rescue overcooked foods.

Although most microwave ovens now have stirrer fans or turntables to help distribute the microwave energy evenly, models may still have individual hot spots – areas in the oven where food will cook faster. To check if your oven has hot spots, put equal amounts of water in nine cups, mugs or other small containers, all made of the same material. Space them out over the base of the oven as shown above right, then turn on to full power. Watch carefully to see which container comes to the boil first and note that this is

the hottest spot in the oven. Techniques like turning the dish, stirring or rearranging the food during cooking (see pp. 198-9) are designed to ensure that all food cooks evenly, despite the existence of any hot spots in the oven.

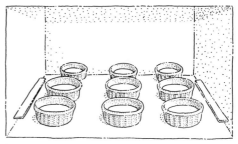

Testing for hot spots
By heating up nine ramekins with equal amounts of water, as described opposite, you can find out your oven's hot spots and then arrange foods accordingly.

Starting temperature of food

The higher the starting temperature of food, the faster it will heat up and cook in the microwave. Foods taken out of the refrigerator and put straight into the microwave will take longer to cook than foods that are allowed to come to room temperature first. You may even find that the same foods take slightly longer to cook on cold days than on hot ones. It is important always to follow the instructions for temperatures of ingredients in recipes, for example, when the addition of boiling broth

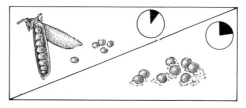

Food temperature
The colder a food is, the longer it will take to cook. Frozen peas need a minute or so more than fresh.

is recommended, do use boiling broth. Adding cold broth will slow down the cooking process and affect all the recommended cooking times in the recipe.

Composition of food

Different components in the food also affect the cooking time. Foods with high fat and sugar contents will reach higher temperatures and cook at a faster rate than other foods because fats and sugars absorb microwave energy more quickly. Consequently, items with a sweetened fruit filling will cook more quickly than similar-sized ones with a low-fat savory filling. Note that particular care is needed when reheating and serving foods with jam-type fillings as the jam will heat up much faster and become scalding hot while the outside remains quite cool.

Foods that have a high liquid content, such as soups, take longer to cook than foods that cook by their own moisture content. Always add the minimum amount of water when cooking vegetables, whether fresh or frozen, as the more water you add, the slower the cooking time will be, and the more vitamins and minerals you will lose in the cooking water.

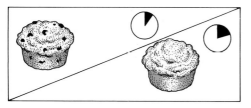

Food composition
A sweetened blueberry muffin will heat up slightly faster than a plain muffin because of its higher sugar content.

Density of food

Density is the most important factor in determining the cooking time of food in the microwave. Dense foods take longer to cook than foods identical in size that have a loose, airy structure; for example, fibrous root vegetables take longer to cook than bread rolls. The dense nature of the food slows down heat conduction. When you are cooking a mixture of dense and light-structured foods, try to arrange the denser

foods around the edge of the dish where they will receive more microwave energy. Place light-structured foods in the center so that they don't cook too quickly.

When you are microwaving a dense quantity of food, such as a lasagne or meatloaf, the center is always the slowest part to cook through because the microwave energy only penetrates the surface to a depth of 2 inches. If possible, use a round, shallow baking dish or a ring mold for such foods. Alternatively, place the dish on an upturned plate or a microwave roasting rask so that more microwave energy can reach the center from underneath.

The density of the container used will also affect the cooking time: Foods take longer to cook in heavy china than in a glass dish or special microwave plastic container.

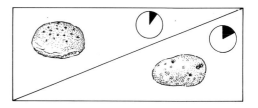

Food density
A light and airy bread roll needs less time to heat up than a potato, which is denser.

Size and shape of food

Always cut food into uniform shapes and sizes for even cooking in the microwave. Small or thin pieces cook faster than large, thick pieces. If cooking irregular shapes, such as broccoli, fish, or chicken portions, place the thinner or less solid area toward the center of the dish and the thick parts to the outer edge of the dish. The same principle applies to delicate foods, such as

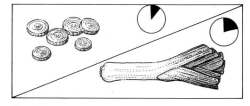

Food size
Vegetables sliced to a similar size cook faster and more evenly than whole vegetables.

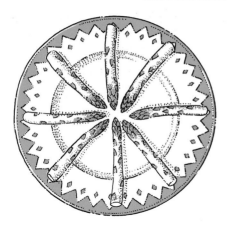

Food shape
Thick areas of food take longer to cook than thin areas.
Put thicker parts around the edge of the cooking dish.

asparagus tips, which would overcook and
spoil if exposed to too much microwave
energy. With these foods, you may wish to
shield the delicate areas from the
microwaves for part of the total cooking time
(see p. 199).

Quantity of food

In microwave cooking, the cooking time is
dependent on the amount of food in the
oven, unlike a conventional oven which will
take the same length of time to cook eight
potatoes as it does one. This is because the
same amount of microwave energy has to be
absorbed by fewer or more items.

Most of the recipes in this book are
intended to serve four people, but you can
reduce the amounts successfully for one or

two people by following certain guidelines
given below. As a general rule, when
reducing the quantity, use a smaller dish so
that the food does not spread out any more
than in the original recipe.

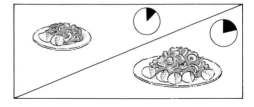

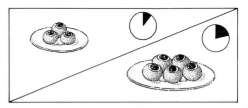

Food quantity
The larger the amount, the longer it will take to cook
by microwave power.

Remember that when the amount of food is
reduced the microwaving time will have to
be reduced too, although not in direct
proportion. If halving a recipe, cook for
approximately two-thirds of the original
time; if quartering it, cook for approximately
one-third of the original time. Always test
the food a minute or two before the
estimated time is up, to avoid overcooking
it. Cover, stir and rearrange the food exactly
as directed in the original recipe.

Microwave cooking techniques

Most of the techniques employed in microwave cooking are similar to those used in conventional cookery. They are designed to promote even cooking, to speed up cooking processes, to accelerate or lessen evaporation and to improve the finish of the cooked item. For the best results, use them whenever a recipe recommends and they'll soon become second nature.

Covering

Covering foods in the microwave reduces the cooking time, helps to retain moisture and prevents spattering of the oven walls. As a general guide, food that is usually covered for conventional cooking is likely to be covered in the microwave, too. Dishes such as vegetables and meat stews are best cooked covered, but items that are meant to have a dry finish, such as cookies or bread, are better left uncovered. Casserole dishes with lids made of suitable (non-metallic) materials are ideal for microwave cooking. If your dish doesn't have a lid, put a plate or a saucer over it. Alternatively, use a microwave bag as a cover.

Some foods that are best cooked without a firm lid or plastic wrap, such as chops, bacon or hamburgers, need to be covered instead with paper towels. The paper doesn't really affect the food, but it does prevent it spattering the inside of the oven as it cooks. Make sure you remove the paper from bacon as soon as it is cooked because the paper has a tendency to stick.

Always take great care when removing a lid or cover at the end of the cooking time because you will release a cloud of scalding steam. Lift it away from you, to avoid any burns to your face or arms.

Instead of cooking vegetables in a covered dish, you can place them in a boiling or roasting bag. Remember to pierce the bag in a few places first, or tie it loosely at the neck so that steam can escape. This is a particularly good method for cooking whole vegetables such as cauliflower.

Uncovering foods
Lift covers away from you to avoid scalding steam.

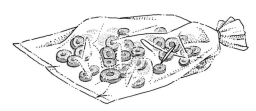

Boiling bags
These are excellent for cooking vegetables.

Waxed paper can also be used for covering foods during cooking, but make sure that it doesn't become loose and flap around, particularly if the oven has a strong fan. You can secure the paper with wooden tooth picks or crumple it if necessary.

Whole fish and fish steaks can be wrapped in waxed paper before cooking. Lay the fish on a large circle or square of paper, and tuck in a few sprigs of herbs and a lemon wedge. Fold the paper in half, then fold the edges over once or twice to seal completely. Place the package in a shallow dish to catch any juices. This is an excellent way to cook fish because the moisture and delicious flavors become trapped inside the paper.

Pastry pie shells cook more successfully when covered with paper towels and a plate. This produces comparatively dry results without the pastry becoming unpleasantly hard.

Piercing

A considerable build-up of steam can occur during microwaving, so any food items with a tight-fitting skin or membrane, such as whole fruit, vegetables, fish, kidneys, chicken livers or raw egg yolk, must be pierced before being cooked in the microwave to prevent them exploding. Fruit and vegetables can be pierced with a fork or the tip of a sharp knife; egg yolks are best pierced with a cocktail stick. Rather than piercing whole fish, slash on both sides at the thickest part; this also helps them to cook more evenly.

As stated above, boiling bags and plastic wrap must either be pierced or secured loosely so some steam can escape.

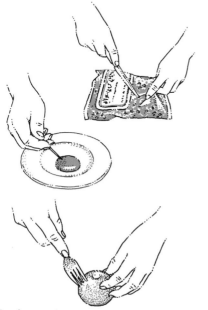

Piercing
Always pierce foods that have skins and membranes.

Wrapping

The microwave process brings out the moisture content of foods, drawing it to the surface. As a result, items that you want to cook with a dry surface, such as baked potatoes, benefit from being wrapped in paper towels while they cook. This soaks up most of the excess moisture produced and helps to spread the heat more evenly over the food. Always remove the paper once you've taken the food out of the oven or it may stick.

For a dinner party, line a basket with cotton or paper napkins before adding the rolls. They can be warmed in the basket, and the napkin will help keep the crusts from becoming soggy.

Wrapping
Wrap foods in paper towels to soak up excess moisture.

Lining dishes

Cake dishes should be lined with waxed paper as specified in the recipe. Remove the lining paper after the standing time has been completed to prevent it sticking to the cake. Do not grease cake pans or coat them with flour as this results in an unpleasant film being left on the cake.

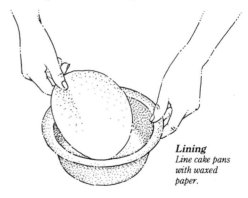

Lining
Line cake pans with waxed paper.

Stirring

Stirring is one of the most important techniques in microwave cooking. As microwaves only penetrate food to a depth of about 2 inches, the food at the edges of the dish may cook before food in the center, especially if the food is dense in structure. To prevent food at the edges overcooking before the center is ready, dishes should be stirred at frequent intervals or as directed in recipes. Stirring should be from the outside edges inward, so that the heat is distributed equally to the center. Stirring sauces in this way also prevents lumps forming, although continuous stirring is not necessary in microwave cooking.

If you are cooking something that requires stirring several times during cooking, one method is to divide the total amount of cooking time and set the timer at regular intervals so you will be reminded to stir enough times.

Even if your microwave has a turntable, it is still a good idea to stir foods when advised to do so.

Stirring
Stir from the edges to the center for even cooking as directed in recipes. Stirring is equally important when reheating and defrosting foods.

Turning or rotating

To ensure even cooking, foods that cannot be stirred, such as lasagne, moussaka, loaves and cakes, need to be given a half or quarter turn at intervals throughout the cooking time as specified in the recipes. This is usually unnecessary if your oven features a turntable.

Turning
Turn cakes, pies, and whole dishes at regular intervals.

Arranging

In microwave cooking, food has to be arranged carefully to ensure even cooking. Always place denser, thicker items at the edge of the dish so they receive more microwave energy. When cooking several items of the same food, arrange them in a circle around the edge of a plate or in a round dish. Space them out evenly so that the microwave energy reaches all sides. Leave the center of the dish empty as this area receives less microwave energy while the edges receive equal amounts. Make sure that the food is an even depth in the dish, and spread it out in a shallow dish rather than piling it up in a deep container. Denser items such as meat loaves and pâtés often benefit from being cooked in a ring mold so that microwaves can penetrate directly from the center as well as from the edges.

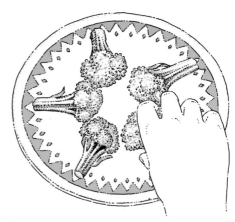

Arranging
Arrange foods in circles, not rows. Place denser areas at the edge and more delicate areas in the center.

When reheating an individual meal on a plate, arrange the food so that it is evenly spread out with denser foods on the outside and more delicate items in the center.

Any small items like cupcakes, cookies, hamburgers, meatballs or individual dishes of food cook much more evenly when arranged in a circle. Remember to rotate individual items a half turn at least once during cooking.

Arrange unevenly shaped foods with the thicker parts to the outside. For instance, arrange chicken portions with thin bony parts to the center, or lay fish fillets in a round dish like the spokes of a wheel, overlapping the thin tail ends in the center where they will cook more slowly. When cooking only two fish at a time, arrange them head to tail and tuck the tails underneath the head of the other fish to protect them from getting burnt.

Turning over

Large solid items, such as baked potatoes, roasts, whole fish or chops or whole cauliflowers, should be turned over halfway through the cooking time to promote even cooking unless otherwise specified in the recipe. This allows all sides and surfaces to receive even exposure to the microwaves.

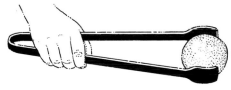

Turning over
Turn over large, whole items for even cooking.

Rearranging

To ensure that no food stays in a hot spot in the oven for the whole of the cooking time, you need to rearrange foods that cannot be stirred. Baked potatoes, hamburgers, sausages and shellfish can be moved around in the dish or on the bottom of the oven at the same time as turning them over. Move items from the edge to the center, from the back to the front, etc, so that nothing remains in the same position throughout the cooking time.

Rearranging
Move foods from the edges to the center.

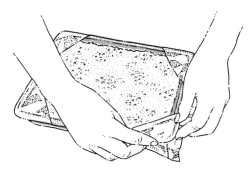

Shielding
Use strips of foil to prevent corners burning.

Shielding

Delicate or thin areas of food that are in danger of overcooking before the rest of the food is ready, can be shielded from the microwaves for part of the cooking time with small, smooth strips of aluminum foil. This is the only time that foil should be used in the microwave, but you should check your manufacturer's instructions before using it. The amount of food left uncovered must be much greater than the area shielded by foil.

You can add the foil at the beginning of the cooking time and remove it halfway through, or it can be added to areas once they are cooked.

Bony ends of large roasts such as leg of lamb and the tails and heads of large fish should be covered for the first half of cooking time. Also, parts of large birds, such as the wing tips, which are cooking too quickly can be covered with small pieces of foil as necessary. However, if you make sure that poultry is trussed into a neat shape before microwaving, wing tips and drumstick ends shouldn't overcook. But the top of the breast may still need to be shielded before the end of the cooking time.

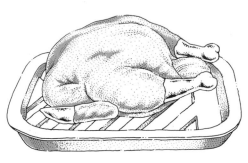

Shielding
Use pieces of smooth foil to prevent poultry wing tips and legs burning.

Shielding can be useful when you are using a square or rectangular container, to prevent the corners from overcooking. Arrange the foil as illustrated.

The foil strips must always be secured firmly. Wooden cocktail sticks are good devices to use. Do not use plastic ones because they could melt from being in contact with the hot food. The foil must never be allowed to touch the sides of the oven cavity or it could cause sparking. If any piece of foil becomes loose, switch off the microwave power immediately and remove it.

Standing time

Standing time is an essential part of microwave cooking as food continues to cook by conduction of heat after it has been removed from the microwave or the microwave power has been turned off. Some foods, such as cakes, may still look uncooked when they come out of the microwave, but will firm up and dry out as they finish cooking through during the standing time. Removing food while it is still slightly undercooked or underthawed and allowing it to finish by standing prevents the edges becoming overcooked by being exposed to further microwave energy before the center has cooked through.

Standing times vary considerably and depend upon the density and volume of different foods. Vegetables need very little standing time; cakes usually need between 5 and 10 minutes. As a rule, the denser the food, the longer the standing time required.

Large roasts and whole birds need quite a long standing time – half an hour or more

for very large birds. This is because the time includes a resting time, just like conventional roasts. If you attempt to carve meat or poultry too soon, you will find that the flesh is difficult to slice and that the cooking juices start to run out of the meat. After a long standing time they are absorbed into the meat so it stays moist and juicy and is easier to carve.

Large fish need 5-10 minutes standing time, whereas small fish, fish steaks and small meat items may only need 3 minutes. Recipes will state when standing times are necessary so follow their recommendations and don't judge a food until after it has completed its standing time. When further cooking is required in the microwave, there is usually no need to repeat the specified standing time.

Tenting

Foods, such as roasts, whole birds and large fish, that require a long standing time to complete the cooking process, should be covered with a tent of foil to maintain their temperature. Smaller items of food such as baked potatoes, stuffed peppers and corn-on-the-cob, can be wrapped in foil, shiny side inward so it reflects the heat, and they will stay hot for at least 20 minutes while

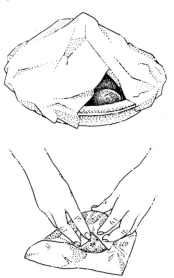

Tenting
Enveloping foods in foil helps to retain their heat once they have been removed from the oven.

other dishes are prepared. The foil must
be removed if they are returned to the
microwave oven.

Don't wrap meat or poultry too tightly in
foil, because this makes them steam,
changing the texture and taste of the flesh.
They also tend to shrink less if they are just
loosely covered.

Browning
Because foods cook so quickly by microwave
energy, the surfaces are not exposed to heat
changes in the normal way so they do not
dry out and brown as they would in a
conventional oven.

Most meats and poultry, especially small
items like chops, hamburgers and chicken or
duck portions don't brown in the microwave,
so they can look quite unpalatable. Cakes and
breads may also look paler and unappetizing
compared to traditionally baked products,
even though their flavor is just as good.

Fortunately, you can improve the
appearance of such foods in several ways:

■ Microwave browning dishes, which have
a special coating that enables the bottom of
the dish to become very hot, can be used for
browning roasts and small meaty items such
as steaks, chops, sausages, poultry portions,
whole fish, and fish steaks and fillets. These
dishes can even be used to shallow fry eggs
and omelets, and to brown microwave
"toasted" sandwiches.

■ Cook roasts and whole birds in roasting
bags to help them brown.

■ Sprinkle poultry skin and meat fat with
special microwave browning agents – or just
use mild paprika – to give food a golden
appearance.

■ Brush chops or poultry portions with a
brown sauce such as Worcestershire or soy
sauce before cooking.

■ Sprinkle fish fillets or steaks with toasted
bread crumbs before cooking.

■ Brown and crisp whole fish, chops,
sausages and poultry portions under a
conventional, preheated broiler after they
have been microwaved.

■ Use whole-wheat flour in cakes, pastry
and bread. These are all items that remain

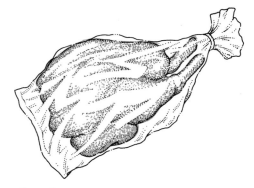

Browning
*A roasting bag will brown meat and poultry while cooking
in the microwave.*

very pale when cooked in the microwave.
Using whole-wheat flour immediately gives
them a better color as well as more flavor
and nutritional value.

■ Add dried fruit, such as apricots or
dates, or chopped nuts and seeds, to breads
and cakes for extra color.

■ Decorate pale cakes with slices of fresh
fruit or a colorful topping using natural fruit
juice and not artificial food coloring.

■ Sprinkle loaves and biscuits with poppy
seeds, toasted sesame seeds, cracked wheat or
oatmeal before baking.

■ Sprinkle cakes or cookies with chopped
nuts, toasted shredded coconut, ground
cinnamon or poppy seeds.

■ Add carob powder, cocoa, or ground
cinnamon to cake and cookie batters with
the flour to make them darker.

■ Put gratin-style dishes with a grated
cheese topping under a preheated
conventional broiler to brown. Deduct this
broiling time from the standing time.

Testing
When testing food to see if it is cooked, it is
important to remember that it continues to
cook for some time after it has been taken
out of the microwave oven. If it is not
cooked enough for your liking after
completion of the recommended standing
time, return it to the microwave oven for

REHEATING FOOD

Cooked food reheats extremely well by a low level of microwave energy. Flavor, color and texture remain as if freshly cooked, and the fast reheating times ensure that fewer vitamins are lost than when food is reheated in a conventional oven. The techniques and procedures used for cooking foods in the microwave also apply when reheating them.

Meat casseroles, fish, poultry or vegetables in a sauce reheat better than foods on their own. Do not put them into too large a baking dish or the sauce will spread and dry out at the edges. Any foods in a sauce should be loosely covered during reheating. Dry foods with a crisper finish can be reheated covered with paper towels.

Soups are easy to reheat in individual portions, either in a mug or a bowl, and take only a few minutes depending on the thickness of the soup. Stir the soup when it starts bubbling up at the edge of the container, then cook for another minute or so to allow it to heat through to the center.

Small containers such as mugs or cups don't need a lid as reheating is so fast, but larger casseroles should be covered to keep in the moisture and speed up the process. Meat and vegetable casseroles reheat more quickly in a shallow baking dish as long as they are spread in an even layer.

Fish cooked by a moist method or covered in a sauce reheats very well on a low power. Make sure that the fish is covered with a lid before microwaving.

Cover slices or small pieces of meat or poultry with gravy or a sauce before reheating – remember to arrange the narrow parts to the center.

Always take care when reheating anything with a jam or other high-sugar filling, such as a pie, as the filling will become very hot very quickly while the outside may still feel cool.

When reheating plates of food, make sure that the food is evenly distributed on the plate, with the thicker items on the outside edge. Up to three plates of food can be heated at a time in an average-sized oven. Position them one on top of the other using special microwave stacking rings. Alternatively, cover the first plate with another upturned plate or large soup bowl and place the next plate on top of this. Avoid positioning the plates so that the same items of food are directly above one another. Give the plates a half turn every few minutes in the same way as you would for other cooking. The food is reheated when the bottom of the plate feels warm.

Stacking rings
Three separate plates of food during reheating.

another minute or two. Use the following guidelines when deciding if items are completely cooked:

■ Microwaved meats and poultry can be tested by piercing the thickest part with a skewer or the point of a sharp knife. The juices will run clear if the meat is well done; slightly pink with a hint of brown if medium; and quite pink if rare. To test more accurately, try using a proper meat thermometer (see p. 189).

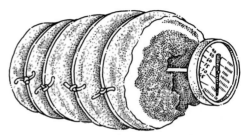

Testing the temperature
Use a meat thermometer to check accurately the temperature of roasting meat.

■ Fish becomes opaque as it cooks and will flake easily. Check the flesh nearest the bone of whole fish, as this is the last to cook, remembering that it will still continue to cook during standing time.

■ Microwave vegetables until they are just tender when pierced with a fork. If you cook them until they are soft, they will have overcooked by the time they are served.

■ Cakes, particularly sponge types, look unpleasantly wet on top at the end of the recommended cooking time. By the end of the standing time they should look dry and be thoroughly cooked. Test them at the end of the time by inserting a wooden tooth

pick or fine skewer into the center. If it comes out clean, the cake is cooked. If it is slightly coated, put the cake back in the microwave for a few minutes more, stand for 5 minutes then test again.

■ Pastry pie shells are cooked when the pastry looks opaque. If cooking in a glass dish, you can double check by seeing if the bottom looks dry from underneath.

■ Quiche fillings may look soft and wet on top after the recommended cooking time, but they soon dry out after a few minutes standing time.

The microwave and the freezer

The microwave and the freezer are perfect partners. Both help to keep flavor, texture and vitamin loss in foods to a minimum and both are great time-savers as well as being economical. The great advantage of using a microwave oven in combination with a freezer is that it can defrost food in a matter of minutes, eliminating the need to pre-plan and take foods out of the freezer hours before they are required in order for them to defrost. Some foods, particularly vegetables, can even be defrosted and reheated in one action. You can also blanch small quantities of fresh vegetables in the microwave in minutes for storage in the freezer as described on pp. 210-11.

The recipes in this book that freeze well are marked with a snow flake symbol. Make sure that all dishes are thoroughly chilled before freezing. Use rigid containers for soups and sauces and allow room for expansion. Seal all items tightly and label. Test for flavor during reheating and add more seasoning if necessary. Seasoning flavors can diminish during freezing.

Defrosting and reheating foods

Most microwave ovens have a Defrost control which allows food to defrost slowly and evenly without danger of it drying out or cooking at the edges. If your microwave oven doesn't have a special Defrost or comparably low setting, you can simulate the Defrost control by turning the oven on to High power for 30 seconds and then off for 1½ minutes. Repeat this process until the food is almost defrosted and allow it to thaw completely by standing. Even with a Defrost control, you'll find that certain, denser foods need additional resting times to prevent the edges cooking while the center still needs to thaw out fully.

Follow the defrosting guidelines below and you should always have perfect results.

■ Defrost food in a container the same size as the block of food. If the food has too much room it will spread out as it melts and the edges will start to cook.

■ Loosen containers, but leave the food covered.

■ Break up food blocks as they start to defrost to bring frozen parts to the edges.

■ Stir suitable foods from the edge to the center as they start to thaw.

■ Foods that cannot be stirred should be separated out, turned over and rearranged to ensure even defrosting.

■ Pies and cakes should be given a quarter turn every minute or so during defrosting.

■ When defrosting food in a bag, pierce or slit the bag to prevent it bursting.

■ Flex bags during defrosting to rearrange the food inside and speed up the process.

■ Shield any delicate areas with small pieces of foil to prevent them cooking while denser parts are still thawing.

■ When defrosting frozen foods that you do not want to cook or reheat, such as soft fruit, use only the Defrost setting. If the food starts to feel warm, leave it to stand for a few minutes, then continue defrosting.

■ Place breads, cakes, cookies or pastry on a double layer of paper towels, so any excess moisture is absorbed and the food does not become soggy.

■ Vegetables can be cooked directly from the freezer without being defrosted.

■ As the defrosting process continues after foods have been removed from the oven, do not wait until foods are completely defrosted before removing them or the outer edges may start to cook.

■ Always remove food from foil containers and remove any metal ties from plastic bags before putting in the microwave to defrost.

Defrosting chart

FOOD	QUANTITY	MICROWAVING TIME	METHOD
Butter or margarine	1 cup	▧ DEFROST for 1½ mins. 600W (*1-1½ mins. 700W; 2-2½ mins. 500W*). Leave to stand for 5 mins.	Remove any foil wrappers. Give a half turn and turn over halfway through.
Cookies	½ lb	▧ DEFROST for 1 min. 600W (*30-60 secs. 700W; 1½ mins. 500W*). Leave to stand for 5 mins.	Turn over halfway through. Remove any wrappings.
Bread, large unsliced loaf	1	▧ DEFROST for 7-9 mins. 600W (*5-7 mins. 700W; 10-14 mins. 500W*). Leave to stand for 5-10 mins.	Stand on paper towels, turn over and rearrange twice.
Large, sliced loaf	1	▧ DEFROST for 11-12 mins. 600W (*9-10 mins. 700W; 15-18 mins. 500W*). Leave to stand for 10-15 mins.	Stand on paper towels, turn over and give loaf a half turn several times.
Dinner rolls	2	▧ DEFROST for 30-60 secs. Leave to stand for 2-3 mins.	Place on paper towels.
	4	▧ DEFROST for 1½-3 mins. Leave to stand for 2-3 mins.	Place on paper towels. Rearrange halfway through.
Fruit cake	1	▧ DEFROST for 5 mins. 600W (*4 mins. 700W; 7 mins. 500W*). Leave to stand for 10 mins.	Give a half turn halfway through defrosting time.
Biscuits	2	▧ DEFROST for 1-2 mins. Leave to stand for 1-2 mins.	Place on paper towels, turn over and rearrange once.
Fruit (soft fruit, eg raspberries, etc.)	½ lb	▧ DEFROST for 3-5 mins. 600W (*2-4 mins. 700W; 4-7 mins. 500W*).	Stir gently once or twice. Leave to stand until completely thawed.
	1lb	▧ DEFROST for 6-8 mins. 600W (*5-7 mins. 700W; 7-10 mins. 500W*).	As above.
Fruit juice concentrate	(7 fl oz)	▧ DEFROST for 2-3 mins. 600W (*2 mins. 700W; 3-4 mins. 500W*).	Remove from container if made of metal. Allow to stand for 3-5 mins.
Fruit paste	2½ cups	▧ DEFROST for 10 mins. 600W (*8 mins. 700W; 12 mins. 500W*).	Stir several times. Allow to stand for about 10 mins.

FISH

FOOD	QUANTITY	MICROWAVING TIME	METHOD
Fish fillets	½ lb	▧ DEFROST for 5 mins. 600W (*4 mins. 700W; 6 mins. 500W*). Stand for 10 mins.	Place in a shallow baking dish and cover. Turn over and rearrange thin parts to the center halfway through.

FOOD	QUANTITY	MICROWAVING TIME	METHOD
Fish steaks	½ lb	🔆 DEFROST for 5 mins. 600W *(4 mins. 700W; 6 mins. 500W)*. Stand for 10 mins.	Place in a shallow baking dish and cover. Turn over and rearrange thin parts to the center halfway through.
	1 lb	🔆 DEFROST for 8 mins. 600W *(6½ mins. 700W; 10 mins. 500W)*. Stand for 10 mins.	
Whole fish	per 1 lb	🔆 DEFROST for 7-9 mins. 600W *(6-8 mins. 700W; 8-11 mins. 500W)*. Stand for 15-20 mins.	Cover, turn over halfway through and shield tails with small pieces of foil, if necessary.
Scallops and mussels, raw, shelled	½ lb	🔆 DEFROST for 3-5 mins. 600W *(2-4 mins. 700W; 4-6 mins. 500W)*. Stand for 3 mins	Cover, break blocks carefully and spread into a single layer, as soon as possible. Stir two or three times.
Shrimp, cooked	¼ lb	🔆 DEFROST for 1½-2 mins. 600W *(1-1½ mins. 700W; 1-2 mins. 500W)*. Stand for 3 mins.	Spread out on a plate and cover. Stir once or twice.
	½ lb	🔆 DEFROST for 3-4 mins. 600W *(2½-3 mins. 700W; 3½-5 mins. 500W)*.	

POULTRY AND GAME

Chicken thighs and legs	4 × ¼ lb	🔆 DEFROST for 8 mins. 600W *(6½ mins. 700W; 10 mins. 500W)* Stand for 5 mins.	Arrange thin ends to the center. Cover and turn over halfway through.
Boneless chicken or turkey breasts	1 × 6 oz	🔆 DEFROST for 6-8 mins. 600W *(5-6½ mins. 700W; 7-10 mins. 500W)*. Stand for 5 mins.	Cover, separate as soon as possible. Arrange thin ends to the center. Turn over and rearrange halfway through.
	2 × 6 oz	🔆 DEFROST for 13-15 mins. 600W *(10-12 mins. 700W; 16-18 mins. 500W)*. Stand for 5 mins.	
Chicken and duck quarters	2	🔆 DEFROST for 7-10 mins. 600W *(6-8½ mins. 700W; 10-12½ mins. 500W)*. Stand for 10 mins.	Arrange in a dish with thin ends to the center. Cover. Turn over and rearrange halfway through.
Rabbit pieces	per 1 lb	🔆 DEFROST for 11-12 mins. 600W *(9-10 mins. 700W; 13½-15 mins. 500W)*. Stand for 10 mins.	Arrange in a shallow baking dish, thin ends to the center. Cover. Turn over and rearrange halfway through.

FOOD	QUANTITY	MICROWAVING TIME	METHOD
Whole birds	under 4 lb	▨ DEFROST for 8-10 mins. 600W (6½-8½ mins. 700W; 10-11 mins. 500W). Stand for 30-45 mins.	Remove any metal ties, place in a bowl. Leave in wrapper or cover. Rotate and rearrange every 5 mins. Remove giblets as soon as possible.
	over 4 lb	▨ DEFROST for 8-10 mins. 600W (6½-8½ mins. 700W; 10-11 mins. 500W). Stand for 30-45 mins.	Defrost as above, but take bird out and stand for 5 mins. several times during cooking.

MEAT

FOOD	QUANTITY	MICROWAVING TIME	METHOD
Steaks and chops	2 × 6-8 oz	▨ DEFROST for 7-8 mins. 600W (6 mins. 700W; 8 ½-10 mins. 500W). Stand for 10 mins.	Separate and arrange in a shallow baking dish. Arrange thin ends to the center. Cover, turn over halfway through.
	4 × 6-8 oz	▨ DEFROST for 9-11 mins. 600W (7-9 mins. 700W; 11 ½-13 ½ mins. 500W). Stand for 10 mins.	
Cubed meat	½ lb	▨ DEFROST for 6 mins. 600W (5 mins. 700W; 7 mins. 500W). Stand for 10 mins.	Spread out in a shallow baking dish and cover. Stir two or three times.
	1 lb	▨ DEFROST for 9 mins. 600W (7 mins. 700W; 11 ½ mins. 500W). Stand for 10 mins.	
	2 lb	▨ DEFROST for 15 mins. 600W (11 mins. 700W; 18 mins. 500W). Stand for 10 mins.	
Ground meat, block	per 1 lb	▨ DEFROST for 6-8 mins. 600W (5-6 mins. 700W; 7-10 mins. 500W). Stand for 10 mins.	Place in a shallow baking dish. Cover. Scrape off soft meat and break up as soon as possible. Stir several times.
Large roasts of meat	2 lb	▨ DEFROST for 18 mins. 600W (15 mins. 700W; 21 mins. 500W). Stand for 10 mins.	Place in a large baking dish. Cover. Turn over and rotate every 5 mins. Shield bony ends and thin parts with foil for half the cooking time.
	3 lb	▨ DEFROST for 25 mins. 600W (20 mins. 700W; 30 mins. 500W). Stand for 15 mins.	
	4 lb	▨ DEFROST for 32 mins. 600W (27 mins. 700W; 37 mins. 500W). Stand for 20 mins.	
Sausage-meat, block	per 1 lb	▨ DEFROST for 3½-4 mins. 600W (3 mins. 700W; 4 ½-10 mins. 500W). Stand for 10 mins.	Place in a shallow baking dish. Cover. Scrape off soft meat and break up as soon as possible. Stir several times.

Reheating from frozen chart

FOOD	QUANTITY	MICROWAVING TIME	METHOD
Vegetable casseroles	4 portions	▣ HIGH for 15-16 mins. 600W *(12-13 mins. 700W; 18-19 mins. 500W).*	Place in a shallow dish and cover. Give the dish a half turn every minute until defrosted enough to stir gently to break up then stir once or twice until hot.
Moussaka, lasagne	4-portion size	▣ DEFROST for 8 mins. 600W *(6 ½ mins. 700W; 12 mins. 500W).* Leave to stand for 6 mins. then ▣ DEFROSTfor 5 mins. 600W *(4 mins. 700W; 7 mins. 500W),* then ▣ HIGH for 9 mins. 600W *(7 ½ mins. 700W; 11 mins. 500W).*	Place in a shallow dish and cover. Give the dish a half turn every 2 mins. until the food is heated through.
Vegetable loaves and meatloaves	1 lb 4-portion size	▣ HIGH for 5-8 mins. 600W *(4-7 mins. 700W; 6-10 mins. 500W).*	Place in a baking dish that fits and cover. Give the dish a half turn every 2 mins. until hot.
Rice, cooked	⅔ cup	▣ HIGH for 1 ½-2 mins. 600W *(1-1 ½ mins. 700W; 1 ½-2 ½ mins. 500W).*	Place in a shallow bowl and cover. Break up with a fork halfway through the time. Stir at the end of the reheating time.
Pasta, cooked	3 cups	▣ DEFROST for 10-12 mins. 600W *(7-10 mins. 700W; 15-18 mins. 500W).*	Place in a shallow baking dish and cover. Stir 2-3 times until hot.
Soup	1 ¼ cups	▣ HIGH for 4-6 mins. 600W *(3-4 mins. 700W; 5-7 ½ mins. 500W).*	Place in a serving bowl allowing room for bubbling. Break up and stir the soup 2-3 times.
	2 ½ cups	▣ HIGH for 7-10 mins. 600W *(5-8 mins. 700W; 8-12 mins. 500W).*	
Sauces	1 ¼ cups	▣ HIGH for 5-6 mins. 600W *(4-5 mins. 700W; 6-7 ½ mins. 500W).*	Place in a baking dish that fits, allowing room for bubbling. Break up and stir the sauce 2-3 times.
	2 ½ cups	▣ HIGH for 10-12 mins. 600W *(8-10 mins. 700W; 12-15 mins. 500W).*	
Fish cakes	2 × 6 oz	▣ HIGH for 4-5 mins. 600W *(3-4 mins. 700W; 5-6 mins. 500W).* Stand for 2-3 mins.	Place fish cakes on a microwave roasting rack. Turn them over halfway through.
	4 × 6 oz	▣ HIGH for 6-8 mins. 600W *(5-6 mins. 700W; 7-10 mins. 500W).*	

FOOD	QUANTITY	MICROWAVING TIME	METHOD
Hamburgers	2	HIGH for 2-3½ mins. 600W *(1½-3 mins. 700W; 2½-4½ mins. 500W)*. Stand for 5 mins.	Preheat a browning dish as manufacturer's instructions, add burgers and press down well. Turn over halfway through.
	4	HIGH for 3-4½ mins. 600W *(2½-3½ mins. 700W; 3½-5½ mins. 500W)*.	
	6	HIGH for 3½-5 mins. 600W *(3-4 mins. 700W; 4½-6 mins. 500W)*.	
Breaded chicken breasts	2 × ¼ lb	HIGH for 4½-5 mins. 600W *(3½-4 mins. 700W; 5½-6 mins. 500W)*.	Preheat a browning dish as manufacturer's instructions, press breasts onto dish. Cook for one-third of the time, then turn over.
Fishsticks	4	HIGH for 2 mins. 600W *(1½ mins. 700W; 2½ mins. 500W)*. Stand for 2 mins.	Preheat a browning dish as manufacturer's instructions. Add fishsticks, press down well. Turn over halfway through.
	6	HIGH for 3 mins. 600W *(2½ mins. 700W; 3½ mins. 500W)*. Stand for 3 mins.	

PRE-COOKED MEALS

Sliced meat in gravy		HIGH for 4-6 mins. 600W *(3-5 mins. 700W; 5-7 mins. 500W)*. Stand for 3 mins.	Pierce bag, place on plate, or place in a baking dish and cover. Turn over and rotate or rearrange two or three times until hot.
Meat casseroles	1 portion	HIGH for 4-5 mins. 600W *(3-4 mins. 700W; 5-6 mins. 500W)*. Stand for 2 mins.	Pierce bag, place on plate or place in a shallow bowl and cover. Turn over bag or stir casserole halfway through.
	2 portions	HIGH for 7-10 mins. 600W *(6-8½ mins. 700W; 8½-12½ mins. 500W)*. Stand for 3 mins.	
Spareribs in sauce	2 portions	HIGH for 5-6 mins. 600W *(4-5 mins. 700W; 6-7 mins. 500W)*. Stand for 2 mins.	Pierce bag, place on a plate or place in a shallow bowl and cover. Turn over bag or stir halfway through.
Roast chicken in gravy	2 portions	HIGH for 5-7 mins. 600W *(4-6 mins. 700W; 6-8½ mins. 500W)*. Stand for 2 mins.	Pierce bag, place on plate or place in shallow bowl and cover. Turn over bag or stir halfway through.

FOOD	QUANTITY	MICROWAVING TIME	METHOD
Dry spicy chicken	2-3 portions 1 lb	▨ HIGH for 6-8 mins. 600W (*5-6½ mins. 700W; 7-10 mins. 500W*). Stand for 2 mins.	Arrange on a plate, narrow ends to the center. Turn over and rearrange halfway through.
Chicken Kiev, raw	2 portions	▨ HIGH for 8-10 mins. 600W (*6½-8½ mins. 700W; 10-12½ mins. 500W*). Stand for 2 mins.	Preheat browning dish as manufacturer's instructions; add 2 teaspoons oil . Press down chicken pieces. Turn over after one-third of the cooking time.
Shrimp curry	1 portion	▨ HIGH for 5 mins. 600W (*4 mins. 700W; 6 mins. 500W*). Stand for 2 mins.	Place in bowl and cover, stir two or three times. Or pierce bag and place in dish. Turn the curry over and rotate halfway through.

Blanching fruit and vegetables for the freezer

A microwave oven takes much of the effort out of blanching vegetables and is a boon to people who grow their own produce. Vegetables can be picked at the peak of perfection and then blanched in small quantities in the microwave. When blanching large amounts, it is usually better to use conventional methods.

Blanching is necessary to stop enzyme activity in vegetables and fruits which would otherwise continue even at freezer temperature, causing loss of flavor and texture. Deterioration is noticeable in some produce after only a few days. Others will last longer but the eating quality will also start to deteriorate.

Before blanching, clean, trim and slice the vegetables to a uniform size. To blanch 1 lb vegetables, place in a casserole dish or bowl with 3 tablespoons water. Cover and cook on HIGH for the time specified on the chart. Stir once halfway through the blanching time.

Drain, then plunge into iced water to prevent further cooking. Once chilled, drain well and pack into freezer bags, or boiling bags if you want to reheat them in the microwave. For smaller amounts, put the prepared vegetables into a boiling bag. Do not add any water. Secure the bag loosely with a non-metallic fastener and cook on HIGH for the appropriate time, turning the bag over halfway through. After the blanching time, put the bag into iced water. Keep the top of the bag above the surface and leave open to allow steam to escape. Once the vegetables have chilled, secure the bag tightly, wipe dry and freeze as normal.

Most blanched produce will keep for up to a year in the freezer. Do not thaw before cooking or more vitamin content will be lost and the texture will be poor.

Blanching vegetables by microwave

1 Clean, trim and slice vegetables evenly into 2-inch pieces.

2 Pack into a boiling bag. Secure loosely. Cook on HIGH as detailed on chart.

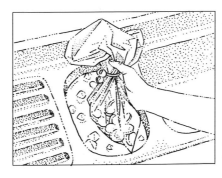

3 Chill thoroughly in iced water. Secure bag tightly, label and freeze.

Blanching chart

VEGETABLE/FRUIT 1 lb	MICROWAVING TIME on HIGH
Asparagus	4 mins. 600W (*3 mins. 700W; 5 mins. 500W*)
Beets, *small*	5 mins. 600W (*4 mins. 700W; 6 mins. 500W*)
Brocolli flowerets	2½-4 mins. 600W (*2-3 mins. 700W; 3-5 mins. 500W*)
Brussels sprouts	5 mins. 600W (*4 mins. 700W; 6 mins. 500W*)
Carrots	3½ mins. 600W (*3 mins. 700W; 4 mins. 500W*)
Cauliflower flowerets	3 mins. 600W (*2½ mins. 700W; 3½ mins. 500W*)
Corn kernals	3 mins. 600W (*2½ mins. 700W; 3½ mins. 500W*)
Corn-on-the-cob (*2*)	7 mins. 600W (*6 mins. 700W; 8½ mins. 500W*)
Green beans, *whole*	3 mins. 600W (*2½ mins. 700W; 3½ mins. 500W*)
sliced	2 mins. 600W (*1½ mins. 700W; 2½ mins. 500W*)
Leeks, *sliced*	2-2½ mins. 600W (*1½-2 mins. 700W; 2½-3 mins. 500W*)
Lima beans	3 mins. 600W (*2½ mins. 700W; 3½ mins. 500W*)
Onions, *sliced*	2 mins. 600W (*1½ mins. 700W; 2½ mins. 500W*)
Parsnips	3 mins. 600W (*2½ mins. 700W; 3½ mins. 500W*)
Peas	2 mins. 600W (*1½ mins. 700W; 3-5 mins. 500W*)
Peppers, *sliced*	3 mins. 600W (*2½ mins. 700W; 3½ mins. 500W*)
Spinach	2 mins. 600W (*1½ mins. 700W; 2½ mins. 500W*)
Zucchini	3 mins. 600W (*2½ mins. 700W; 3½ mins. 500W*)
Apples	3-4 mins. 600W (*2-3 mins. 700W; 3-5 mins. 500W*)
Pears	3-4 mins. 600W (*2-3 mins. 700W; 3-5 mins. 500W*)
Rhubarb	3-4 mins. 600W (*2-3 mins. 700W; 3-5 mins. 500W*)

Hints and tips

BUTTER AND MARGARINE

▧ Use the microwave for softening butter and margarine. For 1 cup, heat on DEFROST for 30-60 seconds. This will speed up the creaming process when preparing cake mixtures.

▧ To melt ½ cup butter or margarine, place in a small dish and ▨ MEDIUM for 1-2 minutes.

BREADS

▧ Heat up rolls and bread before serving with a meal; you can even heat them in their serving basket. Put them in the microwave just before you want to serve them as they soon begin to cool down again, and ▨ HIGH for 1-2 minutes.

▧ You can freshen bread that has gone slightly stale by heating it on ▨ HIGH for about 15 seconds.

▧ Make dry bread crumbs for coating foods by heating a slice of bread on ▨ HIGH for 2-3 minutes. Then crush with a rolling pin or in a blender or food processor and store the crumbs in an airtight container.

▧ You can defrost a single slice of bread in 10-15 seconds. Place it on a paper towel.

MEAT AND POULTRY

▧ Always bring meat to room temperature before cooking to achieve the best results.

▧ If you like a crispy finish to your roast, try cooking it for half the time in the microwave and the remainder of the time in a conventional oven.

▧ Allow 5 minutes additional cooking time if cooking a bird with stuffing.

▧ If cooking poultry portions in a sauce, try skinning them first as this allows the sauce to penetrate right through the flesh.

▧ Chicken, which has been cooked without any additional browning, is particularly suitable for use in salads and sandwiches.

FISH

▧ Some fish have a strong odor which can often linger after cooking. To get rid of this, boil some water and lemon juice in a mug in the microwave for 3-4 minutes. Cooking with wine, vinegar or lemon juice also helps to minimize cooking odor.

FRUIT

▧ Soften dried dates to make chopping easier by heating on ▨ DEFROST for 30-40 seconds.

▧ Microwave citrus fruit on ▨ HIGH for 15-20 seconds to make peeling easier. Prick the skin first.

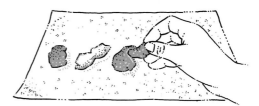

Drying citrus peel

▧ Dry large pieces of peel from citrus fruit to use as a flavoring in teas, cakes and sauces. Orange, tangerine and grapefruit are particularly good. First, make sure that the peel is scrubbed well to remove any traces of chemical pesticides. Lay the pieces out on a paper towel and ▨ HIGH for about 1 minute, until dried and crisp. Rearrange and turn over halfway through the cooking time. Store the dried and cooled peel in an airtight container.

▧ To dry grated peel, place in a bowl and ▨ HIGH for 30-60 seconds, or until dry. Stir once.

▧ To extract more juice from citrus fruit, prick the skin in several different places. For each fruit, ▧ HIGH for about 30 seconds before squeezing.

■ Speed up the process of reconstituting dried fruit in the microwave. For ¼ lb, place in a bowl with 2½ cups boiling water. Cover and ▧ HIGH for 6-10 minutes. Stir, then leave to stand for 10-30 minutes.

HONEY

■ To restore smooth, runny texture to honey that has crystallized in the jar, place in the microwave (after removing the lid) and ▧ HIGH for 1-2 minutes.

SEEDS

■ Bring out the full flavor of seeds by toasting them in the microwave. For ⅓ cup, spread on a dish and ▧ HIGH for about 2 mins. Stir frequently during this time to prevent scorching.

NUTS

■ Toast shredded coconut by spreading 6 tablespoons over a 9-inch plate. ▧ HIGH for 1-2 minutes or until golden brown. Stir at least once.

■ To roast whole nuts, spread ⅔ cup over a medium-sized plate. ▧ HIGH for 3-4 minutes and stir at least twice.

DESSERTS

■ Soften ice cream before serving by warming on ▧ DEFROST for between 30 and 60 seconds. This timing should also enable you to loosen gelatin salads and mousses from their molds.

SAUCES

■ Save on dish washing by making sauces in what you wish to serve them in. Select a container large enough to allow for any bubbling and liquid expansion.

■ To prevent sauces from cooking unevenly and lumps forming, watch for the mixture thickening around the edge of the bowl or jug. As this happens, open the door and stir the sauce briskly.

■ Bring starch-thickened sauces to a boil and remove from the microwave as soon as they have thickened. Overcooking will destroy the thickening agent and the sauce will start to thin.

TOMATOES

■ To make peeling tomatoes easier, put them into a bowl, cover with boiling water and ▧ HIGH for about 30 seconds. Drain and then peel.

PASTRY

■ Bake pastry dough shells by covering with paper towel and a plate. This helps to keep the pastry crisp and dry. Avoid adding very moist fillings or the pastry will absorb the moisture and become soggy.

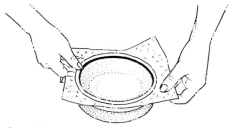

Covering pastry

EGGS AND CHEESE

■ Always pay special attention when cooking eggs in the microwave as timings will vary according to the size, composition and freshness of the eggs. It is better to take them out of the oven slightly undercooked, then they can finish cooking in the standing time.

■ To soften cream cheese for easier spreading or mixing, just ▧ DEFROST for 30-60 seconds.

CAKE MAKING

■ Tap the sides of cake dishes during the standing time to help loosen the cake and bring it away from the edge.

■ The inside diameter of a cake container should not exceed 8 inches, or the center will probably not cook through. Use a tube pan or Bandf pan for larger cakes.

To melt chocolate, put 2 squares in a dish and ⊠ MEDIUM for 2-3 minutes.

When baking cakes in the microwave, only half fill the container as the batter will rise considerably in the oven and cause a mess if it overflows.

DRYING HERBS

Fresh herbs can be dried effectively in the microwave for use all the year around. Dry about ½ cup at a time. Remove the stalks from the leafy herbs. Rinse the leaves carefully, then pat dry with paper towels. Place the herbs between two sheets of paper towels on the floor of the oven. Add a small bowl of water as a safety measure: The moisture content in this small amount of herbs is very low and the water will prevent the paper towels scorching. ⊠ HIGH for 4-6 minutes, depending on the type of herbs, until they lose their bright color and become brittle to touch. Rearrange the herbs several times and watch them carefully throughout the cooking time. Leave them to cool, then press through a strainer. Store in an airtight jar in a cool, dark place.

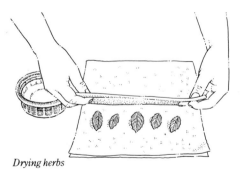

Drying herbs

JARS

■ To scrape the last of the contents from preserves and jams in jars, remove lids and ⊠ DEFROST for 30 seconds.

■ To heat baby foods in the jar, remove the lid and ⊠ MEDIUM for 40-60 seconds. Always test the temperature before serving.

WINE

■ To bring red wine to room temperature, pour into a suitable pitcher, and ⊠ HIGH for 10 seconds. Do not heat in the bottle.

FROZEN FOODS

■ Cook frozen vegetables in their own bags. Simply pierce the bag first and place it on a plate.

■ Freeze foods in small or individual portions for speedier defrosting.

■ When freezing a casserole, it is a good idea to insert an empty paper cup in the center so food isn't concentrated there and the defrosting process takes less time.

REHEATING PASTA, GRAINS AND DRIED BEANS

■ With the microwave you can reheat pasta, grains and dried beans so that they keep their texture and flavor in full. For one or two servings, place in a dish, toss in a little oil, cover and ⊠ HIGH for 1-2 minutes.

IMPROVIZING CONTAINERS

■ To make your own tube pan for cooking cakes and grain dishes, stand a glass tumbler in the center of a round dish. Hold in position when adding food.

■ Unusually shaped cardboard boxes can be used to make interesting cake containers. Line the box with waxed paper first. Do not use boxes with wax coatings or any metal trimmings.

GLOSSARY

Arcing
Small sparks that occur in the oven cavity during cooking when an electric discharge is conducted from one surface or electrode to another. This may be caused by metal being introduced into the oven either as foil, a utensil or a container. Never use metal utensils in a microwave. Also, be careful to use only smooth foil in small amounts as advised in the manufacturer's instruction manual, and never let it come near to or in contact with the oven walls.

Arcing may also be the result of scratches or indentations on the oven cavity's surfaces; care must be taken when cleaning the oven interior. Always wipe or soak off spilt foods (see pp. 184-5) as carbonization can cause sparking.

Audible reminder
A bell or buzzer that sounds to let you know when the cooking time that you have set has been completed.

Blanching
Process of boiling vegetables or fruit for a brief period to halt enzyme activity before freezing. See pp. 210-11 for detailed directions on blanching vegetables in the microwave.

Browning dish
A special dish with a tin-oxide coating on its bottom designed to brown foods in the microwave oven. The coating absorbs microwave energy and becomes very hot when preheated in the oven. These dishes come in a variety of shapes and sizes and can be used with a lid for sautéing and simmering. Each type of dish is supplied with a set of directions which should be followed when using.

Browning broiler
Some microwave ovens incorporate a radiant electric broiler which is usually sited in the roof of the cooking cavity. This can be used to crisp or brown foods after cooking or, in some of the models, during cooking.

Combination oven
As the name suggests, combination ovens incorporate microwave power with conventional cooking facilities. Depending upon the model, these can be operated either separately, in sequence, or at the same time, combining the speed of microwave energy with the browning and crisping qualities of conventional cooking by heat.

Conduction
The way heat spreads from one layer to the next. This is an important part of the microwave cooking process and is how foods continue to cook after being removed from the microwave. It is also the reason why microwave-proof plates get hot in the microwave oven – it is not the plate that is being heated up by the microwaves but the food it contains, and the heat generated by the hot food heats up the plate.

Defrosting
The process by which ice crystals revert to moisture as food thaws. As the pattern of ice crystals in foods is not uniform, thawing is often uneven. For even thawing, set the microwave on Defrost. This pulses out energy at regular intervals so the temperature of the food evens out between bursts.

Density
The density of different foods affects the length of time they need to cook, defrost and reheat. The denser the food, the longer the cooking time it will require. Similarly, the density of containers also affects cooking times.

Door seals
Although microwave ovens vary in design, all have door seals which run around the perimeter of the door's interior. The seal consists of a metal channel filled with absorbent material to reduce the risk of any microwaves escaping while the oven is in use.

Hot spots
Although modern microwave ovens incorporate at least one device to help distribute the microwave energy evenly throughout the cooking cavity, hot spots may still exist. Find out where your oven's hot spots are by following the test on p. 193. The existence of hot spots necessitates food being turned, stirred and rearranged for even results.

Magnetron
A high-frequency radar tube that converts electrical energy into microwave energy.

Microwave thermometer
A thermometer especially designed for use in the microwave. Traditional thermometers cannot be used because the mercury is affected by microwaves.

Piercing
Any item covered by a membrane or skin must be pierced before being microwaved. This is to allow steam to escape during cooking and to prevent anything bursting from the pressure. Any boiling bags used in the oven should first be pierced to prevent too much steam building up inside of them.

Rearranging

Some items need rearranging in the microwave oven in order to cook evenly (see p. 199).

Shielding

A technique used to protect delicate areas of food from receiving too much microwave energy during cooking, by covering them with smooth strips of foil. Always follow your oven's manufacturer's guidelines when employing this technique and only use the minimum amount of foil.

Splash guard

Some wave stirrers are protected from food spatterings by a splash guard. This should be cleaned regularly according to the manufacturer's directions.

Stacking

Plates of food being reheated should be stacked one above the other using microwave-safe stacking rings or upturned plates as separators (see p. 202).

Standing time

This is an essential part of microwave cooking and allows food to continue cooking by conduction after the microwave energy has been turned off.

Stirring

A most important technique used in microwave cooking to distribute heat and help foods, particularly liquids, cook evenly. Always stir from the edges of the container to the center (see p. 198).

Tenting

This is the method of covering foods with foil once they have been removed from the oven so that they keep their heat during their standing time.

Variable power

A setting control that offers a range of energy outputs for different functions. The different powers available may be expressed in numerals, words, or percentages (see p. 179). The lower powers are usually achieved by pulsing the energy on and off for varying lengths of time.

Wave guide

A metal duct that directs microwave energy produced by the magnetron into the cavity of the oven.

Wave stirrer

A device sited close to the wave guide outlet, designed to distribute the emerging microwaves evenly throughout the cooking cavity.

INDEX

Acknowledgments

Dorling Kindersley would like to thank the staff who worked on the original title **Sarah Brown's Vegetarian Microwave Cookbook:** Carolyn Ryden, Felicity Jackson and Anita Ruddel.

Designer: Mick Keates

Editor: Mary Lambert

Americanization: Elizabeth Wolf-Cohen

Editorial Assistance: Julia Harris-Voss

Design assistance: Mark Regardsoe

Photographer: Clive Streeter

Home economist: Linda Fraser

Stylist: Sue Russell

Illustrator: John Woodcock

Studio: Del & Co

Typesetter: Bournetype, Bournemouth and MS Filmsetting Limited, Frome

Reproduction: Colourscan, Singapore